CAPITAL, COERCION, AND POSTCOMMUNIST STATES

Capital, Coercion, and Postcommunist States

Gerald M. Easter

CORNELL UNIVERSITY PRESS ITHACA AND LONDON

Cornell University Press gratefully acknowledges receipt of a subvention from Boston College which helped in the publication of this book.

First published 2012 by Cornell University Press

First printing, Cornell Paperbacks, 2012

Printed in the United States of America

Library of Congress Cataloging-in-Publication Data

Easter, Gerald, 1959–
    Capital, coercion, and postcommunist states / Gerald M. Easter.
        p. cm.
    Includes bibliographical references and index.
    ISBN 978-0-8014-5119-5 (cloth : alk. paper)
    ISBN 978-0-8014-7824-6 (pbk. : alk. paper)
    1. Finance, Public—Poland. 2. Finance, Public—Russia (Federation)
3. Fiscal policy—Poland. 4. Fiscal policy—Russia (Federation)
5. Post-communism—Economic aspects—Poland. 6. Post-communism—
Economic aspects—Russia (Federation) 7. Poland—Economic
conditions—1990– 8. Russia (Federation)—Economic
conditions—1991– I. Title.
    HJ1213.E27 2012
    339.5'209438—dc23   2012014475

| Cloth printing | 10 | 9 | 8 | 7 | 6 | 5 | 4 | 3 | 2 | 1 |
| Paperback printing | 10 | 9 | 8 | 7 | 6 | 5 | 4 | 3 | 2 | 1 |

To the memory of EAGL81, my friend Rob Farrell

Contents

Preface

> **The [Russian] government should assure that in all public institutions transparency and accountability prevail; debts are paid and arrears eliminated; the tax system is fair, simple and efficient, based on transparent laws and effective administration.**
> Michel Camdessus (St. Petersburg, 1999)

> **Man walks into a doctor's office and says, "Doc, it hurts when I do this." Doctor replies, "Don't do that."**
> Henny Youngman

Why invoke the words of Henny Youngman on the subject of the postcommunist state, when his main body of work was in the area of intrahousehold relations? Because they capture so well the gist of the advice on tax collection that capitalist custodians, such as IMF head Michel Camdessus, had for postcommunist governments, like Russia's. Of course, Camdessus had a pretty good idea of what Russia was doing or, in the case of tax collection, not doing, and he had a clear image of what Russia should be doing. But what one does not get from his remarks is a sense of why Russia was doing what it was doing. His advice repeats the monotonous mantras, based on idealized depictions of capitalism and governance in the West, which an international brigade of economic advisers chanted to Eastern European public officials throughout the 1990s. Regarding public finance, in particular, policy expertise invariably rested on assumptions of public choice theory, a conceptual world of rational economic actors where political and cultural phenomena were unwelcome intruders. By contrast, fiscal sociology represented an alternative conceptual framework, where state finances are enmeshed in a larger sociopolitical context, promising a richer explanation of the fiscal fates of postcommunist states. But as the Russian state succumbed to financial collapse, transition technocrats for whom fiscal sociology was as remote as the medieval chronicles were left wanting for analysis, and could only offer admonition: "Don't do that."

I was living in Yekaterinburg, Russia, when the 1998 financial crisis struck. I was studying regional governors, not fiscal policy. But I had managed to figure out that the Sverdlovsk regional administration was financing its budget through a pyramid scheme of short-term debt issues. In August 1998, when the Kremlin declared it was out of rubles and reneging on its outstanding debts, I realized that this local financial scheme was a replication of fiscal policy at the state center. Within days, I witnessed a bank run, featuring an angry mob, broken windows, and roughed-up bank manager. A few weeks later, I happened to be in the office of an ex-pat friend when her business was raided by the tax police, who that summer had become notorious for contrived sting operations. It was most interesting, quite sad, and very much at odds with the optimistic assessments of the Russian economy touted by self-congratulating international advisers only six months earlier. I wrote up what I knew about it and submitted it to a journal, which rejected it, saying it would be so much better if it were comparative. As fate would have it, next summer I visited Poland for the first time, where I discovered how differently they do state financing there. Good-bye regional governors, hello tax collectors.

For those who have not yet had the pleasure, a thorough immersion into the intricacies of tax policy and tax collection offers the most fascinating and penetrating insights into the workings of political power and interactions of state and society. At first, I envisioned a quick and tidy comparison of Russian and Polish tax politics leading to the 1998 financial crisis. I learned some public finance theory and Polish, one of which, at least, was comprehensible ... *polski oczywiscie*. Before I could finish, however, both Russia and Poland introduced major new tax reforms; and just when that was digested and incorporated, both Russia and Poland were hit with a second international financial crisis, with different outcomes from the first. Thus, I learned the hard way that the tax system, any tax system, is an object in perpetual motion. Now, after more than a decade, I must bring this project to conclusion (despite the interesting piece today in the *Krakow Post* concerning a crackdown on tax-evading prostitutes). Next time, I plan to study only retired and dead people.

So who has abetted my fiscal fetish for the past ten years? Those who provided income of course should go first: I received financial support (and many follow-up e-mails) from the Smith-Richardson Foundation; a wonderful one-year appointment at the Davis Center at Harvard University; a one-year sabbatical and some summer travel money from Boston College; a teaching Fulbright at the European University in Saint Petersburg; and a Social Science Research Council postdoctoral research grant (sorry about the regional governors). Opportunities to speak come next: I received a lot of encouraging comments and useful criticism from panelists and audience members while doing the American Political Science Association and American Association for the Advancement of Slavic Studies annual meetings circuit. In addition, several special presentations and workshops stand out for the collection of talent that lent its attention to my research efforts: none more near and dear than the Davis Center's Post-Communist Workshop, where this project first got off the ground and finally returned home seven years later, almost finished; a workshop on Tax Evasion and State Capacity at the University of St. Gallen, Switzerland; a conference on Post-Communist State Building at Yale University; a Society for the Advancement of Socio-Economics (SASE) panel on tax compliance at the Central European University in Budapest; a collaborative Russian-American workshop, sponsored by the Carnegie Foundation, on Governance in Russia in New York and Moscow; and an invitation to the Center for Russia, East Europe, and Central Asia (CREECA) at the University of Wisconsin, Madison.

Finally, without sorting the time or place or division of services rendered, the people who helped along the way: Hilary Appel, Bob Arnot, Margarita Balmaceda, Marc Berenson, Michael Bernhard, George Breslauer, Martino Bridgeman, Timothy Colton, the Comparativisti, Elitsa Daneva-Molles, Grzegorz Ekiert, Steven Fish, Timothy "Kid" Frye, Scott Gehlbach, Marshal Goldman, Dmitry Gorenburg, Robert Faulkner, Nicolas Hayoz, Yoshiko Herrera, Elzibeta Hinke, Steve Holmes, Simon Hug, Jan Jurek, Mark Kramer, Marc Landy, Margaret Levi, David McDonald, John Micgiel, Burton Miller, Mick Moore, Stanislaw Owsiak, David Quigley, Joe Quinn, Tom Remington, Neil Robinson, Kay Schlozman, Klaus Segbers, Oxana Shevel, Brian Silver, Lis Tarlow, Caitlin Tomae, Lucan Way, and David Woodruff. In addition, it is my pleasure to join the long line of scholars indebted to editor Roger Haydon. Meanwhile, back at the pink house, I am forever captivated and comforted by Mara Lynn; as for Shay and Van, t'anks fer nuttin, but I love you anyway.

CAPITAL, COERCION, AND POSTCOMMUNIST STATES

CAPITAL, COERCION, AND POSTCOMMUNIST STATES

"The revenue of the state is the state," Edmund Burke said.[1] From Caesar's renderings to Cicero's sinews to Franklin's fatalism, a symbiotic relationship has long been recognized between tax collection and state capacity. Yet for some time Burke's taxing maxim remained obscure to contemporary comparative politics. Since the 1990s, however, the trend has been reversed with a rash of new studies on the politics of taxation. Coincidently, just as comparativists were developing a taste for taxes, state finances in the postcommunist world took a turn for the worse. In August 1998 the Russian government announced that for lack of means it must renege on its outstanding debt obligations. The postcommunist state was in fiscal collapse. Scholars of the transition hastily redirected attention to the pyramid scheme that was financing the Russian government. This confluence of academic trends and real world events could only mean that a new literature on the comparative politics of the postcommunist tax state was not far off.

This is a book about power and wealth, the essence of the modern state. Yes, the modern state provides public goods and shapes social identities. But in its origin, and still at its core, the state is the institutional embodiment of coercion, hopefully in the interest of the greater good of the society within which it presides. To support coercion, the state makes claims on capital in society. The analytical framework rests on the assumptions of a "realist" intellectual tradition, which leans more toward Weber than Smith or Marx.[2] In this scheme, the state is not depicted as neutral, but as an actor in its own right and in competition with societal actors over power resources, namely capital and coercion. Capital here refers to the means of economic existence as manifested in kind, cash, or credit;

1

while coercion refers to the means of inflicting punishments of a physical, economic, or social sort as manifested through agents of violence, bureaucracy, and law.[3] State and society are distinct units of analysis, but there is no assumption that they are inherently autonomous. From its early modern emergence to its postmodern perseverance, the state has been sustained principally by its ability to lay claim to the power resources of capital and coercion. And so this study of postcommunist states takes its analytical cue from Charles Tilly, who stated simply that "various combinations of capital and coercion produced very different kinds of states."[4]

State building is about the accumulation of power resources. At one level, the general features of postcommunist state building appear to fit a familiar pattern. It involves the same set of interrelated processes that characterize state-building experiences in other historical periods and regional contexts: monopolizing violence, extracting revenue, administering territory, cultivating loyalty. Yet the postcommunist experience provides its own unique variation. It does not fit with the early modern pattern, associated with Western Europe, in which state builders incrementally extended their claims on the use of coercion and access to capital against the competing claims of societal actors, eventually consolidating the decentralized power structures of feudalism under the aegis of state-building monarchs while leaving intact an autonomous, property-based civil society.[5] In this process, ethnoregional identities and personal allegiances eventually were subsumed under an encompassing national identity attached to the modern state. Nor does it fit with the late modern pattern of state building, associated with postcolonialism, in which would-be state builders did not fully realize their claims on the use of coercion and access to capital against rival societal actors, and instead created power arrangements in which the public offices of the state either coexisted with or were penetrated by autonomous societal actors and regional "strongmen."[6] In this pattern, subnational identities, based on region, tribe, or religion, remained salient, while national identities proved ephemeral; political fidelity was more personal than institutional.

By contrast, the process of postcommunist state building begins with the state already in possession of an abundance of power resources in relation to society—the inheritance of the old regime. Communist states came as close as any modern states in history to realizing a monopoly on coercion and capital in their societies, hence the "totalitarian" designation they earned. They were, of course, much less successful in monopolizing normative resources, in cultivating loyalty, especially in those countries where communist regimes were propped up by Soviet Russia's iron glove. Deep-rooted national identities existed across much of Eastern Europe, but they were mostly detached from and antagonistic to the communist state. Because postcommunist states start out with this preponderance of power resources in relation to society, state builders did not have to make and realize claims on capital and coercion. Postcommunist society, meanwhile, was lacking in economic and coercive resources and remained in certain critical respects dependent on the state. Thus, postcommunist state building was not about the *accumulation*, but rather the *redistribution*, of power resources—between state and society and within the state itself.[7] In this sense, postcommunist state building is more a matter of state re-formation, or even society building, than it is about state building in the conventional historical sense.[8]

The redistribution of capital and coercion in postcommunist state building began during the breakdown phase of the old regime. The process was marked by conflict as state and societal actors made competing claims on the power resources amassed by the communist state. In some cases of regime breakdown, representatives of society through collective actions were able to break the state's unchecked monopoly over coercion and capital. In other cases, capital and coercion were traded within the state and between state and society as part of a negotiated settlement. In still other cases, capital and coercion were simply seized by renegade state or society-based actors. Ultimately, the malleable and protracted transition process led to the reconfiguration of capital and coercion into new institutional forms. As it turns out, there are not a lot of intermediate cases among the postcommunist states. The tendencies in the redistribution of capital and coercion reveal a predominance of two ideal-typical postcommunist states: "contractual" and "predatory."

In contractual states, the power resources of the old regime were redistributed and reconsolidated, and the boundary lines between state and society regarding coercion and capital were clearly marked. Coercion was tamed. The state's coercive resources were depoliticized and subordinated to institutional checks and civilian political control. As a consequence, capital was transformed. Economic resources were transformed into legally protected private property, and new sources of entrepreneurial wealth were created. Contractual states evolved with greater checks on political power, internally through institutional checks and balances and externally through legal mechanisms that protect society's autonomy. Finally, contractual states were more successful in establishing consolidated democratic political regimes.[9] By contrast, the predatory states had unchecked access to coercive resources. Coercion remained in the service of politics, while civilian control and legal constraints were ineffective and weak. As a result, capital was vulnerable to state predation. The boundary lines between public and private, and between state and society, were never clearly defined. Some economic resources were transformed into private property, but the most valued assets were instead made into economic concessions, which the state did not fully relinquish its claim to. In addition, predatory states evolved with fewer constraints on political power, internally through the rise of strong executives and externally through weak legal mechanisms. Finally, predatory states tended toward competitive authoritarian and neotraditional authoritarian regimes.[10]

Across the postcommunist realm, states in East Central Europe (ECE) and the Baltics more closely resemble the "contractual" state, while states in the former Soviet Union (FSU) more closely resemble the "predatory" state. ECE includes Poland, Hungary, the Czech Republic, and Slovakia. The FSU includes Russia, Ukraine, Belarus, Armenia, Georgia, Azerbaijan, and the Central Asian states. Although part of the FSU, the postcommunist Baltic states have evolved in a manner closer to the ECE states. Although part of the war-torn Balkans, Slovenia also resembles the ECE variant. In the early 1990s, these alternative state building trajectories were not so obvious. The outcomes were not predetermined by geography or history. In the first years, political power was fluid, and capital and coercion were yet to be organized in new arrangements. The ECE and FSU postcommunist states evolved in different ways through incremental and contested processes. The eventual institutional shape in each case was determined by the cumulative results of numerous political battles over the redistribution of capital and coercion, among actors within the state and between the state and society. The effort to build new systems of taxation was one of the crucial arenas of conflict in postcommunist state building.

A realist approach to the state assumes that power will inevitably find wealth. What power does to access wealth once it is found, however, is not inevitable. The history of the means by which power acquires wealth—plunder, tribute, rents, taxation—is the history of the rise of the modern state. And "fiscal sociology" is the study of the social implications of the means by which power acquires wealth. Following communism's collapse, power was forced to devise new means of accessing wealth, which, in turn, affected state-society relations. In this book I explain this process through a focused comparison of two cases, representing contrasting types of postcommunist states—Poland and Russia. Both Poland and Russia begin the transition from similar starting points: a political-economic institutional inheritance, a failed democratization from above, an incapacitating fiscal crisis, and radical policy reform. But they soon end up on different transition paths, leading to different postcommunist places: Poland constructs a rule-of-law-based state, a civil society, a consolidated democracy, and market capitalism; Russia reverts to a rule-by-law state, a dependent society, competitive authoritarianism, and crony capitalism. Fiscal sociology helps to explain this divergence by focusing attention on the battles between state and society over the redistribution of capital and coercion.

The book is organized into six chapters that illuminate the interconnected stages of the state-building process. The first chapter situates the study in the comparative social science literature on state building, the comparative politics of taxation, and postcommunist studies. It offers a critique of the neoliberal-influenced conceptualization of "the state," whose society-centered assumptions dominated postcommunist studies to the detriment of the early research agenda. As an alternative, the chapter elaborates a state-centered approach, which draws from Schumpeterian fiscal sociology and Tillyesque political development. Chapter 2 lays the empirical groundwork with a historical overview of the systemic fiscal crisis that triggered communism's collapse. Postcommunist state building starts amid fiscal crisis. The communist state effectively restructured its revenue base to gain direct access to societal wealth. Socialism's command economy is depicted as an industrial form of feudal-like rent-seeking. The Polish and Soviet states entered a fiscal abyss, formed by the old regime's attempt to sustain a reward-based political-compliance strategy with an economic system incapable of regenerating growth.

Chapter 3 focuses on the politics of tax reform. Why were some postcommunist states able to enact fundamental tax reform, while others were not? The initial conditions shaping tax reform were an inherited economic structure, regime-breakdown politics, and an early-transition fiscal crisis. Three rounds of tax reform in Poland and Russia are compared, showing that the degree of political contestation in each country determined the success or failure of tax reform. I go beyond the formal tax code to reveal the underlying informal revenue bargains. The new revenue claims of postcommunist states initially met societal resistance, which was overcome by revenue bargaining. Although revenue bargains helped the new states to survive early fiscal crises, they became enduring political constraints on the tax policy process. Revenue bargains embodied a mix of political, economic, and fiscal resources that were exchanged among select groups of state-societal actors. In Poland, a "state-labor" revenue bargain was crafted between public sector workers and public welfare recipients and the ex-communist social democrats, which became an embedded feature of domestic political competition. In Russia, a "state-elite" revenue bargain was formed between regional and economic elites and the ruling party of power, which lasted until the 1998 financial crash, after which it was forcibly broken. Revenue bargains, in turn, provided the foundation for transitional tax regimes.

Chapter 4 asks: Why do people pay taxes? It examines the way in which the state interacted with society in the transitional tax regime. The concept of tax regime goes beyond formal tax policy and informal revenue bargains to include the means of extraction and patterns of compliance. The Polish transitional tax regime was based on "legalistic consent." Here the means of revenue extraction were deliberately designed to protect capital from coercion. The formal limits on coercion in tax collection were well defined and well regulated. Bureaucratic and legal checks were built in to the system to guard against attempts to exceed those limits or to politicize tax collection. Even when it was apparent that tax evasion was on the increase, the greater concern was not to give too much power to tax enforcers. Society responded with widespread avoidance, violation of the spirit of the law while adhering to the letter of the law, but limited evasion, violation of both the spirit and letter of the law. Legalistic consent was a minimalist form of quasi-voluntary compliance. Russia's transitional tax regime was based on "bureaucratic coercion." The state's revenue agents were not effectively constrained by legal-institutional checks. Unlike Poland, the Russian state sought to build compliance through fear, rather than through consent. In response, society did not just engage in tax avoidance, but in widespread tax evasion by moving into the shadow economy. The 1998 fiscal collapse became the opportunity to bring together coercion and capital. When a former policeman, Vladimir Putin, became president, coercion became a more credible component of tax collection. Transitional tax regimes, in turn, directly influenced the institutional outcomes in the postcommunist transition.

Chapter 5 is a study of institutional performance, namely state fiscal capacity. For postcommunist states, the main fiscal challenge is to expand the narrow revenue base inherited from the command economy and develop new dependable sources of income. The contagion effects of two international financial crises twice put Polish and Russian fiscal capacity to the test. In the 1998 financial crisis of emerging markets, Polish state finances held firm because of a steady stream of income flowing into the state treasury. The Russian state, meanwhile, was still dependent on a narrow revenue base that was more lucrative, but less reliable. The state was forced to declare bankruptcy, renege on its debts, and devalue its currency. By contrast, when the 2008 global financial meltdown reached Eastern Europe, both Poland and Russia displayed sufficient fiscal strength to fend off a collapse of state finances, unlike most of their postcommunist neighbors. Chapter 6 is concerned with institutional outcomes, namely the reconfiguration of state-society relations. Taxation plays a decisive role in the process of redistributing power resources between state and society. In Poland, coercion was tamed and subordinated under the "rule of law," while capital was protected by private property in a "social-market economy." In addition, the legalistic-consent tax regime bolstered a societal basis for elite status, organizational capacity, and moral authority, which upheld a nascent "civil society." In Russia, coercion remained politicized and an instrument of "rule by law," while societal capital was exposed to state predation in a "concessions economy." Russia's bureaucratic-coercive tax regime undermined the societal basis for elite status, organizational capacity, and moral authority, which, in turn, perpetuated a "dependent society."

The materials to construct the case studies are drawn from an assortment of primary, secondary, and statistical sources. Indicators of tax collection, criminal enforcement, tax evasion, and compliance are collected from government agencies, economic policy institutes, and international financial organizations. Assessments of the actors and their motives are derived from public statements and written accounts, local press and mass media coverage, and political party and lobby group literature, supplemented by personal interviews. To gauge societal dispositions toward the state and tax policy, this book uses surveys conducted by government agencies, public opinion organizations, and social science barometer studies. Although this book includes a wealth of statistical material, it is very much a qualitative approach.

Postcommunist state building, more than anything else, is about the reconfiguration of capital and coercion. What happened to capital and coercion in the transition process dictated whether a postcommunist society was able to defend itself against the postcommunist state. In this book I illustrate this proposition through a focused comparison of the contrasting cases of Poland's "contractual" state and Russia's "predatory" state. By examining the cumulative results of numerous state-society revenue battles, the research findings show how microlevel political conflicts shape macrolevel institutional forms. To more fully understand the implications of this dynamic, this book employs a fiscal sociology approach that harkens back to Burke's taxing maxim; that is, the way in which a state collects taxes has a profound influence on the strength and character of both state and society.

TOWARD A FISCAL SOCIOLOGY
OF THE POSTCOMMUNIST STATE

The unexpected collapse of the communist regimes of Eastern Europe was an event not to be missed by social scientists. The once-feared Soviet Leviathan and its formidable totalitarian bloc crumbled into two dozen independent nation-states, rechristened the "ideal laboratory," wherein social science theories on markets and democracy could be applied. Most influential in this endeavor were neoliberal economists, behavioralists, and transitologists, none of whom made the state a central feature of analysis. Instead, they shared expectations about individual and elite behavior that rested on a "liberal" conceptualization of state and society. But early postcommunist reform experiments produced unantici-pated and disappointing results. Democracy was derailed, capitalism was cor-rupted, financial systems failed, and criminal rackets thrived. In the time it takes to publish a dissertation, scholarship on the postcommunist transition experi-enced an abrupt shift in focus. The ideal laboratory was closed, and the state was brought back in.

The second wave of postcommunist scholarship pointed to the "weak" state to explain Eastern Europe's wayward transition outcomes. But while scholars now agreed that a "strong" state was a necessary component in making markets, crafting democracy, and upholding the rule of law, they still disagreed over the principal sources of "weakness" of the postcommunist state. Was the state too accommodating, too avaricious, or just too inept? The real-life event that prompted a social science return to the postcommunist state was the 1998 financial crisis, which wreaked havoc on state finances across the region. Indeed, this event led some scholars to identify underdeveloped fiscal capacity as the

principal source of state weakness. From this observation emerged a lively literature on the comparative politics of the postcommunist tax state. It is upon this
foundation that this book builds a fiscal sociology framework. Fiscal sociology
was originally devised as a state-centered conceptual alternative to Marx and the
Market. Although long missing from contemporary social science, recent scholarly efforts have begun to elaborate a *neo*-fiscal sociology, which this book contributes to through a comparative case study of the postcommunist state.

Leviathan Once Lost, but Now Found: In Search of the Postcommunist State

In September 1993, as a newly minted PhD and visiting professor at Georgetown
University, I was invited to a meeting of Washington-area political scientists to
discuss the ongoing political crisis in Moscow, which had just turned violent.
A most reputable senior political scientist, though not a Russian specialist, clearly
exasperated by what he was hearing, pulled out a copy of the U.S. Constitution
and exclaimed: "Here is a constitution that works, all Russia needs to do is to
adopt it." In retrospect, this advice does not quite seem sufficient to have brought
resolution to Russia's protracted transition crisis, though implicit versions of this
point of view were entrenched in the first wave of postcommunist political and
economic scholarship; that is, the notion that a new set of institutions and rules
would promote new behavior by individual actors. It is a notion associated with
the "neoliberal" paradigm.   *new rules→ new behavior*

The collapse of communism fundamentally changed political life in Eastern
Europe as well as political science about Eastern Europe. Regional specialists
came in for harsh criticism for being too insulated by theoretical generalists, who
reorganized the research agenda of postcommunist studies. This scholarly regime
change incorporated the "neoliberal" paradigm.[1] It was delivered by neoliberal
economists and economics-influenced political scientists, whose policy and academic influence were ascendant in a moment of triumphant global capitalism.

The neoliberal paradigm contained several basic assumptions about human
nature, society, and the state: All humans possess similar desires and fears, and
are thus susceptible to similar incentives and threats. All humans are capable
of reasoning their way to actions that will realize their desires and minimize
their fears. Society is an aggregate of self-interested individuals, at least some of
whom figure out that their particular interests are better served through selective
associations, from which are derived both market and state. Because the market is driven by private interests, as opposed to the public interest-driven state,
it is a more efficient, and thus, a preferred form of association. Neoliberalism

neoliberal paradigm views

prefers a minimalist utilitarian state, which comprises politically neutral institutions charged with private conflict resolution and public safety.[2] The first wave of scholarship on the postcommunist transition assumed features of this worldview: individual rationality, blank-slate institutions, state-societal autonomy, and universal applicability.

The influence of neoliberalism is especially noteworthy, since the stakes were more than academic.[3] Early assessments of the postcommunist transition were based on assumptions of an ideal neoliberal state. The main concern was the creation of a conducive macro-setting for the market. The state was viewed as inherently antagonistic to the market, which could take care of itself. In 1993, Anders Aslund and a leading cast of neoliberal economist-advisers to Russia published a two-hundred-page collection of essays commenting on the initial progress of economic reform and discussing designs for the next phase; the role of the state consumed just three pages.[4] Similarly, in an early evaluation of Polish reforms, Jeffrey Sachs identified "five pillars of an economic transition to a market economy," including stabilization, liberalization, privatization, a social safety net, and Western economic aid. His analysis had no role for the state, although he cautioned that politics, in the form of "demagogues ready to seek political power by playing on the public's fears," posed the "hardest part of the transformation."[5]

According to the neoliberal script, the transition economy was supposed to follow a "U-curve," with a steep drop in production as the old state sector wilted, followed by a precipitous upturn as a new private sector blossomed.[6] But expectations for the spontaneous emergence of Western-like markets were dashed as economies in East Central Europe only slowly improved, the former Soviet Union languished in depression and financial collapse, and the war-wracked southern tier became a smugglers' paradise of black market banditry. Unleashing individual incentive in the service of market capitalism was a more complex task under postcommunist conditions than theoretical generalists had assumed. The neoliberal script needed a rewrite.

critique of neoliberalism

The critique of neoliberalism is now its own sizable literature, in four varieties: denial, repentance, vindication, and scorn. "Denial" is expressed by those who long insisted that, as messy as things might look, most of Eastern Europe had in fact constructed market capitalism. Growth and prosperity were being concealed by deliberately deflated economic statistics; any persisting problems were not due to neoliberal plans per se, but to the bad intentions of those who implemented them.[7] "Repentance" is expressed by economists who early on advocated macropolicy radical reform, only to later acknowledge its shortcomings in the absence of accompanying institutional and cultural support. "Vindication" is expressed by economists with area studies training, who were consistently skeptical that manipulations of macrolevel incentive structures would cause a shift in individual behavior, which cumulatively would lead to the emergence of market capitalism. "Scorn" is expressed by analysts who view Russia's neoliberal experiment as an imperialistic sham, which some of its leading academic proponents used to enrich themselves personally.[10]

The neoliberal autopsy on the socialist economy attributed the main cause of its miserable demise to state suffocation of society's natural economic inclinations. Thus, the disentangling of the state from the economy to uncover the suppressed markets within was the priority task of the transition. "Many economic problems solve themselves," assured Jeffrey Sachs. "Markets spring up as soon as central planning bureaucrats vacate the field."[11] But the departed communist state bequeathed more than just economic planners. The ideal neoliberal world may be one of butchers, bakers, and candlestick makers—those who create capital—but the real postcommunist world was one of cops, colonels, and racketeers—those who trade in coercion. History is replete with examples of demobilized agents of coercion who, once official political hostilities have ceased, managed to adapt their violent skills to unofficial economic activities. The end of the cold war brought one of the largest demobilizations in history, which was ignored because coercion was not an essential component in making markets in the neoliberal lexicon.[12] Coercion was not subordinated and tamed in a legal system. The coercive talent of the communist state did not fade away like an old soldier; instead, it became a defining feature of many transition economies in the region.[13] Postcommunist scholars who wanted to follow the lead of economists might have profited more from reading Schelling's cool appraisal of "criminal enterprise" than Friedman's warm praise of "free enterprise."[14]

The second wave of postcommunist scholarship was launched in reaction to the transition's deviant outcomes: reinvigorated authoritarianism, crony capitalism, criminal rackets, and social decline. These negative phenomena were blamed on a series of institutional weaknesses—contested laws, ineffective enforcement, broken bureaucracies. The tasks of the state, that is.[15] The second wave began with a scholarly consensus that an enfeebled state is not an asset, but a liability to a transition economy. Disagreement existed over the sources of state weakness, however. To explain postcommunism's wayward development, analysts compiled three competing conceptualizations of the postcommunist state: captured, incapable, and grabbing.[16]

In the second wave, the conceptual heir to the neoliberal state is the "captured state," in which the public powers of the state are in service to private interests.[17] From this perspective, the state is weak and society is strong, or at least a segment of society is strong. The state is effectively seized by special interests, who use its rule-making, administrative, and coercive agencies for their personal benefit, instead of for the public good. Accordingly, postcommunist reforms went awry when narrow cliques high-jacked the transition for their own selfish ends. The concept was inspired by the rise of the Russian "oligarchs" in the mid-1990s, a small group of newly rich business tycoons, whose political influence peaked during President Boris Yeltsin's wobbly second term. Curiously, the concept has endured, even though under President Vladimir Putin it seems increasingly clear that it is the "oligarchs" who have been captured, figuratively and literally. The concept was fundamentally flawed because of implicit "liberal" assumptions: first, its presumption that society-based capital was autonomous from the state; and second, its neglect of the enormous reserve of coercive resources possessed by the state. To be captured and to be for sale, as it turns out, are quite different situations.

Second, some scholars instead conceptualized an "incapable state," redirecting attention to issues of implementation, enforcement, and compliance.[18] From this view, both state and society were weak—disconnected and disorganized. The source of weakness was institutional underdevelopment, which caused postcommunism's dysfunction, disparities, and disappointments. The incapable state could not perform the most basic tasks associated with the modern state. Its claim as rule-maker was disputed. Its claim to monopolize the means of violence was challenged. And, its claim on society's resources was disregarded. Economic transactions were badly regulated, contract enforcement was in doubt, financial investments were vulnerable, and property rights were unsecured. Criminal protection rackets and private police forces supplanted the state's monopoly on coercion. Operating in an institutional void, state and societal actors fell back on survival strategies learned under the old regime: building patron-client networks. In so doing, personalistic practices of the past persisted and corrupted institutional development in the present.[19] The incapable state concept also underestimated the potential for state-directed coercion to shape institutional outcomes, and did not give enough credit to the actors themselves for their strategic, though incapacitating, choices.

The third concept is the state as "grabbing hand," as opposed to the market's "invisible hand."[20] From this view, the state was strong and society was weak. No shortage of coercion here. The grabbing state is part of an intellectual tradition that goes back at least as far as Machiavelli. Its contemporary "neorealist" incarnation fancies sinister-sounding metaphors: the state as predator, bandit, and racketeer.[21] This state was capable of making policy and setting rules with minimal interference from societal actors. Moreover, it maintained the infrastructural capabilities to implement policy and enforce the rules when it so desired. Postcommunism's protracted economic crisis was attributed to the state's resilient capacity for distortion and extortion through interventionist and regulationist forays. The state employed its coercive and rule-making powers to exact rents from the business sector. In so doing, it undermined market development by creating perverse incentives. To avoid the grabbing hand, transactions took cover in the shadow of the unofficial economy and investment capital sought safe haven beyond the state's reach. By manipulating the redistribution of resources, the state designated victors and losers in the transition economy. The problem of the grabbing state is not ineptitude, but its blatant disregard for the public good. It confiscates, coerces, and connives for its own advantage, with little regard for even its own rules. The main weakness of the grabbing state concept is that it sometimes exaggerates the capability and coherence of the postcommunist state.

Of course, there really is not one type of postcommunist state. Cross-national observation reveals varying degrees of capture, incompetence, and grabbiness, as well as efficiency, accountability, and service. Most analysts recognize that each of the above characterizations can be found in one place or another within any particular state's multiple spheres of activity. The state is not a single entity, nor is it Janus-faced. The state is a multifaceted institution, whose representative human agents often act at cross-purposes. What is called the state for the sake of analytical convenience is a complex organization riven with horizontal and vertical, external and internal, formal and informal cleavages. Each above conceptualization, however, highlights what is suspected to be the root political-institutional cause for postcommunism's divergent outcomes. On this point, this book leans decidedly toward a "realist" perspective, emphasizing the interaction of capital and coercion in the state-building process. Given that at the time of its collapse the communist state was flush with economic as well as coercive resources, it is surprising that early analysis of postcommunist transitions was so indifferent to the postcommunist state's unique inheritance of power resources. In this regard, it seems especially appropriate to invoke Charles Tilly's emphasis on capital *and* coercion, since so much of early transition scholarship turned out to be studies of capital *without* coercion.[22] And, nowhere in the state-building process do capital and coercion come together more often and with more lasting effect than in the area of taxation.

Return of the Fisc: Comparative Politics of the Postcommunist Tax State

During the first wave of postcommunist scholarship, the issue of taxation did not receive much attention from comparative political scientists; rather, the subject was confined to policy-oriented economists, whose findings tended to depict "incapable" states.[23] Then, in August 1998, the Russian state with much fanfare declared bankruptcy, setting off an economic and political crisis. "Power in the country is weak," lamented ousted vice premier Boris Nemtsov. "Power cannot collect taxes and cannot implement its own decisions."[24] The event refocused the attention of comparativists. The ensuing scrutiny of Russian state finances revealed a maladapted and malfunctioning system that rested on a pyramid scheme of short-term credit. Analysts quickly concluded that underdeveloped fiscal capacity was a contributing, if not the leading, cause of state weakness across Eastern Europe. Invoking Burke's taxing maxim, Thane Gustafson noted that "the less people pay, the weaker the government gets; and the weaker the government gets, the less people pay."[25] The financial crash spurred research advances into the postcommunist tax state, guided by a recent comparative politics revival of interest in the fisc.

In older scholarship comparative politics meant studying the formal institutions of government, thus state budgets and taxation were viewed as practical means of gaining insight into patterns of power and wealth in different countries.[26] This line of inquiry, however, became muted in midcentury American political science, where attention turned to interest group behavior and later to individual rational actors. Even when the state made its clamorous return to political science in the late seventies, it did not stir an immediate renewal of interest in taxation.[27] After a lengthy absence in comparative politics, the fisc returned to prominence. The continued interest of comparativists in the state has now yielded a substantial literature on the politics of taxation and fiscal capacity. This literature includes four distinct analytical approaches: political economy, political institutions, political culture, and political development.

The most influential works comprise a comparative *political economy* of taxation, which stresses an "exchange" between state and society. First, the state is conceptualized as a rational actor that seeks to secure access to revenue from society. Second, state actors are embedded in structures with societal actors, which serve as constraints on state strategies of revenue extraction. Third, given such constraints, revenue claims are realized through bargains in which targeted societal actors give up economic resources to the state in exchange for something valued, such as private property rights or political representation. Margaret Levi's seminal *Of Rule and Revenue* is still the most encompassing and nuanced analytical framework in comparative politics that explains taxation as a form of state-society exchange.[28] The political economy of taxation goes back at least as far as Montesquieu. It contends that an economic base rich in mobile assets, which can be moved or hidden, will force rulers to make concessions on political rights as part of a revenue bargain; by contrast, an economic base rich in fixed assets, which cannot be moved or hidden, will be more easily exploited by rulers without mutual consent or political concessions. From this premise, taxation explains the rise of modern democracy as well as the persistence of resource-cursed authoritarianism.[29] For postcommunism, the political economy approach was best represented in the work of Scott Gehlbach, who with methodical neatness investigated the economic structural determinants of tax policy across postcommunist states and explained the uneven distribution of public goods.[30]

Whereas the political economy approach looks for the political effects of revenue gathering, the *political institutions* approach sees things in reverse. These scholars emphasize power arrangements to explain differences in taxation patterns. Political competition is at the forefront of this analysis, as opposed to the economic rationalism in the political economy approach. In the words of Sven Steinmo, "the structure of a polity's decision-making institutions" explains variation in the distribution of tax benefits and burdens.[31] Three versions of the political institutions approach can be discerned: domestic politics, regime types, and international forces.[32] Postcommunist scholarship has produced several exemplary studies using a political institutions approach, including Anna Grzymala-Busse on political incentives for rent-seeking in East Central Europe, Dan Treisman on "perverse incentives" for tax collection caused by ill-defined federalism, and Hilary Appel on international institutional pressures on tax policy reform.[33]

A third approach is *political culture*, which stresses social identity and norms to explain variation in tax systems. Social identity suggests that paying taxes is a collective norm that is influenced by a sense of group belongingness and a desire to remain in good standing among peers. Evan Lieberman, for example, produced an innovative example of this approach with a comparison between race-based inclusive compliant Afrikaner elites in South Africa and region-based exclusive noncompliant Brazilian elites.[34] Other work has shown a positive correlation between sociocultural norms of civic duty and higher levels of tax compliance.[35] As yet, no Lieberman-like study of elite identity and taxation has been attempted for the postcommunist states. There is, however, a growing body of work on the "tax morale" of Eastern European citizenries, which shows that higher levels of social capital and trust are consistent with higher social norms of tax compliance. In these efforts, Marc Berenson has gone the furthest in elaborating the political implications of the findings to the comparative politics audience.[36]

Each of these approaches contributes to a better understanding of the postcommunist tax state. There are, however, several recurring analytical limitations: politics, crisis, coercion. First, anyone who has ever spent time studying tax systems quickly realizes that their subject refuses to stay still. Tax policy has an immediate effect on personal wealth, and therefore it is the object of constant political conflict and compromise over the allocation of the burden. Tax systems do not change only as a result of major legislative reform, but exist in a condition of perpetual transmogrification through less conspicuous acts of haggling with

[margin note: Fiscal crisis ↓ tax constraint]

officials and finagling with rules. This dynamic generally is not captured in the political economy and political culture approaches, which tend to gloss over the microlevel domestic politics that directly shapes macrolevel tax systems.[37] Second, the above approaches, especially political culture and political institutions, generally do not take into account the extraordinary constraint on tax policy caused by fiscal crisis. Yet crisis conditions had considerable influence on the initial efforts to create as well as to reform the new tax systems in the postcommunist states. Third, with some notable exceptions, the above approaches fail to incorporate coercion into the analysis.[38] Yet coercion is an essential element of all tax systems, even ones based on quasi-voluntary compliance. If you missed coercion in the analysis, then you probably got it wrong.

[margin note: Political development]

These particular shortcomings, however, are directly addressed in studies employing a _political development_ approach. Political development provides path-dependent, historical-institutional analysis of fiscal practices and institutional outcomes in particular states. The political development approach includes social scientists and historians, who are not strictly speaking comparative politics scholars, though their work is widely cited in comparative politics literature. Exemplary of this breed is Charles Tilly, whose "protection racket" model remains a syllabus staple in comparative politics.[39] Tilly explains the rise of the modern state as a political-institutional product of the interplay of the dual processes of raising revenue and making war. At the core of the political development approach is the notion that revenue enhances state strength, and strong states claim more revenue; or, as Gabriel Ardant put it, "each increase in the power of states was linked to an increased possibility of levying taxes."[40] The political development literature provides rich case studies that explain institutional variations among early modern states as a consequence of the efforts of capital-starved rulers to realize new tax claims on society, the implications of which remain relevant to contemporary would-be state builders.[41]

The present study of the postcommunist tax state is unique for elaborating a political development approach. In this framework, comparative investigation of the politics of taxation is embedded in a sociohistorical context, allowing for a deeper and wider perspective. As such, it helps to overcome the analytical shortcomings of the alternatives approaches. First, political development moves beyond political economy's state/society conceptual dichotomy, and is more directly focused on the goals and strategies of actors in the revenue process. Second, political development emphasizes the causal effects of fiscal crisis, the solutions for which create unintended political constraints on state actors and revenue-based path dependency that shape institutional outcomes. Finally, political development explicitly takes into account the interconnected relationship between coercion and capital as well as the political effects of consensus-based versus coercion-based tax regimes. With its emphasis on historical-institutional framing and sociopolitical context, the political development approach is akin to that of fiscal sociology.

Toward a Fiscal Sociology of the Postcommunist State

The origin of fiscal sociology is associated with a pair of Austrian economists, the well-known Joseph Schumpeter and the not so well-known Rudolf Goldscheid, who watched and wrote as Central Europe's traditional world of empire and aristocracy gave way to the modern forces of nationalism and capitalism.[42] They saw fiscal sociology as an approach that could reconcile the distinct but interrelated ways in which political-institutional and sociocultural factors influenced one another as part of a larger process of historical change.[43] They resisted liberal market-based as well as socialist class-based conceptualizations of the state. Instead, they worked in the "continental" intellectual tradition, where the state could be an actor unto itself and state-society relations were not unilateral, but interactive.

In Schumpeter's enduring essay, "The Crisis of the Tax State," he provided the analytical contours of fiscal sociology. He started by giving credit to Goldscheid for being "the first to broadcast the truth" that "the budget is the skeleton of the state stripped of all misleading ideologies."[44] From this premise, Schumpeter drew a historical sketch of the transition from the feudal prince to the modern state, stressing the dynamic role of fiscal developments. Schumpeter began with feudalism's fiscal crisis of princely rule, which resulted from the declining ability of the manorial economy to meet escalating revenue demands caused by warfare and self-indulgence. The process of change was incremental—the feudal prince does not set out to destroy feudalism. The prince invented and operated the apparatus of a protostate to encourage and exploit private enterprise. There subsequently emerged two parallel realms, a private economy and public authority, interpenetrated by a fiscal system. Initially the instrument of feudal princes, the state apparatus eventually became autonomous and brought unintended consequences, namely the reordering of society from a collective to an individual basis, ultimately destroying feudalism. "We have seen," Schumpeter stated, "that without financial need the immediate cause for the creation of the modern state would have been absent."[45] The essay concluded by suggesting that the modern tax state, exhausted by the revenue demands of the Great War, was itself in crisis.[46]

Even though Schumpeter relocated to American academia, fiscal sociology was overtaken by rival trends in American social science. The grand-scale

Schumpeterian fiscal model of historical change was not part of the discussion. The study of taxation passed into the domains of public finance[47] and development economics.[48] In the 1970s, neo-Marxists appropriated Schumpeter's conceptual themes in premature anticipation of capitalism's demise.[49] The renewal of interest in the state in the 1980s led some social scientists back to Schumpeter.[50] With adherents scattered across disciplines and continents, however, the field of fiscal sociology still "remained in its infancy."[51] Now a *neo*-fiscal sociology has begun to take shape, with Schumpeter's essay as the obligatory point of departure.[52] But as Mick Moore rightly noted, the essay offers a kind of macrohistorical paradigm or, more simply, "a way of looking at things," rather than a conceptually tight framework for comparative research.[53] It constructs a conceptual framework that suggests a sequence of causality, but the explanatory particulars remain case specific. Given its multiple stages of interactive causal inferences, this approach is simply too messy for at least some contemporary social scientists. Rather than providing theoretical parsimony, fiscal sociology embraces empirical clutter, but on the assumption that you can't get your theory tight until your case study's right.

What precisely is entailed in a fiscal sociology of the postcommunist state?[54] Schumpeter's model is both historically sweeping and analytically unwieldy. This book recognizes the limits in devising a model that can capture it all, and therefore sets a more modest agenda. I elaborate a four-part state-building process that includes (1) initial conditions; (2) politics of revenue bargains; (3) transitional tax regimes; and (4) institutional outcomes.

Initial conditions include three particular features of the institutional inheritance of the old regime: the crisis of state finances, the structure of capital, and the disposition of coercion. First, following Schumpeter, we start with fiscal crisis. Empty coffers, exhausted credit, and overdue debt lead some communist rulers down uncharted political paths in search of revenue, which instead lead to regime breakdown. Postcommunist states emerged amid fiscal crisis. While budget deficits are a characteristic feature of a transition economy, they do not in themselves indicate a fiscal crisis. A fiscal crisis exists when budgetary expenses exceed income, alternative sources of revenue are unavailable, and the ability to borrow is exhausted. The fiscal crisis of the postcommunist state derives from three sources: the enfeebled fiscal-administrative structure of the old regime, the budgetary politics of regime breakdown, and the fiscal traps of economic restructuring. In postcommunist transitions, fiscal crises typically begin to unfold at the outset of the reform process. At this point, these three factors converge to cause a rapid revenue shortfall, threatening to destabilize the transition economy and bankrupt the postcommunist state. But there are degrees of need, and not all the postcommunist states begin the transition in a full-blown fiscal crisis. The need to steady state finances was more urgent in Poland and the Soviet Union, for example, than it was in Czechoslovakia and Hungary. The degree of urgency, in turn, affected the early strategic decisions of policymakers regarding the allocation of the tax burden and the granting of economic concessions or political rights.

2 Second, the structure of the economy is a critical initial condition. Postcommunist states start out revenue-dependent on a small number of large enterprises. The command economy concentrated economic activity in industrial complexes in order to facilitate planning and management. Postcommunist state builders face the challenge of expanding the base through the cultivation of new revenue sources, and the need to refurbish the fiscal-administrative apparatus designed for the command economy. But within this general structural constraint, particular variations existed concerning the location of revenue in transition economies. In some countries, capital was concentrated, while in others it was dispersed. It was generated by a quasi-private sector in some countries, and by the public sector in others. In Poland and Hungary, for example, the revenue base lacked significant income-generating enterprises, although it did include an already established and growing private sector of small businesses. By contrast, the revenue base in Russia and Kazakhstan lacked a developing small-business private sector, but it did contain very lucrative income sources in the energy and metallurgy export sectors.

3 Third, the disposition of state coercion was an institutional inheritance, influencing the initial conditions. Although the particular way in which coercion is practiced in the postcommunist states is mostly sorted out as part of the politics of the transition phase, this outcome is strongly influenced by events during the breakdown phase. Notable here is whether old regime elites or new counterelites, who each bring different experiences and inclinations about coercion, end up occupying positions of power in the postcommunist state.[55] Variant elite configurations affected the reorganization of state coercive resources. In places where old regime elites prevailed, such as Russia, Belarus, and the nations of Central Asia, state coercive resources tended to be placed under executive control with weak political-institutional checks; in places where counterelites prevailed, such as Poland, Hungary, and the Czech Republic, state coercive resources tended to be subjected to parliamentary control with stronger institutional checks.

These initial conditions are the inheritance of the old regime. They will constrain political maneuvering and policymaking early on. They are by no means insurmountable, imposing an inevitable transition destiny of democracy or despotism. But their influence is weighty and needs to be accounted for, especially regarding the fiscal strategies of postcommunist state builders. In particular, the variations in initial conditions directly shaped the particular makeup of the revenue bargains, which arose from the adoption of tax policy reforms for the transition economies.

Politics of revenue bargains refers to the exchange of political and economic re-sources among discrete sets of state and societal actors related to the distribution of the tax burden. What potential revenue sources are available in the transition economy? Who stands between them and the state? And what power resources can be mobilized to prevent the state from taking them? The model for new postcommunist tax systems was borrowed from the advanced market economies, which evolved incrementally, often with sustained challenges, over the course of a century. The new revenue claims made by postcommunist states likewise provoked societal resistance, threatening political conflict and fiscal crisis. As a result, revenue bargains were struck between the postcommunist state and soci-ety. Revenue bargains helped to bring about political peace and provided states with income. We use the term bargain in a broad sense. Revenue bargains were not negotiated at one defining moment or even in one forum; rather, they were pieced together incrementally, the product of the outcomes of a series of interac-tions, both confrontational and cooperative, between state and society over taxes, wealth, and the transition economy.

Revenue bargains arose from a political process, wherein competing economic interests sought to influence tax policymaking, the distribution of the tax bur-den, and the means of tax collection. Societal tax resistance was reconciled in the different arenas of political conflict, including elections, lobbying, protests, and noncompliance. In this way, revenue bargains became entwined with patterns of political competition. In places where elite consensus existed over the broad parameters of political and economic reform, such as in Poland and Hungary, political competition tended to be channeled into election campaigns, providing the opportunity for fiscal populists to influence tax policy. In places where elite conflict persisted over the basic direction of the transition, such as in Russia and Ukraine, the patterns of political competition tended to create an opportunity for corporate and regional elites to exert greater control over tax policy. Even if intended only as short-term solutions, revenue bargains often became an endur-ing political constraint, giving shape to transitional tax regimes.

Transitional tax regime includes three elements: tax policy, the means of ex-traction, and patterns of compliance. First, tax policy refers to official legislation that sets tax rates, assigns tax obligations to individual and corporate actors, and allows for special exemptions and tax relief. Tax policy entails the distributional effects of political power: Who in society is saddled with the tax burden and who receives special privileges to avoid the burden? Second, the means of extraction refers to the administrative infrastructure of state finances. In order to locate, claim, and collect revenue, postcommunist states had to establish new systems of monitoring and extraction that could operate across the different realms of a transition economy. Was there institutional coherence or fragmentation in the

conduct of state finances? Was the administrative-bureaucratic structure of revenue flows centralized or decentralized? What was the skill level and professional
ethos of the state's tax collectors? Third, patterns of compliance refer to the strategies employed by the state to realize its revenue claims on society as well as to
society's response to these efforts. Tax compliance strategies differed across the
postcommunist states. In East Central Europe, for example, the Czech Republic
and Poland offered the exchange of revenue for public goods; while the former
Soviet Union, Russia and Ukraine raised the coercive risk of evasion.

The notion of a "transitional" tax regime draws attention to the special circumstances of the postcommunist states. It may be true that no tax system is
fixed, but instead is subject to constant incremental change, including those in
the market economies of the West. The tax regimes of the postcommunist states,
however, were created practically from scratch. The opportunities for political wrangling and the amount of administrative learning were considerable by
comparison. The variant tax regimes observable across Eastern Europe can be
distinguished into two broad types: consent-based and coercion-based. In turn,
transitional tax regimes directly influenced the divergent macroinstitutional outcomes of the postcommunist transitions.

Institutional outcomes include two types: performance and form. Institutional
performance in this case refers to state fiscal-administrative capacity. In the modern state, the basic elements of fiscal capacity have not changed much over time:
currency, credit, and, at the foundation, income. If a state develops sufficient
and reliable sources of income, then it is more likely to have good credit and a
stable currency. For postcommunist states, however, the need to break out of the
inherited constraints of a narrow revenue base and weak tax administration to
enhance income potential was a formidable challenge. To gauge fiscal capacity,
Eastern Europe's postcommunist states were tested on two occasions, in 1998 and
in 2008, when international financial crises moved across the region, causing a
run on foreign capital. Those states whose transitional tax regimes managed to
overcome inherited constraints and to cultivate new income sources were most
likely to survive these events without succumbing to fiscal crisis.

Institutional form refers to the organization of power resources. Postcommunist state building is not about the accumulation of power resources, but rather
about their redistribution. The process entails the reconfiguration of capital and
coercion in new institutional forms, redefining the boundary line between state
and society. The process is driven by cumulative outcomes of numerous political conflicts over capital and coercion that are waged by actors within the state
and between the state and society. Conflicts involving transitional tax regimes
were especially influential in determining the forms in which capital and coercion were reconsolidated. Out of this process emerged two distinctive types of

postcommunist state: <u>contractual and predatory.</u> In contractual states, coercion was tamed by the rule of law and capital was protected by private property. In predatory states, coercion was an instrument of rule by law, while capital was vulnerable to political power. In general, postcommunist states in East Central Europe (ECE) and the Baltics more closely resemble the "contractual" state, while states in the former Soviet Union (FSU) more closely resemble the "predatory" state. Moreover, the "contractual" ECE states have been more successful at building consent-based state-society relationships, while the "predatory" FSU states rely more on coercion-based state-society relationships.

Eastern Europe's variant transitional tax regimes directly led to variant state-building outcomes. This is not to argue that conflicts over new revenue claims were the only influence on postcommunist states. Other factors, such as geography, culture, and society, also contributed to the process. I do not take a naive view, for example, that if Russia had tried harder to establish a personal income tax in the 1990s, then it would have been a consolidated democracy in the 2000s. However, the success or failure to construct effective checks on coercive power and to formalize private property rights, determined in political battles over taxation, stand out as perhaps the most crucial developments in the reconfiguration of power resources between state and society. In this way, fiscal sociology potentially offers a more comprehensive and more insightful framework than the alternative analytical schemes for understanding the origin and character of the postcommunist state.

THE FISCAL CRISIS OF
THE OLD REGIME

The English Civil War, the American War of Independence, and the French Revolution are among the featured episodes adorning the syllabus of Western Civ, and they all have one thing in common—*fiscal crisis*. To be clear: fiscal crisis did not create these illustrious upheavals, but it was the instigating cause that set in motion a sequence of events that led to the dramatic demise of an established order. Many regimes experience fiscal crisis and survive. But broken regimes—that is, political power arrangements wherein institutions can no longer contain social antagonisms and legitimating symbols have lost emotive appeal—are especially vulnerable to fiscal crisis. To this list add the Collapse of Communism.

Looking back, if the communist regimes of Eastern Europe were to endure, they would have had to overcome two entwined dilemmas of rule. First, how do you get people to go along with the Communist Party's monopolistic claim on political power? Second, how do you get the command economy to regenerate economic growth? The first dilemma is the classic question of political compliance. All systems of political authority must devise ways to legitimate their rule, drawn from a combination of three distinctive strategies: coercion, reward, belief. In Stalin's time, coercion figured prominently as a communist compliance strategy, as an unchecked and well-armed political police force terrorized society, as well as state elites. With Stalin's successors, communist regimes scaled back coercion, moving from arbitrary lethal terror to predictable thuggish oppression. They delicately dabbled with alternative, normative-based compliance strategies. But "national communism" and "humane socialism" proved untenable, going beyond the parameters of imperial acceptability and prompting full-scale

displays of more sinister coercion. In the end, Eastern Europe's communist regimes settled on the promise of a better standard of living, that is, reward-based
compliance strategies, epitomized by Hungary's "goulash communism."

The second dilemma of rule involved the command economy. It is routinely
noted that the command economy was riddled with inefficiencies and disincen-
tives. True enough. It is rarely mentioned that the command economy could do a
few things well. Putting aside the matter of means, the command economy built
the foundations of industrial society in rapid fashion, outperformed the Nazi
German war machine in World War II, and sent the first satellite into space. Yet, the
same economy that put a rocket on the moon had trouble moving a potato twenty
miles. The command economy was good at realizing big state-directed industrial projects; it was bad at satisfying basic society-driven consumption needs. In
order to maintain an expansive bureaucratic-coercive apparatus and satisfy mass
consumer expectations, the communist state needed economic growth. But the
rigidly centralized and tightly interconnected design of the command economy
left little room for manipulation, experimentation, or innovation. There was no
creative destruction in the command economy, only bureaucratic stultification.
And here is where communist Eastern Europe's twin dilemmas of rule met: What
is the fate of a political regime that employs a reward-based compliance strategy
if it rests on an economy incapable of regenerating growth? Welcome to Poland.

Stalin once said that imposing the Soviet command economy on Poland would
be like fitting a saddle to a cow. He did so anyway, and proved himself right. The
collapse of communism began in Poland, where persistent protest politics at last
compelled the Communist Party to relinquish monopoly rule. Poland's political
breakthrough inspired oppositionists across East Central Europe and the Baltics
to take up movement politics against moribund regimes, which in an accelerat-
ing swirl of events culminated in the collapse of communism. To be sure, the
collapse was rooted in long-term, multilayered structural decline; however, the
precipitating cause that sparked 1989's revolutionary conflagration was the fiscal
crisis of the Polish communist state.

The process was familiar to students of revolution: a bankrupt old regime in
a desperate bid to gain revenue makes limited political concessions to societal
actors who possess capital; and, using this political leverage, newly empowered
actors succeed in usurping the authority of the old regime.[1] King Charles and
King Louis called their legislatures into session for the express purpose of securing access to more revenue, but the maneuver instead became the fatal first step
on a path that led political rivals to seize power and royal heads to roll.[2] Late
communist experiments in limited democratization followed a similar path. Poland's Roundtable Accords and Russia's New Union Treaty were contemporary
counterparts to Britain's Long Parliament and France's Third Estate, marking the

critical moment when would-be usurpers were legitimately empowered by the same political authorities that they soon would overthrow. And, like their historical counterparts, Eastern Europe's communist regimes by the 1980s were broken, and thus vulnerable to fiscal crisis.

The origin of the fiscal crisis of the communist state was in its partly modern, partly feudal command economy. By design, the command economy was an industrial *demesne* political economy. Before the capitalist revolution, the demesne was those manorial lands and enterprises directly owned by the lord.[3] The feudal lord was a premodern political figure who also embodied legal and economic power. The property rights of the lord were superior to all, and they empowered the lord to claim revenue and service from those who lived and worked therein. The demesne properties generated surpluses for reinvestment in the lord's personal household, ruling court, and warrior retinue. Feudalism's demesne economy shared several key features with the modern command economy. Political power and economic wealth were not separate, but coterminous, except that industrial workers and scientific-technical specialists replaced tenant farmers and skilled craftsmen. Political power, economic activity, and social life were not distinct areas of existence, but rather were integrated as organic wholes. Political and economic needs compelled society to be organized into discrete collective bodies, which defined roles and conferred status on individuals. The command economy particularly resembled a demesne economy in capital and coercion: corvée-like forced labor of the peasantry; diminished role of money and reliance on barter, and economic surpluses reinvested into war-making.[4]

Through the command economy, the communist state devised a system of revenue extraction that effectively adapted the rent-seeking practices of early modern agricultural-based autocracy with a late modern industrial-based society. In terms of classifying systems of revenue extraction, demesne-style rent-seeking differs fundamentally with capitalist-style modern taxation: (1) property ownership—politically owned versus privately owned means of wealth; (2) organization of means of production—corporate-organized versus market-organized units of production; and, (3) state-society fiscal relationship—indirect fiscal relations with society through collective intermediaries versus direct fiscal relations with society through individual households and enterprises. The limits of the communist state's revenue strategy would become glaringly apparent when confronted with the twin dilemmas of rule.

Extra! Extra! Superstructure Bites Base

Communist societies were among the most heavily taxed in the world, although the ways by which communist states extracted revenue concealed the crushing fiscal burden. Ironically so, since radical socialists going back to Karl Marx consistently advocated transparent taxation, so that the workers could more clearly see the repressive social effects of the capitalist state's fiscal practices. Radical socialism first came to power in Russia, which had its own particular fiscal problems. The country was a latecomer to industrialization, and the tsars long relied on rents from agriculture and raw materials for revenue, preferring to interact with society through centralized collective bodies. The efforts of modernizing ministers to create a modern tax system, whereby the state would directly engage entrepreneurs and households, did not get far. When the Bolsheviks took charge, they too found it hard to raise revenue for their ambitious history-making agenda. The postrevolutionary state lacked the capacity to locate and claim revenue in a mixed-market peasant economy. The Bolshevik solution was to go back to collecting rents from the properties of the realm, but this was a very different kind of realm than that of the tsars. Rather than build a system of modern taxation, the communist state molded a new type of industrial economy from which it could directly extract revenue. The Bolsheviks turned Marxism upside down: the superstructure transformed the base.

Karl Marx was unambiguous on the subject of taxation: "Taxes are the source of life for the bureaucracy, the army, the priests and the court, in short, for the whole apparatus of executive power. Strong government and heavy taxes are identical."[5] He railed against indirect taxes on commodities as a bourgeoisie-imposed burden on the proletariat and the poor. "The modern fiscal system," he wrote in *Das Kapital*, is formed from "taxes on the most necessary means of subsistence, thereby increasing their price. Over-taxation is not an accidental occurrence, but rather a principle."[6] Thus, the transition from capitalism to socialism must be facilitated by a direct, progressive, and steep income tax. This recommendation was repeated by his leftist disciples. Austrian Marxist economist Rudolf Hilferding, in one of twentieth-century socialism's most influential works, *Finance Capital*, reaffirmed that under capitalism "taxes are borne mainly by the workers."[7] Rosa Luxemburg, in a widely cited essay, *The Accumulation of Capital*, wrote that "indirect taxes extorted from the workers are used for paying the officials and for provisioning the army, meaning that the workers rather than the capitalists were made to pay for the personal consumption of the hangers-on of the capitalist class and the tools of their class-rule."[8] And, Russian Bolshevism's leading economic theorists, Nikolai Bukharin and Evgeny Preobrazhensky, described the bourgeois state as "a huge mass of individuals who never produced so much as a bushel of wheat," living off the "surplus value of the workers and peasants in the form of taxation."[9] When socialism finally came to power, however, the appeal of indirect taxation proved strong.

Marx was certainly wrong about one thing: socialist revolutions were not likely to occur in the late stages of capitalism, but in the early stages. Imperial Russia was a latecomer to capitalism and industrialization. The tsars long subsisted on rents collected from the properties of the realm, in an enduring feudal-style demesne economy. In the late medieval period, the tsars claimed ownership of the vast northern forest, profiting from furs and other woodland commodities.[10] In Russia, almost any wealth-generating enterprise—market stalls, manufacturer shops, mining operations—was owned and "rented" as royal property. Early modern Russian state building was whipped forward by Peter the Great, whose avaricious revenue demands led to taxes on bricks, bathhouses, and beards. Peter's most important fiscal act, however, was to impose a direct "soul" tax on the adult male population, most of whom were peasants. To assure that the peasants would continue to provide income, the tsars took away their freedom and bound them to a fixed location, giving their lords the legal right and economic incentive to keep track of them. This serf-based manorial economy, where tsar played overlord to the landed gentry and wealth was extracted from agricultural production and peasant labor, served as the revenue base of the imperial administration for two centuries.[11]

But collecting taxes in Russia's far-flung empire proved no easy task. To overcome the challenge of monitoring and enforcing revenue claims across a vast territory with dense forests and open frontiers, the state center relied on a system of collective responsibility, in which community revenue quotas were collected by local elites, operating between the broad constraints of threat of punishment from above and opportunity for self-enrichment from below.[12] The state also derived income from its control of production and sale of life's basic necessities—salt, sugar, and alcohol. The fiscal system of rents, however, was at last exhausted by the demands of industrialized warfare.[13] In 1814, the Russian army pushed Napoleon's *grande armee* all the way back to Paris; in 1854, it was being pushed around by the French and British on the Crimean Peninsula. Henceforth, to fight the wars of the modern age, the autocracy would need modern armies and weapons, and modern revenue sources to pay for it.

From the 1880s, the government included a succession of savvy ministers—Nikolai Bunge, Sergei Witte, Pyotr Stolypin—who sought to modernize Russian state finances.[14] They acquired the bureaucratic accessories of modern state finance, a state bank and a finance ministry.[15] They attempted to restructure state-society fiscal relations by way of a modern tax system. In the countryside, the fiscal burden on the peasantry shifted from soul tax to sales tax.[16] Further agricultural reforms sought to generate wealth by promoting smallholding, profit-motivated peasant farms. The reform may have prompted a boost in productivity among better-off peasant households, but the top-heavy state apparatus lacked the capacity to collect its share. In the urban areas, the government had a bit more luck introducing a modern income tax and consumption-based excise taxes, targeting the nascent commercial, middle, and worker classes. Indirect customs and excise taxes eventually accounted for 80 percent of the tsar's total revenue take.[17] The state vodka monopoly provided as much as one-third of the revenue collected by the imperial treasury.[18] By bringing state and individual directly together, these fiscal reforms threatened to undermine Russia's long-standing estate-based social hierarchy, and so they were resisted by the guardians of the old order, the nobility and clergy. On the eve of war and revolution, tsarist "fiscal practice," as described by one historian, "was a regime of compulsion tempered by the bureaucracy's recognition of its own ignorance."[19] When the tsarist autocracy finally fell, it was bankrupt.

Vladimir Lenin suggested that "the best way to crush the bourgeoisie was to grind them between the millstones of taxation and inflation." Upon taking power, the Bolsheviks put this proposition to the test.[20] They imposed confiscatory taxes that stripped bare the wealthy. In December 1917 the government enacted a direct tax on the profits of trade and manufacturing enterprises as well as on the income of industrialists, applied at high rates with harsh sanctions for noncompliance. It did not stop there: bank accounts were broken into, and properties were seized and sold off. Only when there was nothing left to grab did Lenin suggest building a more conventional tax system, "a regular and constant collection of property and income taxes that would bring the greatest returns to the proletarian state."[21] But these taxes proved nearly impossible to collect, especially from peasants and workers. The government next announced an "Extraordinary Revolution Tax" that was supposed to whoop up ten billion rubles worth of proletarian enthusiasm, but it mustered less than a billion instead.[22] Without revenue to support a regime, now entrenched in civil war, the Bolsheviks turned on the printing press and flooded the market with paper money. The new Soviet notes quickly became worthless, and caused demonetarization. By October 1920 the purchasing power of the ruble was less than 1 percent of what it had been in October 1917.[23] Society turned to barter and black markets to survive; the state resorted to requisitioning, and even refused to accept its own currency for tax payments.[24] The policy of fiscal desperation lasted until the end of the civil war.

Victorious in political revolution, Bolshevik ambitions were redirected to industrial revolution. To accomplish this, the proletarian state opted for a bourgeois strategy. It would raise investment capital by encouraging a little capitalism. In April 1921, the Soviet government announced the New Economic Policy (NEP). "We must do everything possible to develop trade at all costs," Lenin explained. "We must not be afraid of capitalists."[25] The Bolsheviks now tried what the tsarist government had previously tried, and failed to do—to secure state finances to a modern revenue base of private business and household incomes. The Bolshevik plan was to encourage private actors—manufacturers, retailers, traders—to start profit-making enterprises. Individual incentive would facilitate economic growth. The state would then create a new revenue source by taxing the profits of business activity. Of course, the main source of wealth in postrevolutionary Russia was still agriculture. The NEP introduced an obligatory tax-in-kind on peasant villages, beyond which individual peasant households could sell their surplus harvest in open markets for profit. The government wagered that a stratum of go-getter peasants would seize the opportunity to become rich. They would create a rising pool of wealth in the countryside, which state tax collectors could draw from.[26] In addition, the government invited foreign capitalists to invest in the socialist state, believing that inherent bourgeois greed would overcome ideological taste.

The introduction of the NEP brought the restoration of a money-based economy and the resumption of commercial activity.[27] The Bolshevik state, however, was incapable of making any credible commitment to entrepreneurs and investors. The state bureaucracy created a multiplicity of business categories, and a multiplicity of tax rates and regulations to go with them. The tax burden on NEP entrepreneurs grew heavier throughout the decade, killing what little incentive existed to comply with state revenue claims. So many rules and rates created ample opportunity for tax avoidance.[28] Meanwhile, in the countryside, peasants reported paltry harvests when paying the tax-in-kind, but appeared with bulging sacks at the profitable farmers' markets. The tax administration was overwhelmed by the connivance of taxpayers and the complexity of tax policy. It did not help either that many tax inspectors were corrupt and drunk.[29] The situation was exacerbated by the lack of loans and investment from abroad. Having contemptuously repudiated all tsarist-era debts and seized foreign-owned factories, the Bolsheviks found that the reopening of the economy brought only a dribble, and not the expected flood, of foreign capital.

The fiscal premise of the NEP was to skim wealth from private actors through taxation, which would be reinvested in state-managed development. But the state's revenue take from commercial activity could not cover the costs of industrial investment.[30] Further, a main source of revenue during the NEP was excise taxes, which was rather embarrassing in light of socialism's harsh critique of capitalism's reliance on indirect taxation.[31] And, even more troubling, the proletarian state was fiscally dependent on the peasantry. Between 1923 and1927, the agricultural tax accounted for nearly half of total revenues collected for the state budget.[32] The limits of NEP revenue extraction were especially exposed in the 1928 grain procurement crisis.[33]

Taxation troubles set off a rancorous rift in the proletarian party: Why was the state still too poor to build socialism? The debate focused on the principal source of wealth in postrevolutionary Russia—agriculture—and the uneasy coexistence between proletarian state and peasant society.[34] The gist of the debate was whether more revenue could be raised through material incentives or physical compulsion. The pro-NEP side argued: Remember what peasant rebellion did to the tsarist regime, remember what the peasants almost did to us at the end of the civil war; we can assure political peace and raise the revenue necessary for industrialization as long as we provide economic incentive for peasants to comply. The anti-NEP side countered: Remember what peasant rebellion did to the tsarist regime, remember what the peasants almost did to us at the end of the civil war; we will never have political peace and we will never raise the revenue necessary for industrialization as long as we refrain from forcing peasants to comply. In 1925, the pro-NEP side was ascendant, when Bukharin urged the peasants to "enrich themselves." In the late 1920s, two successive years of bad harvests and lower-than-expected grain collections tipped the party faithful toward Stalin and the anti-NEP position. Rates and penalties were pushed upward not for the purpose of collecting revenue, but for confiscating property and destroying the private sector.[35] The brief experiment with modern taxation was over; the Bolshevik state was about to return to the long-favored revenue strategy of Russian rulers—rents.

In 1929, the Soviet government launched the "Great Breakthrough," a state-directed campaign of radical economic reform that was supposed to lead society to the socialist epoch. The irony was that the state's revenue strategy to support its futuristic campaign was derived from the past. The modernish taxation-based revenue strategy of the NEP was abandoned. Taxation stopped being used as a means to raise revenue, and instead became an instrument of expropriation and destruction. The dwindling ranks of private traders were decimated by aggressive new revenue demands. Instead of modern-style taxation, the emerging command economy featured a feudal-style rent-based revenue strategy. Economic activity was concentrated in a relatively small number of sprawling industrial conglomerates. In this way, state economic planners might have the chance to track the flow of capital in a rapidly industrializing economy, from investment to output, from surplus to reinvestment, from production to consumption. Through the command economy, the communist state forcibly restructured its own revenue base, so that it could directly access the economic wealth generated by society.

Taxation and the Command Economy

The Soviet command economy was an alternative path to industrial development, by which the state assumed near total responsibility for economic activity in society. The role of taxation in the command economy differed in key

aspects from taxation in capitalist states. Like capitalism, taxation was the economic means that supported the political, coercive, legal, and administrative
organs of the state. Unlike capitalism, taxation was also the principal means of
accumulating investment capital for economic development. The formal tax
system in the command economy served mainly as a financial-administrative
complement of industrial planning. The central state's phalanx of fiscal planners
struggled mightily to balance investment demands and military capacity with
consumption needs and political stability.

To accompany Stalin's state-driven industrial revolution, in 1930 a major tax
reform was enacted. The reform dismantled the NEP tax regime, as the private
sector shrank as a source of revenue. Individual state firms, meanwhile, were assigned to collective industrial associations, whose responsibilities included tax
collection for the state budget.[36] The 1930 reform introduced two new taxes for
the rapidly expanding state sector: turnover and profits.[37] These taxes were used
by central planners to capture excess capital for reinvestment elsewhere. The
turnover tax was a sales tax on enterprises, applied usually at the point of production. The initial attempt to simplify and consolidate turnover tax rates did not
last long; by decade's end fiscal bureaucrats had created more than a thousand
different rate categories. The profits tax applied to all state enterprises, with most
firms subject to high rates of 80 percent or more. Over time, profit tax rates were
modified, and firm managers were allowed to negotiate for even lower rates as an
incentive to boost productivity. The turnover and profits taxes formed the fiscal
foundation of the Soviet state; by the mid-1930s they combined to cover more
than three-fourths of all taxes collected.[38]

The main source of capital for the Soviet state before World War II was still the
agricultural sector. Hence, state tax policies reflected an extreme "urban bias" by
placing a severe fiscal burden on the peasantry.[39] After the unsuccessful experiment with peasant markets during the NEP, the government briefly employed a
"contract" system with collectivized peasant villages, based on future portions
of the harvest. Contract fulfillment varied wildly across provinces, according to
climate conditions and administrative arbitrariness. Neither state procurers nor
peasant contractees knew what to expect from one another. And so, in 1932, contracts were replaced by a system of fixed "obligatory deliveries," which imposed
greater order and predictability on the state-peasant fiscal relationship.[40] Delivery "norms," or quotas, were set by the state, supposedly taking into account local
growing conditions. By the mid-1930s the new delivery norms were, in general,
markedly lower than the initial outrageously unrealistic quotas, which devastated
the country's richest grain-growing regions in Ukraine, the northern Caucasus,
and the lower Volga. Delivery norms varied by type of agricultural enterprise:
state farms were assigned the lowest percentage of the harvest, collective farms

turned over a higher percentage, and the few remaining independent farmers were hit with the highest percentage. Because the norms were fixed, revenue burden on peasants were lower in seasons of plenty and higher in seasons of dearth. In practice, the obligatory deliveries were a kind of property tax-in-kind that ignored one's ability to pay.[41]

The state also imposed personal income taxes (PIT) directly on individuals. These taxes counted for little of the total revenue take; instead, they were used to redistribute household income, modify individual behavior, and signify social status. The application of personal income tax differed by occupation and place of residence. In urban areas, state enterprise workers, public employees, and students were assigned the lowest rates, while professionals, artisans, and priests were assigned the highest rates.[42] For rural residents, an agricultural tax, to be paid with money, was levied on peasant households for income earned from private plots and livestock. Once again, the rates varied according to bureaucratically assigned status: the tax paid by private farmers was 100 percent higher than that paid by collective farmers. The personal income tax also was used to nudge people to behave in state-approved ways. For example, highly productive "hero laborers" were given income tax exemptions, while population losses during World War II prompted a surtax on bachelors and couples with fewer than three children.

Although household income contributed only a small portion of state revenue, state revenue claims took a large portion of household income. The proletarian state imposed a heavy fiscal burden on its worker citizens. Before the war, the main source of state revenue, the turnover tax, was collected overwhelmingly from the consumer goods and food sectors, while heavy industry contributed only about 10 percent.[43] Soviet households were continuously pressed to give back to the state, rather than to accumulate personal wealth. Taking into account both direct income and indirect consumption taxes, the estimated percentage of household wealth returning to the state via taxation generally ranged from 50 percent to 65 percent. The amount was even higher during the war years.[44] The special wartime income tax, applied at high rates to the entire adult population between 1942 and 1945, was second only to the turnover tax as a revenue source. On top of this, individuals were approached in the workplace for "voluntary goodwill contributions" to the armed forces, which during the war brought in an additional one hundred billion rubles.[45]

The fiscal obligations on households did not end with taxes and donations. Strong social pressure was exerted on workers to purchase government bonds. Roughly three-quarters of government bonds were sold to individuals, and one-quarter to institutions. The purchases were directly deducted from paychecks, like taxes. They could not be cashed in before maturity, while the government sometimes extended maturity periods and lowered rates without the consent of bondholders. During the war, the number of individuals purchasing bonds rose from nearly eleven million to twenty-seven million.[46] Following the war, the government enacted a currency reform that effectively canceled two-thirds of the value of its outstanding debt obligations to the public. Surely, the old socialist critique of capitalism's indirect and hidden taxes on the workers was even more apt for the communist state.

The general pattern of taxation, worked out in the 1930s, endured with only minor revision for more than fifty years. The command economy was a self-contained autarky, in which values on goods and services were bureaucratically determined. The state's major sources of revenue proved steady from year to year. Excepting the war years, the Finance Ministry operated with either a balanced budget or a small surplus.[47] There were a few accounting tricks, to be sure, such as including bond sales as revenue, but overall, Soviet state finances were stable from the mid-1930s through the 1970s.

After the war, the command economy expanded to Eastern Europe. At first, a one-size-fits-all approach was taken regarding the imposition of Soviet-style economic reform; but in the post-Stalin period, the trend was toward greater variation among Eastern European economies. But even accounting for those satellite states that moved from a command economy to market socialism, the organization of taxation was similar across the region (see table 2.1). The table also highlights the contrast between the command economy's industrial rent-seeking and the advanced capitalist states' modern tax systems. First, communist states relied more on enterprises for tax revenue in comparison with OECD states. The profits tax on enterprises accounted for one-third of all revenues collected, while OECD states on average took in less than 10 percent in corporate income taxes.

TABLE 2.1   Breakdown of tax revenues as % of total taxes collected—1988

	PROFITS	TRANSACTIONS**	PERSONAL INCOME	SOCIAL SECURITY
Bulgaria	45	26	8	20
Czechoslovakia	32	35	8	13
Hungary	16	48	9	27
Poland	30	32	9	20
Romania	36	28	16	19
USSR	35	45	10	9

	PROFITS/CORP INCOME	TRANSACTIONS*	PERSONAL INCOME	SOCIAL SECURITY
Communist states				
(average)	32	36	10	18
OECD	8	31	31	20

*Refers to VAT and other sales and excise taxes. **Refers to the turnover tax and customs duties.

Source: OECD: Role of Tax Reform in East Central Europe (Paris: OECD, 1991).

Second, it shows how OECD states effectively established a claim over the income of households through direct personal income taxes, which communist states tended to avoid. Third, the table draws attention to the dependency of both OECD and postcommunist states on taxation of transactions. But the table does not show that transaction taxes were collected in the command economy mainly from large enterprises at the point of production. Transaction taxes collected by OECD states were paid by individuals and small businesses, as well as by large firms, at the point of consumption.

The forcible integration of postwar Eastern Europe into the command economy was a temporary boon to the Soviet Union. Cross-national economic ties provided Soviet state planners with direct access to highly valuable resources: raw materials, manufactured goods, cheap labor. But the short-term gains of economic plunder brought long-term costs for political survival. The great irony was that at the moment of Soviet Russia's greatest triumph, when it defeated Nazi Germany, the seeds were sown for its future demise, when it reclaimed Poland.[48]

Fiscal Costs of Political Compliance

For four decades, Polish society challenged its communist viceroys with collective action protest. State officialdom responded to these challenges with a mix of coercion and concession. Demonstrators risked truncheons and bullets, while strike leaders were denied jobs and kept in jail. But coercive punishment was tempered with economic concession. Social subsidy was exchanged for political peace. The cycle of protest, punishment, and concession was replayed in each chapter in the history of Communist Poland: Poznan worker strikes in 1956, student demonstrations in 1968, shooting deaths of striking shipyard workers in Gdynia and Gdansk in 1970, crippling strikes in the central industrial regions in 1976, and finally the nationwide Solidarity movement in 1980–81. Each time the cycle was repeated the fiscal burden on the state grew heavier. By the 1980s the strategy of "buying" compliance was spent: protest politics could only be contained by coercion, which General Wojciech Jaruzelski announced to the nation via television in December 1981.[49]

Much had changed in the ways of state finance by the time Poland was restored to independence on the map of Europe. In the early 1920s, the Second Republic had a rough time recovering from the ill effects of "great power" partition, warfare, and diplomacy. The economy was devastated: tax revenues covered less than 10 percent of government expenses, while hyperinflation made money transactions worthless. By mid-decade, however, Prime Minister Wladyslaw Grabski, a historian and political economist by training, righted state finances.

The talented Grabksi introduced the institutional foundations of a modern fiscal system, including a state bank, a national currency, tax reform, and good credit. The budget operated in surplus.[50] Then, in 1939, the short-lived Second Republic was attacked and dismantled. Forced to become a battleground in World War II, Polish society and economy were tragically transformed. Poland's population fell from a multinational thirty-five million to an ethnically homogenous twenty-five million. Borders were redrawn, residents relocated. Before the war, agriculture accounted for two-thirds of economic activity; after the war, industry was boosted by factories and mining operations acquired in the Silesian territories.

Postwar Poland lay in ruins. In 1947, the West enticed Poland to join the Marshall Plan for European economic recovery; still under Red Army occupation, the government was forced to decline. Instead, Poland followed a Kremlin-dictated plan for economic rebuilding. In the first years after the war, moderate leftists controlled economic policy, but Moscow's malicious meddling soon put radicals in charge.[51] A Soviet-style command economy was fitted to Poland—like a saddle on a cow. In 1949, an ambitious Six-Year Plan of state-directed economic growth was launched, which squeezed the private sector, collectivized the agricultural sector, and shoved forward the industrial sector. Poland's command economy experienced rapid heavy-industrial development, while the rest of the economy languished.

In postwar economic debate, radical leftists insisted that rapid industrialization could be achieved from the "mobilization of the masses, whose creative energy and enthusiasm are the most important factor."[52] Once in charge, however, they conceded that tax revenue would be helpful too. State fiscal policy was redesigned to enable central planners to get ahold of sufficient capital to fund their audacious development goals. The Finance Ministry enacted a major tax reform that was similar to the 1930 Soviet reform. The main sources of revenue came from the socialized industrial sector through turnover and profits taxes. Like the Soviet Union, the state squeezed capital from urban households. Personal income tax and indirect sales taxes accounted for more than 20 percent of all taxes collected by the central state.[53] Household consumption was suppressed to make more capital available for industrial investment. Unlike the Soviet Union, Poland managed to raise little capital from agriculture. The Polish state lacked the means and will to undertake the forceful reorganization of the countryside for the direct extraction of peasant surplus.

The Stalinist strategy of accumulating capital for economic growth included keeping Eastern European workers in semiservitude. Labor norms were excessive, wages were taxed away, and basic goods were rationed. The heavy fiscal burden on worker households could not be sustained, and small steps were taken to ease the strain, but only after Stalin's death. Payment of wages-in-kind was replaced by cash, the extensive rationing system was mostly abolished, and more consumer goods were made available.[54] It was not enough to soothe disgruntled workers.[55] In 1956, Poznan workers at the Josef Stalin (soon to revert to its original name, Cegielski) Metal Works petitioned managers and ministers to redress their economic grievances, foremost being the extra tax imposed on the extra pay awarded for overfulfillment of production norms. The request was refused. Three-quarters of the factory went on strike. More than one hundred thousand people gathered in Poznan's main square in a protest that turned violent. Only a Soviet-led force of armored vehicles managed to restore order after killing an estimated fifty protestors.[56]

The Poznan riots forced a fundamental change in the regime's compliance strategy. Erstwhile Stalinist victim Wladyslaw Gomulka was returned to power, promoting a policy of tentative liberalization, known as "national communism," which was supposed to help legitimate the communist regime by showing its tolerance for particular features of Polish national identity, such as the Catholic Church, smallholding peasantry, and statues of Adam Mickiewicz, Poland's national poet. The regime also moved decisively toward a reward-based compliance strategy. The rejected demands of Poznan metal workers were conceded, and then some; workers' wages increased across the country. In the agriculture sector, collectivization was formally abandoned. The government next unveiled the Kalecki Plan, an ambitious fifteen-year program to raise household consumption to a level comparable with Western Europe and make "significant improvement" in urban and rural housing conditions by 1975.[57] The Soviet leadership reluctantly supported "national communism." Khrushchev canceled more than $500 million worth of outstanding foreign debt, which Poland owed as a result of the unequal terms of trade imposed under Stalin. The consumption boom was supposed to be financed with domestic resources, although the Soviet Union chipped in $250 million in low-interest loans and allowed for a small amount of Western credit to import food.[58]

The protest-coercion-concession cycle turned again in the late 1960s. The limits of "national communism" were reached in March 1968, when the government banned a performance of Adam Mickiewicz's patriotic poem, *Dziady* (Forefathers), prompting protests by university students.[59] Fearful of the contagion effects of the Prague Spring, party leaders acted quickly to suppress the demonstration. Workers were rewarded for not joining the protest with another wage increase. But when economic growth slowed, the government targeted labor productivity. It introduced a "new incentive" system that effectively raised work norms by tying individual wages directly to individual output. The government also sought to squeeze additional capital from households by raising prices for basic goods. A steep increase in meat prices just before the Christmas holiday in

1970 sent Baltic coast shipyard workers into the street to protest. Overwhelmed and confused soldiers in Gdynia fired on the demonstrators, and the conflagration spread across the country. Forty people were killed and three thousand arrested. Out with Gomulka; in with Gierek. Poland's new communist leader, Eduard Gierek, immediately reversed the price hikes, canceled the "new incentive" system, and raised workers' wages. Invoking his own working-class roots, Gierek promised that the government would be more accountable to the people. The Polish state was now even more deeply committed to a reward-based compliance strategy. The question remained, however—how to pay for it?

In the early 1970s, a confluence of external factors provided a new source of capital for the Polish state. A political thaw in the cold war allowed for more interaction between East and West, at a time when capital-rich commercial bankers were looking for higher returns on investment. Eastern Europe seemed a sure thing, with a developed industrial infrastructure, a skilled labor force, and reliable authoritarian rule. Poland became a favored borrower of Western lenders. The subsequent infusion of foreign credit was used for importing technology to modernize industry and foodstuffs to raise household consumption. The "new economic strategy" was supposed to work as follows: imports would increase industrial productivity, which would increase exports of manufactured goods, which would increase revenue to state coffers. And, it worked, by half. In the early seventies, Polish workers were better fed and Polish industry was more productive. The big payoff in foreign currency earnings, however, was less than expected.[60] Industrial exports went mostly still to the socialist bloc; meanwhile, what had been the economy's main export to the West, meat and food products, was now being served in Polish kitchens. The promise of prosperity could not be kept. Even more worrisome, the government had to repay Western loans in hard currency, which it simply did not have. In 1971, the state's total debt service was $291 million; in 1979, debt service climbed to $6.1 billion.[61] The Polish state was falling into fiscal crisis.

The Gierek regime was caught in the twin dilemmas of communist rule. It lacked the resources to maintain its reward-based compliance strategy. In 1976, the government sharply cut consumer imports and hiked meat prices. The cycle of protest-coercion-concession began once more. Angry strikers were again subdued with force, while the government again retreated from fiscal austerity measures. State and society were locked in stalemate as the economy deteriorated. Production and consumption declined, and the government accumulated more debt. Unable to collect income, state financial planners manipulated the currency, making more money in an effort to gain access to household wealth through extraction by inflation. Wages went up, but household consumption went down.[62]

In 1980, Gierek's ten-year tenure ended the way it began, with Poland on strike.[63] The regime resorted to familiar divide-and-rule tactics, but now society was better organized and more astute about using collective action. Protest politics crossed regional and social lines in the nationwide Solidarity movement. Gierek was replaced by former interior minister Stanislaw Kania, who made the historic decision to give legal recognition to the workers movement. In the Gdansk Accords, the government tried to buy political peace with Solidarity in exchange for a long list of economic concessions, including reducing the standard work week from six to five days; exporting only commodities that were in surplus on the domestic market; limiting price increases; raising the minimum wage and retirement benefits; and instituting three-year paid maternity leaves. It was all quite generous—and quite unaffordable. Economic concessions were made in political desperation, without regard for state finances.

The regime's recognition of Solidarity as an autonomous sociopolitical entity was a landmark event in Communist Eastern Europe. Unfortunately, for Polish Communists, it did not achieve its two intended goals: halting the momentum of social mobilization and creating the opportunity for economic reform. Fearful of economic downturn and political upheaval, capitalist and socialist lenders shut off short-term credit to the Polish government. State finances slipped over the edge. In 1981, the Polish government reneged on its debt obligations. It was forced to reschedule 95 percent of its outstanding debt to the West. But even this reprieve was not enough to avert financial collapse.[64] At the source of the Polish state's fiscal crisis was a compliance strategy based on rewards and a treasury out of zloty.

The Soviet Union relied on a different mix of compliance strategies. Under Stalin, coercion was the principal means of political compliance. Unlike Poland, the Soviet state also succeeded in cultivating normative-based compliance. For the postrevolutionary generation, at least some upwardly mobile citizens embraced the state-constructed image of a "new Soviet man" and gladly participated in building the socialist future. The mobilizing oomph of revolutionary rhetoric diminished over time. A more effective normative-based strategy was the commingling of Russian nationalism with Soviet patriotism. When Hitler's tanks came rolling into Russia, Stalin summoned the ghost of medieval Prince Alexander Nevsky before entrusting the defense of Moscow to living Red Army generals. From the time of the Great Patriotic War, the Soviet state openly tried to legitimate itself with selected images and themes of Russian national identity, mostly to good effect, among ethnically Russian citizens anyway.[65]

In March 1953, as the last breath passed from the Georgian generalissimo, Stalin's successors introduced a fundamental change in compliance strategy: coercion was downplayed and reward was upgraded. The new prime minister,

Georgy Malenkov, acted quickly to ease the fiscal burden on households. Workers' wages were increased, peasants' obligations were lightened, direct taxes were decreased, food prices were lowered, compulsory bond sales were curtailed, and investment capital was reallocated to the light-industrial consumer sector.[66] Malenkov eventually lost the political leadership struggle, but his consumerist policy agenda ultimately prevailed. In 1956, First Party Secretary Nikita Khrushchev boisterously proclaimed that "history is on our side, we will bury you." The remark was about welfare not warfare, and presumed that socialism would prove superior to capitalism in making a better life for people. The Soviet state thereafter embraced a reward-based compliance strategy.

In the mid- to late fifties, the command economy grew enough to improve urban living conditions, including food supply and housing space, while still accommodating the military-industrial complex.[67] But this dual development could not be sustained over the long term. Khrushchev's tumultuous tenure was famous for impulsive quick-fix, low-cost policy solutions, which too often backfired. In May 1960 the populist premier announced the abolition of personal income taxes for more than 99 percent of the workforce, a thirty-five-hour work week, and a sixty-ruble-per-month minimum wage.[68] The political gesture was generous to a fiscal fault; budgetary income and expenses could not be reconciled by state financial planners. A year later, the government was forced to retract its promises and instead unexpectedly raised basic food prices and briefly restored compulsory bond purchases, causing deep resentment in society.

More than a decade after the communist collapse, a majority of Russian citizens still said that they lived better during the Brezhnev years. Although Leonid Brezhnev is often remembered as the chief octogenarian of the late Soviet gerontocracy, the first half of his tenure saw dynamic growth in global military capacity as well as domestic mass consumption. The problem, however, was that the command economy could not maintain both for more than short spurts. By the 1970s, most Soviet citizens were better off materially than at any time in their lifetimes, and better off than their parents and grandparents too. But this economic fact was not cause for consumer satisfaction. In urban areas, in particular, better-informed professionals made unfavorable comparisons between their lives and those of people with similar educations and careers in the West, rather than favorable comparisons with their own family past. The late Soviet state's explicit endorsement of a reward-based compliance strategy only produced pervasive cynicism in society, summed up in the oft-quoted quip about the Brezhnev social contract: "They pretend to pay us, and we pretend to work."[69]

In March 1985 the Soviet politburo chose its youngest member, Mikhail Gorbachev, as new leader. Gorbachev inherited a stagnant economy, but not a fiscal crisis. He came to power with an elite consensus to reverse economic decline, but without a consensus as to how this might be done. Gorbachev opted for a politically loaded strategy to regenerate economic growth, which called for the unleashing of the "human factor" in society.[70] Instead of the usual reform recipe of bureaucratic reorganizations and exhortative campaigns, Gorbachev proposed individual material incentives and cultural liberalization.[71] To reinvigorate Soviet socialism, Gorbachev hoped to show that the state existed for the benefit of society, not to spite it. At a party meeting on economic reform in June 1987, Gorbachev explicitly faulted the fiscal practices of his predecessor for relying too much on oil exports and for concealing budget deficits.[72] But it was mostly Gorbachev's own policies that plunged state finances deep into the red.

Gorbachev's promotion prompted a big increase in state subsidies in the 1986 budget, especially in food processing, social services, and the defense sector. But there was no accompanying boost in revenue to pay for the GenSec's largesse. Indeed, several of Gorbachev's early policy initiatives undercut budgetary income. Most notably, teetotaler Gorbachev was determined to sober up society. In 1986, he launched an anti-alcohol campaign that cost the state an estimated thirty-seven billion rubles in lost tax revenue between 1986 and 1988.[73] Next, Gorbachev curtailed the import of food products and consumer goods, ending a scheme by which the state profited from steep price markups for domestic consumers. The market for imported goods was not quashed, however; it simply moved into the unofficial "shadow" economy, and out of reach of tax collectors.[74] The state budget also took a hit from a sudden drop in world energy prices. Between 1982 and 1984 the state received on average about $15 billion in income annually from oil exports, but in 1986 it collected only $7 billion from this source. Last, but by no means least, the state industrial sector was in systemic decline, which Gorbachev's policies seemed to only make worse, as state enterprise profits plummeted in the second half of the 1980s.

Nineteen eighty-nine is famous as the year communism fell in Eastern Europe; it is also the year that the Soviet Union fell into fiscal crisis. In Soviet politics, the incredible regime-changing events across the border redefined the parameters of political possibility. Movement politics came to the fore in the non-Russian republics, as Gorbachev's vision of reform socialism was rejected in favor of national independence. The Baltic states led the way, openly contesting the Soviet state center over the most basic power resources, coercion and capital: protecting young men from military conscription and withholding taxes from the central budget. Unlike Poland, there was no all-embracing labor movement, but there were still some formidable displays of worker protest. In July, coal miners went on strike. In what was the largest labor action in Soviet history, more than four hundred thousand miners closed down more than two hundred enterprises in West Siberia and Ukraine.[75] Given his own inclination toward Prague Spring–style democratic socialism, Gorbachev was hesitant to use coercion to bring society to heel. Instead, the government responded by desperately trying to buy political peace, although it lacked the economic means to do so. The combination of declining income and uncontrolled spending led to the highest budget deficits since the war. As a percentage of GDP, the deficit climbed steadily under Gorbachev. Before Gorbachev's tenure: 1981, 1.75 percent; 1983, 1.5 percent; 1985, 1.8 percent; during Gorbachev's tenure: 1987, 6.4 percent; 1989, 8.7 percent; 1991, 12–14 percent.[76]

Soviet fiscal managers were inexperienced with deficit financing, and immediately made the classic mistakes of a government in denial. First, the government's foreign exchange and gold reserves were depleted.[77] Second, the state sought to supplement the budget with credit. The government first looked to the domestic economy to raise additional capital. The government issued a new domestic savings bond to the public, redeemable in ten years at 4 percent interest. Between 1985 and 1988, the internal debt rose from 11.7 billion rubles to 90.1 billion rubles.[78] The Soviet Union also borrowed heavily from Western banks; it took Gorbachev less than four years to double the government's foreign debt obligation, from $30 to $60 billion. In January 1988, the Soviet Union issued its first ever international bond sale, for one hundred million Swiss francs, in Zurich. Second, as expenses rose and income fell, the Finance Ministry chose to make up the difference through currency manipulation. The State Bank was instructed to issue credits to cover budgetary expenses that went beyond the means of the treasury. The practice fueled inflation, and caused an unofficial devaluation of the ruble. Finally, in December 1990, the government announced a set of tough fiscal measures aimed at getting ahold of income needed to finance the 1991 budget. A wide range of price subsidies, including for basic food products, were eliminated, with consumer costs quadrupling for some items. The government relaxed its anti-alcohol campaign in order to boost tax receipts. And, by special decree, Gorbachev enacted a 5 percent sales tax, which was applied to almost all goods and services. The "president's tax," as it came to be known, quickly became a tangible target of popular scorn.[79]

The government's get-tough fiscal stance was consistent with a sudden hardline political lurch by Gorbachev, in an attempt to reassert central state authority by compulsion.[80] It was also a rare attempt by Gorbachev to place state fiscal need above free-spending politics; it did not last long. By March, Soviet society was mobilized against the state's new tax demands and austerity measures. In West Siberia, coal miners went back out on strike, closing more than a quarter of the nation's mines. In Minsk, tens of thousands of public employees walked off the job in protest. Gorbachev retreated. In April, he signed a new decree, cancelling the 5 percent sales tax.[81] Prime Minister Valentin Pavlov announced wage increases to compensate for price rises, and the government printed more money to pay for it. In the Soviet Union's last year, the supply of rubles circulating in the economy increased by 70 percent.[82] Still worse, Pavlov was then forced to renege on the promised wage increases, because the government was flat broke.[83]

The scholarly debate over the Soviet collapse treats Gorbachev as a controversial figure, inspiring ardent defenders and cynical detractors. For good reason, these debates tend to focus on political reforms and nationality conflicts. By redirecting attention to state finances, however, it should become less puzzling to Westerners why Gorbachev has remained for so long so detested by his own countrymen. He was after all in charge when the government lost control of fiscal affairs, and people lost their livelihoods, life savings, and self-worth. Gorbachev's reckless policies of borrowing, spending, and printing money destabilized Soviet state finances. For certain, Gorbachev was not responsible for the deep structural flaws in the command economy, but just as certain he does not get nearly enough credit for his decisive role in fomenting the final fiscal crisis of the old regime.[84]

Empowering the Usurpers: Fiscal Crisis and Communist Collapse

In history's great revolutions, the critical point for broken regimes in fiscal crisis is when they are forced to negotiate with previously disenfranchised actors for more capital. This is the moment when the usurpers are empowered. The Polish communist state desperately needed to squeeze more income from Polish worker households. To get it, in 1989 the communist regime consented to recognize the Solidarity trade union as a legally autonomous sociopolitical body and official opposition; soon after Communists and Solidarity were sharing power. And, in the Soviet Union, in 1991 the bankrupt central government reluctantly agreed to renegotiate a new division of power with its brassy national republics, only to be left with the crumbling façade of a federal state.

The breakdown of the communist regime in Poland offers a textbook case of a failed attempt at limited democratization from above. The events of the breakdown marked the culmination of a long-term, incremental process by which protest politics eroded the power resources of the communist regime. Solidarity's eighteen-month aboveground movement, in 1980–81, forever changed state-society relations in communist Poland. As society was politically energized, the state was economically depleted. Finally, under pressure from the Kremlin, Poland's Communist Party leader, Stanislaw Kania, was pushed aside in favor of an army general, Wojciech Jaruzelski, who managed at least temporarily to interrupt Solidarity's unfinished revolution.

In December 1981 the communist regime shifted from an openhanded reward-based approach to a heavy-handed coercion-based compliance strategy. Jaruzelski's martial law declaration signaled a temporary "militarization" of the economy.[85] The state resorted to coercion to suppress the labor movement and restore discipline in the workplace. Martial law also enabled the state to impose a set of emergency fiscal measures to stave off financial collapse. The year and a half of labor turmoil took a heavy toll on the economy. As measured by GDP, the Polish economy shrank 5 percent in 1980, 10 percent in 1981, and 5 percent in 1982.[86] Correspondingly, tax revenues declined and budget deficits increased. Foreign debt rose from $20 billion in 1979 to $25 billion in 1982; the value of the zloty was eroded, as inflation soared past 100 percent in 1982.[87] To raise more income, the state introduced confiscatory taxes on individuals and firms. A punitive payroll tax was imposed on enterprises that raised wages because that contributed to inflation, and a gouging sales tax was applied to enterprises that showed profits. Tax breaks, however, were offered to any firm earning hard currency by exporting goods to the West.[88] Meanwhile, state subsidies for household expenses were drastically cut back. Price controls on food and other necessities were removed, and the cost of living rose by more than 300 percent. In 1982, household consumption was nearly 20 percent lower than what it had been two years earlier.[89] The state's program of coercion-imposed austerity succeeded in stopping protest politics, but it failed to fix state finances.

Polish leaders looked to their international connections to help escape the vise grip of fiscal crisis and political stalemate. The government presumed that foreign creditors would be impressed by its firm policy stance and offer fresh financial assistance. Western commercial bankers, however, refused even to talk to the Polish government for almost two years, and then only to sort out repayment schedules. Western political leaders were adamantly opposed to conducting normal relations under the abnormal conditions of martial law, and linked financial assistance to political liberalization.[90] Poland's Soviet patrons were just as adamantly opposed to political liberalization, although they did not offer any new credit either. Finally, in 1985 a leadership change placed a reform socialist in the Kremlin, and provided the opportunity for political compromise in Poland. In the summer of 1988, Mikhail Gorbachev visited Jaruzelski in Warsaw and made clear that Poland must find its own solution, promising that Moscow would not interfere.

Responding to these cues, in the fall of 1988 the communist regime devised the Rakowski Plan. Named for the new prime minister, Mieczyslaw Rakowski, the strategy entailed an explicit endorsement of capitalism and a vague promise of democracy. The plan rested on an assumption that the best means for regenerating economic growth was to create the conditions for private enterprise.

A long-time antagonist of the workers' movement, Rakowski at first hoped to pursue this plan by going around the banned Solidarity trade union, rather than through it. The new minister of industry, Mieczyslaw Wilczek, spoke contemptuously about the banned trade union: "The future of Poland will not be decided by these people."[91] Rakowski even threatened to close down the Lenin Shipyard in Gdansk, where the Solidarity movement had started, on the pretense of fiscal prudence. But there could be no economic reform without political peace, and no political peace without Solidarity's consent. In January 1989, Jaruzelski told a meeting of the central committee that if the party refused to endorse a plan to reinstate the banned trade union, he would resign from office. The party relented, and Solidarity was legal once more.

The regime offered the opposition limited democratic reform in exchange for a labor truce, while the government implemented cost-saving reforms that effectively lowered household living standards. The details were worked out in the Roundtable Agreement, which was signed in April 1989. The compromise called for new semi-open elections that would include Solidarity candidates, and for a new bicameral legislature, where a fixed number of seats would be reserved for the Communist Party, assuring that they would remain in charge.[92] The lower house, the Sejm, would then elect the president, who would appoint a government. The political reform was rigged so that the communists could not lose: Jaruzelski would be elected president and Solidarity would have a voice in the policy process. From this semidemocratic arrangement, Jaruzelski hoped to see economic reform finally go forward. The June 1989 Polish elections went as planned, except Jaruzelski was denied his legitimating mandate. The defeat of the communists in every seat that was openly contested only underscored the political isolation of the communist regime. As the new Sejm got under way, the opposition was emboldened to obstruct communist plans and demand a greater role in policymaking. Amid the political uncertainty, the fiscal crisis deepened.

Rakowski's economic reforms caused a financial collapse. The flow of income to the state budget was completely turned off, and the budget deficit reached all-time highs, approaching 10 percent. Many enterprises simply stopped paying taxes, without retribution. Those tax payments that were made were immediately devalued because of hyperinflation. Wages increased, despite attempts by the government to keep them in check, contributing further to the inflationary spiral. The government printed money to cover budgetary expenses, and it continued to subsidize insolvent state enterprises. In what turned out to be his last act as prime minister, Rakowski raised food prices by 200 percent. The Sejm started discussion about impeaching Rakowski and his finance minister.[93] Instead, Jaruzelski nominated a new communist candidate to head the government. In early August, Jaruzelski proposed Czeslaw Kiszczak as prime minister. Despite the communists' built-in majority, the nomination process proved contentious. Kiszczak's credentials were not in state finance, but in state coercion. He was a former army general and trusted colleague of Jaruzelski, who since the declaration of martial law he had overseen the police apparatus as head of the Interior Ministry. He was personally well acquainted with opposition Solidarity leaders, both as police chief and political negotiator. The appointment was supposed to project an image of order, so that the government could move forward with economic reform. It did neither.

The government's first small steps toward economic liberalization caused big social reactions—panic buying in the markets and labor unrest in the factories. Kiszczak lasted only two weeks. Jaruzelski was at last persuaded that no communist government could successfully oversee the painful economic reforms that state finances desperately needed. He relented in favor of a more radical solution—political cohabitation. By the end of August, Solidarity took control of the government under the premiership of Catholic dissident intellectual Tadeusz Mazowiecki. Solidarity was now in charge of economic policy and state finances. Cohabitation proved to be a short-term arrangement. Before the year was out, Jaruzelski announced his resignation as president. At its final central committee meeting, in January 1990, Poland's Communist Party voted to disband. The events in Poland incited protest politics elsewhere. By year's end, almost all of Eastern Europe's single-party communist regimes had either been toppled or had given up power. And, it all started when Polish communist rulers empowered the Solidarity opposition movement in order to find a way out of the fiscal crisis.

At the same time that Poles were gathering around the roundtable, Mikhail Gorbachev was devising his own version of limited democratization for the Soviet Union. Gorbachev's reform package included four parts: (1) a reorganized Supreme Soviet with enhanced legislative powers; (2) partially competitive elections for the new Supreme Soviet; (3) a strong chief executive attached to the new Supreme Soviet; (4) the replication of parts 1–3 in the national republics the following year. In spring 1989, Gorbachev's reforms, parts 1–3, went into effect, successfully shifting the locus of power in Soviet politics away from the Communist Party's central executive bodies. However, before part 4 could be acted upon, the unexpected occurred in Eastern Europe. At this point, even Gorbachev's supporters were cautious and urged the postponement of the republican-level reforms. But Gorbachev was intent on seeing them through, and in spring 1990 the national republics elected newly reorganized Supreme Soviets, as the legislative body in the republics also was named. With varying assertiveness, these legislatures began to act as the preeminent political-legal authority in the territory of the national republics. In the second half of 1990, several republican legislatures directly challenged the Soviet center for control of the state's most precious power resource—tax revenue.

Already by this time, tax policy was a source of friction between the state center and national republics, setting the scene for the final showdown. In 1988, a new law legalized private entrepreneurship, overturning sixty years of strict state ownership; however, the Finance Ministry slapped a steep progressive income tax (with a top rate of 90 percent) on the new cooperatives. Led by Estonian and Belorussian delegates, the Supreme Soviet overturned the tax, marking an unprecedented act of defiance by the usually compliant legislature.[94] In November 1989, the three Baltic republics negotiated a special deal with Gorbachev for greater control over local finances, including a "one channel" tax reform by which locally collected revenue would be sent to the central budget in one big annual transfer. To the center's dismay, the Baltic republics then took more revenue than they were entitled to under the agreement.[95] The big prize for republic authorities was the income generated by centrally administered all-union enterprises located on their territory. By the end of 1990 the Baltic republics had prevailed in a contest with the center for a greater share of this lucrative revenue source, with Estonia to receive 84 percent, Lithuania 78 percent, and Latvia 57 percent.[96] What started as a seemingly small concession to local autonomy became the first step toward the collapse of the fiscal infrastructure of the Soviet state.

Nowhere was the diffusion of power away from the Soviet state center to the constituent national republics more clearly observable than in the wrangling over the 1991 federal budget. The national republics now viewed their territories as sovereign economic spaces; they asserted rival claims to the economic resources contained therein. If the Soviet center wanted access to their economic space, it would have to be negotiated. It came as a shock to Gorbachev that the newly empowered republican legislatures refused to go along with the state center's revenue claims on the economic resources in their territory. At first, Gorbachev in disdain rejected the notion of republican economic autonomy, and in disregard imposed the revenue prerogatives of the state center. But the national republics successfully resisted. It was 1 January 1991, and Kremlin coffers were still empty.

In early January 1991, Boris Yeltsin declared a "war of budgets" between his Russian Federation and Gorbachev's Soviet Union. Yeltsin's choice of weapons showed how shrewd a political tactician he was. Yeltsin sought to mobilize the power resource of capital by stealing the Soviet state's revenue base. He consistently promised Russian-based enterprise managers and regional governors a better fiscal deal in his Russian state than in Gorbachev's Soviet state. In 1991, the Soviet state corporate income tax rate was set at 45 percent; Yeltsin offered enterprise managers a 38 percent tax rate, if paid to the Russian budget, instead of the Soviet budget.[97] In August 1990 Yeltsin famously urged regional leaders to "take as much sovereignty as you can swallow." He followed up by negotiating special tax deals with commodity-rich regions, by which a greater share of tax wealth stayed in the locality.[98] Finally, in late 1991 he exempted Russia's regional governments from turning over their collected tax receipts to the Soviet central budget, effectively starving the state of revenue and hastening its demise.[99] The 1991 Soviet state budget, meanwhile, was set at R276 billion in proposed expenses and R250 billion in projected income, with foreign borrowing making up the difference. The Russian Federation was expected to provide almost half the total revenue. But Yeltsin led a revolt of the republics to withhold revenues, and force the center to negotiate. The immediate dispute was resolved by mid-January with a temporary compromise. The republics agreed to put up R42 billion to keep the Soviet state going for a few months while a new fiscal arrangement was sorted out.[100]

With the threat looming of another republic revenue boycott, Gorbachev agreed to negotiate a major redistribution of power between the state center and the national republics, effectively empowering the would-be usurpers of the soon-to-be old regime. From April to July, the details were worked out for a new territorial division of power, in which taxation was the most controversial item.[101] Gorbachev pushed for a two-channel tax system, by which the center and the republics would have their own revenue claims, separate from one another. The Russian Federation and Ukraine instead espoused a one-channel system, by which all revenues were claimed by the republic, which then would turn over a negotiated amount to the center. Gorbachev strongly resisted the one-channel scheme, which would make the state center fiscally dependent on the republics. "The existence of a federal state," Gorbachev reasoned, "is of course unthinkable without federal taxes."[102] In late July, a hard bargain was struck over taxes: the state center was assigned a fixed quota of 10 percent of all revenue collected, thus guaranteeing a source of income; in exchange, the national republics were given proprietary claim over revenues from nearly all the economic enterprises and natural resources on their territories.[103]

The formal enactment of the New Union Treaty, however, was preempted by a political farce, otherwise known as the August Putsch. In late August, old regime hardliners placed Gorbachev under house arrest and ordered the Russian Supreme Soviet shut down, in an attempt to prevent the reformation of the union. At the point at which Boris Yeltsin climbed atop a tank and dared KGB snipers to shoot him, and they did not, the Soviet Union was done for. The failed coup revealed that the old regime could no longer rely on coercion to compel political compliance. Gorbachev's efforts to revive the union treaty were mostly ignored by national republic leaders, who could neither be persuaded of the benefits of staying together nor frightened by the consequences of going it alone. More important, they simply stopped sending revenue to the central budget.[104]

Meanwhile, the Soviet state fell into fiscal collapse. The government lost control of spending.[105] By the end of the summer the 1991 budget was well ahead of proposed expenses, and well behind in expected income. The budget deficit was supposed to be about twenty-five billion rubles, but it now reached two hundred billion inflated rubles, almost 20 percent of GDP![106] Gorbachev's still tight foreign connections enabled the government to get a one-year reprieve from paying back the principal on foreign debt obligations to the G-7 nations.[107] The state bank proposed a bailout package to the Supreme Soviet worth more than R90 billion, which was to finance Soviet state operations for the fourth fiscal quarter. But the emergency measure was rejected in the legislature, on the advice of the Russian Federation's deputy prime minister, Yegor Gaidar, who said that "we are not prepared to sign a blank check guaranteed by an institution which has no resources." At the end of November, central bank head Viktor Gerashchenko publicly declared the Soviet state was indeed bankrupt.[108]

Of course the Soviet state was bankrupt—Yeltsin had stolen its revenue base for his Russian state. He successfully claimed the income generated by economic enterprises on the territory of the Russian Federation. He secured control over Russia's lucrative natural resources, such as gold, diamonds, and oil. He seized a portion of the Soviet state's hard currency foreign reserves. He banned Communist Party cells from the workplace, undercutting the revenue base of the Communist Party as well. And, now in December 1991, Yeltsin stepped forward to bail out the destitute Soviet state. The last vestiges of Soviet fiscal independence were quashed. The Soviet budget was merged with the Russian budget. The Soviet Finance Ministry was subordinated to the Russian Finance Ministry. Yeltsin promised to cover the salaries of all federal employees, including President Gorbachev, whose stingy expense allowance was personally overseen by the vindictive Russian president.[109]

On December 25, with the stroke of a pen, Mikhail Gorbachev consigned the Soviet state to history. In the end, the great nemesis of market capitalism, the socialist command economy, was incapable of regenerating sufficient levels of economic growth to enable the Soviet Union to compete as a military superpower abroad as well as sustain a reward-based compliance strategy at home. It was Gorbachev's search for a solution to this dilemma that eventually led him to empower rival political actors, who then conspired to destroy the Soviet state. It was an act of political desperation forced on the last Soviet leader by fiscal crisis.

Fiscal Crisis of the Postcommunist State

Postcommunist states were born amid fiscal crisis. New state leaders were persuaded that the best solution to this crisis was to raze the command economy and build a market economy. But in the short run this dramatic structural transformation caused a further deterioration in state finances. Economist Janos Kornai revealed the hidden "fiscal traps" contained within the radical economic reform program that the Western financial community pressed on Eastern Europe.[110]

The main policy features of macroeconomic restructuring inadvertently subverted the flow of income to the postcommunist states. First, price liberalization called for an end to the command economy's bureaucratically assigned values for goods and services; prices controls would be lifted and market demand would determine economic worth. This reform, however, caused the "Tanzi effect" (named for IMF economist Vito Tanzi), which said that liberalization leads to inflation, which in turn leads to a devaluation of tax receipts. After an initial but brief surge in revenue, inflation overtakes and consumes the revenue base.[111] Second, monetary stabilization entailed the freezing of the money supply, so that liberalization did not fuel hyperinflation. Stabilization meant that the state could no longer print money or issue credit to sustain unprofitable public enterprises. The state industrial sector was deprived of investment capital at the same time that it suffered a loss of trading partners and protected markets, causing a sudden and steep drop in production. Thus, the postcommunist state was deprived of in-

TABLE 2.2   Fiscal crisis of the postcommunist Polish and Russian states compared

	POLAND			RUSSIA		
	1990	1991	1992	1992	1993	1994
GDP*	89	93	102.6	85.5	91.3	87.3
Industrial output**	−12	−8	−4	−18	−14	−21
Tax revenue***	32.5	25.6	27.2	29.5	25.5	24.5
Budget deficit***	+0.4	−3.8	−6	−8.8	−9.5	−10.1
Inflation****	586	70	43	2,521	840	215

(* based on previous year as 100%; ** % change from previous year; ***as % of GDP; **** CPI annual % change)

Sources: Stats for Poland: OECD Economic Survey: Poland (Paris: OECD, 1992), 17 (chart 1); OECD Economic Surveys: Poland 1994 (Paris: OECD, 1994), 12 (table 1); Alain de Crombrugghe and David Lipton, "The Government Budget and the Economic Transformation of Poland," in The Transition in Eastern Europe, ed. Oliver Blanchard (Chicago: University of Chicago Press, 1994), 129–32 (tables 11A.1, 11A.2); Daniel Gros and Alfred Steinherr, Economic Transition in Central and Eastern Europe (Cambridge: Cambridge University Press, 2004), 92 (table 3.6), 95 (table 3.7). Stats for Russia: OECD Economic Surveys: Russian Federation (Paris: OECD, 1995), 23 (table 7); Rossiia v tsifrakh: Ofitsial'noe isdanie (Moscow: Goskomstat, 1999), 28, 31, 308 (table 22.2).

come from what had been the old regime's most reliable revenue source. Finally, privatization increased economic activity beyond state oversight. New private entrepreneurs, widely dispersed in smaller units, overwhelmed state capacities for monitoring and enforcement of revenue claims.

Table 2.2 shows several key indicators of the fiscal crises faced by the post-communist Polish and Russian states. The negative fiscal trends that instigated the collapse of the old regimes were exacerbated by political upheaval and economic transformation. The industrial sector, once the mainstay of budgetary income, was in rapid decline. Inflation soared, production plunged, and consumption dropped well beyond initial expectations. As a consequence, both states experienced a precipitous revenue drop after the introduction of radical reform.

New state actors in Poland and Russia were pressed to find a way out of fiscal crisis. This daunting task demanded a fundamental restructuring of the old regime's system of revenue extraction: from rent-seeking in an industrial demesne-style economy to modern taxation in a market-based economy. No less, the implementation of the new revenue system further demanded a fundamental restructuring of state-society fiscal relations: from hidden, indirect, and collectively based extraction to transparent, direct, and individually based extraction. For Poland, this project would find state leaders trying to reconnect to their precommunist Second Republic past. For Russia, it would mark the third time in the twentieth century that state leaders tried to build a modern taxation system. It was a political challenge as much as an economic one.

POLITICS OF TAX REFORM
Making (and Unmaking) Revenue Bargains

Postcommunist states faced the same challenge as their fiscally inept communist predecessors—raising sufficient revenue from society to cover expenses and debts. To meet this challenge, a new approach to revenue extraction was needed. In the command economy, the state was financially sustained by industrial rents; in the transition economy, the state would have to rely on modern taxation. Two waves of tax reform surged across Eastern Europe in the postcommunist transition. First, in the early 1990s most postcommunist states adopted macrolevel tax policy reforms modeled after the advanced capitalist states. These reforms aimed to redirect the state's fiscal focus from the point of production to consumption, from corporate to individual taxpayers, from big to small entities, and from closed to open markets.[1] Second, in the 2000s some postcommunist states initiated a comprehensive revision of the advanced capitalist macropolicy design, fashioning more streamlined and simplified tax systems, best exemplified by low-rate flat taxes. This second reform was intended to overcome a set of obstacles to revenue extraction that were particular to transition economies: low tax morale, weak tax administration, and scarce investment capital.[2]

Whereas nearly all postcommunist states participated in the first reform wave in the early 1990s, only about half participated in the second reform wave in the 2000s. The variant patterns of tax reform among postcommunist states are best explained by their variant configurations of political constraints. Political constraints affect the level of contestation: if a government is relatively insulated from political pressures—meaning that its ability to survive politically is not threatened by the enactment of reform—then contestation is low; by contrast, if a government cannot enact reform without incurring risk to its political survival, then contestation rates are high. Not surprisingly, tax reform was more likely to occur in conditions where political contestation was low, and less likely where contestation was high. Postcommunist fiscal engineers had their best successes when the targets of taxation were either not alerted to or not able to fend off the state's new revenue claims. Several political paths led to the "more likely" scenario: nascent democracies with weakly organized opposition, consolidated democracies with bipartisan elite consensus, and façade democracies with hegemonic political parties. By contrast, the "less likely" scenario unfolded in conditions of mobilized societal opposition or with elites in conflict, and, especially, in consolidated democracies with genuinely competitive elections. It was in the consolidated democracies that the second reform wave, the flat-tax revolution, was most actively resisted.

Once reform is enacted, however, tax systems remain works in progress, undergoing constant small changes, overt and covert, by those from whom revenue is sought. This ongoing process gives rise to revenue bargains involving political and economic actors. Structural variation existed across transition economies concerning the location of capital. In some transition economies wealth was highly concentrated, while in others it was widely dispersed. These variations in economic structure gave rise to different sets of actors—industrialists, entrepreneurs, traders, and wage earners—who stood between societal capital and state claims. To make matters more complicated, the fiscal architects of postcommunist states had to persuade the very same societal actors who had brought down the revenue-starved communist regimes to pay their taxes. At the start of the transition, these societal actors were still in a position to mobilize power resources to resist state revenue claims. As a result, the competition for capital in the transition economy created an opportunity for forging revenue bargains between state and society. Revenue bargains involved select groups of actors from state and society whose particular interests were tied up with the distribution of the tax burden. These interests were the economic interests of certain societal actors, the political interests of certain elected state actors, and the fiscal interests of certain appointed state actors.

Poland and Russia exhibited similar outcomes in the first wave of tax reform and contrasting outcomes in the second wave. Following the collapse of the old regime, both countries experienced "low" contestation regarding tax reform. The enactment of major tax reforms in the early transition quickly led to the rise of revenue bargains with those groups on whom the new tax burden fell. In Poland, a "state-labor" revenue bargain was pieced together, wherein a social democrat/ peasants party coalition managed to dominate parliamentary competition, while their public-sector worker and farmer supporters were accorded tax exemptions and fiscal subsidies. In Russia, a "state-elite" revenue bargain unfolded, wherein the president's government fended off a hostile parliament by securing political support from regional and economic elites, who in exchange held on to a significantly higher share of revenue through negotiated deals and lax enforcement.

Even when it became apparent in both cases that the fiscal interests of the state were suffering, revenue bargains acted as a political constraint on further tax reform. Both Poland and Russia, in a condition of "high contestation," failed to enact corrective tax reforms in the late 1990s. In the early 2000s, however, the condition of contestation changed: by consensus in Poland and by coercion in Russia. As a result, Poland enacted partial tax reform, as the state-labor revenue bargain survived, and Russia enacted a major tax reform, as the state-elite revenue bargain was sundered.

Staking New Revenue Claims: From Tax Reform to Tax Resistance

According to Polish finance minister Leszek Balcerowicz, the opportunity for radical economic change in a postcommunist transition was created by a unique political situation, a moment of "extraordinary politics." Part hangover, part honeymoon, "extraordinary politics" referred to a brief phase in which the new government was able to enact fundamental policy reform without significant political opposition.[3] But as Balcerowicz well knew, "extraordinary politics" was temporary, an abnormal condition that would soon give way to "normal politics," as the inevitable effects of radical reform—soaring inflation, plunging production, decreasing consumption—shocked society back into politics. "Extraordinary politics" was an example of "low contestation" in a nascent democracy where organized opposition was weak. Both Poland and Russia experienced "extraordinary politics," during which fundamental tax reforms were enacted. And, accordingly, both Poland and Russia soon reverted to "normal politics," which included societal resistance to the state's new revenue claims.

Poland: From Extraordinary Politics to Collective Protest

In the fall of 1989, Prime Minister Tadeus Mazowiecki declared that he needed to find a Polish Ludwig Erhard, the economic architect of the postwar "German Miracle." He approached Leszek Balcerowicz with the task. At the time, Balcerowicz was barely known outside Poland, though his name soon became synonymous with "shock therapy." Trained in socialist economics, Balcerowicz had earlier organized a secret circle of young economists who discussed the inherent

flaws of communism and forbidden works of capitalism. In 1980, he was com-
missioned by the communist government to design a Polish transition to
Hungarian-style market socialism. But these plans were quashed by martial law.
Balcerowicz concluded that half measures could not fix the command economy,
and he became a passionate proponent of free market capitalism. Balcerowicz at
first declined Mazowiecki's invitation. Ludwig Erhard had it easy, he said: in Germany, capitalism was only suspended; in Poland, it was destroyed.[4] Assured of the
prime minister's commitment to radical change, Balcerowicz finally accepted the
positions of finance minister and deputy prime minister. He recruited his former
circle of clandestine capitalists to form a team of free-market technocrats who
were ensconced in the finance ministry.[5] The goal was to enact drastic policy-
institutional reforms that would change social-psychological attitudes.[6] Balcerowicz not only wanted to promote a private sector but to demolish the state sector.

In January 1990, the Solidarity-led government accomplished what had long
been impossible for the communists—introducing comprehensive economic reform without immediately provoking worker protests. As part of the package,
Balcerowicz's team outlined a macrolevel tax reform copied from the mature
capitalist economies.[7] The corporate income tax (CIT)—introduced in 1988,
modified in 1990, codified in 1992—consolidated a single tax rate on business
profits of 40 percent. Temporary exemptions, however, usually for three years,
were allowed for firms with foreign capital investment and new start-up small
and medium enterprises (SMEs).[8] The personal income tax (PIT), which went
into effect in January 1992, shifted the tax burden from the corporate sector to
individual households. It combined five different payroll taxes with rates as high
as 90 percent into one income tax with three rates of 20, 30, and 40 percent. Exemptions were permitted for the self-employed and, after much debate, for pensioners. The value-added tax (VAT), which went into effect in 1993, retargeted tax
collection efforts from production to consumption. Balcerowicz used tax policy
as a means to cultivate capitalism. It favored individual entrepreneurs and foreign investors in the nascent private sector with incentives and exemptions.

Balcerowicz's tax reform was intended to encourage private entrepreneurship,
as well as to discourage public employment. It did so through two punitive taxes
on state enterprises—the excess wage tax and the dividend tax. Known by its
acronymic nickname, *popiwek*, the excess wage tax, was enacted as a fiscal check
on inflation. A similar tax had been tried earlier by the communist government
to regulate labor costs, without success. The *popiwek* was brought back by Balcerowicz to accompany price liberalization, as a disincentive to state enterprise
managers to give in to pressure for pay increases.[9] The use of an excess wage tax as
an inflation deterrent was common practice in postcommunist Eastern Europe,
but no one applied the measure with more zeal than Balcerowicz. Enterprises

exceeding the government-established wage standard by up to 3 percent incurred a 100 percent penalty on their tax bill; by 3 to 5 percent, a 200 percent penalty; and by more than 5 percent, a whopping 500 percent penalty.[10] The dividend tax, meanwhile, was a kind of surtax on the working capital of public-sector firms.[11] The amount of the dividend surcharge initially was capped at 25 percent of enterprise profits, but this ceiling later was removed.[12] The *popiwek* was supposed to hasten the demise of the public sector by forcing insolvent firms into bankruptcy and harrying public employees into the private sector. Instead, it aroused the return of protest politics.

In less than six months, extraordinary politics gave way to collective protest.[13] Given the unfamiliarity and incoherence of the new political institutions, collective protest provided society with a familiar and tested strategy for how to engage in politics. The living legacy of protest politics provided the "repertoires of contention and frameworks for collective action" that were employed in response to radical restructuring.[14] Industrial workers, farmers, and public employees resorted to protest actions—work stoppages, street demonstrations, roadblocks, and hunger strikes—to force their concerns into the policy process. The number of strikes recorded by the government shows the spike in labor protests: there were 250 strikes in 1990, 305 in 1991, 6,362 in 1992, 7,444 in 1993, and 482 in 1994.[15] It should be noted, however, that the postcommunist strike movement paled in comparison with the Solidarity strikes against the communist regime. Unlike their predecessors, the new regime's leaders did not resort to coercion in response to protest actions. Indeed, Poland's counterelites had already dismantled the ZOMO brigade, the armored antiriot police force.[16] Like their predecessors, they engaged protesters in discussion and compromise. In this way, the new regime's leaders, many of whom had only recently been on the same side as the protesters, accepted protest politics as a legitimate form of interest representation.[17]

"Away with the *popiwek*" was the slogan that got thirty thousand demonstrators to take to Warsaw's streets on a cold February morning in 1991.[18] In the recharged political atmosphere, the unequal tax burden between the private and public sectors was a tangible target for embattled state workers. Workers made a cognitive connection between plummeting living standards and the excess wage tax, which animated the strike movement. As Mark Kramer observed, the "reviled" *popiwek* was the "main grievance" in worker protests and strikes.[19] And David Ost identified the *popiwek* as the "most detested (and most contested) part of the entire Balcerowicz Plan."[20] In May 1990, protest politics returned in dramatic fashion when eleven railroad workers from Slupsk staged a hunger strike to publicize their demands for wage increases and the elimination of the *popiwek*. In November 1990, sixty-six out of the seventy coal mines in Poland went out on strike to protest the government wage and tax policies. Also that month, workers at the Gdansk port began a strike in opposition to the *popiwek*. In December, the head committee of the Solidarity trade federation issued a public plea to the government to stop penalizing wage increases through taxation. Next, the postal workers joined the ranks of public employees demanding an end to the *popiwek*. In early 1991, the All-Poland Trade Union Alliance (OPZZ), the former main communist trade union, joined a series of work stoppages and public demonstrations against the *popiwek*. Tens of thousands of workers from more than two thousand enterprises participated in these antitax, economic protests, which continued from February to April.[21] In May, more than five thousand Solidarity-organized demonstrators encircled the Sejm, demanding the repeal of the *popiwek*.[22] Even farmers denounced the *popiwek*, and organized a tax protest in 1991, in which they paid taxes with agricultural products instead of money.[23]

Meanwhile, societal tax resistance took the form of noncompliance. Enterprise managers and workers acted together in refusing to go along with the punitive public sector taxes. After initial reluctance, state enterprise managers began to increase workers' wages in disregard of the *popiwek*. Firms were accordingly assessed stiff tax penalties by the tax administration. But these fines often went unpaid, as many enterprises opted to be tax delinquents. Still other state firms, constrained by the *popiwek*, provided alternative forms of social benefits, in defiance of government austerity policies.[24] By the end of 1991, the Ministry of Finance (MinFin) estimated that the total tax arrears owed to the state budget amounted to more than fifty trillion zloty, or 70 percent of the budget deficit; unpaid *popiwek* taxes accounted for thirty-one trillion zloty of this debt.[25] Poland's postcommunist state lacked both the administrative techniques and the coercive temperament needed to overcome societal tax resistance.

Besides collective protest, electoral politics also provided a means for public workers to register discontent with the Balcerowicz Plan in general, and with his tax policies in particular. The first postcommunist presidential and parliamentary elections heightened political contestation. The *popiwek* was a prominent issue in Poland's first postcommunist presidential campaign in late 1990. The only candidate that did not strongly denounce the unfair tax burden, Prime Minister Mazowiecki, was forced to resign after a poor showing in the first round. In December, Lech Walesa decisively defeated Polish-Canadian businessman Stanislaw Tyminski. In the campaign, both candidates railed against the social and fiscal costs of radical economic reform and the inherent unfairness of the *popiwek*. Despite Walesa's populist campaign rhetoric, Balcerowicz remained as finance minister.

In the midst of a severe revenue shortfall, Balcerowicz persuaded Walesa that it was not feasible to give up the *popiwek* just yet, and so punitive taxes continued to be applied to the state sector. Following a meeting at Belweder Castle, the presidential residence, Balcerowicz agreed to form a task force with trade union representation to discuss government wage policies.[26] The task force decided that the *popiwek* would be phased out—gradually. In 1991, the government showed greater flexibility in its application of the *popiwek*, issuing more exemptions and lowering the upper marginal rate from 500 to 400 percent.[27] Minister of Labor Michal Boni brokered negotiations that lightened the wage tax burden for state firms that reduced their labor force and funded social programs.[28] In parliamentary elections in the autumn of 1991, the *popiwek* again was a campaign issue. Of the six parties that scored higher than 3 percent in the Sejm vote, five explicitly called for either relief from or elimination of the excess wage tax.[29] In late 1991, the new left-of-center prime minister, Jan Oleszewski, kept at least one campaign promise—he fired Balcerowicz.

Russia: From Extraordinary Politics to Cadre Defection

"Power was lying in the street," Leon Trotsky said to explain how communism came to power in Russia. But it sure didn't leave that way. The fall of Soviet communism had less to do with angry masses, and more to do with opportunist elites. Amid political uncertainty, some communist cadres remained loyal, others voiced criticism, and still others headed for the exit, making off with the valued resources of the old regime as they went. Power was not lying in the street, but in the capital stock of the command-administrative state.

In December 1991, the Soviet state passed into history with the stroke of a pen. Russia entered its own short-lived phase of "extraordinary politics." Domestic contestation was low in the aftermath of the old regime's collapse. Buoyed by his victory over the once formidable Communist Party, President Boris Yeltsin was handed emergency powers to sort out the wreckage of the Soviet collapse. With the Supreme Soviet temporarily in retreat, policymaking was entrusted to Yeltsin, including special powers to govern by decree. Taking advantage of "extraordinary politics," Yeltsin enlisted a little-known economist, Yegor Gaidar, to lead the transition. Descended from an elite Soviet lineage (both grandfathers were acclaimed writers and his father was a rear admiral), Gaidar seemed an unlikely capitalist.[30] He graduated from the Economics Faculty of Moscow State University and served as editor of *Kommunist*, the Communist Party's main theoretical journal; he later insisted that his views on economics were influenced mostly by Adam Smith.[31] In November 1991, Gaidar assumed the positions of deputy prime minister and minister of economics and finance, with a personal mandate from Yeltsin to work out a program for a rapid transition to a market economy.

Like Poland, Russia introduced tax reforms modeled after the mature capitalist states. The main features included a valued-added tax (VAT), replacing the
old turnover tax on enterprises; a new corporate income tax (CIT), replacing the
old profits tax in 1992; a new excise taxes on the business sector; and a revamped
personal income tax (PIT) on households, which came into effect in1992.[32] Tax
rates were high, but consistent with the rates throughout Europe. The legislation
transposed over society a set of categorical assignments denoting the legal status
of taxpayers, but it did not provide a set of countervailing legal protections for
society against state revenue claims. In principle, the new tax system fit with a
market economy; in practice, it retained features of the command economy.

Unlike Poland, the state's new tax policy did not attempt to cultivate the nascent
small-business sector with temporary exemptions or reduced rates.[33] Instead, the
government used the new excise taxes to target a couple dozen large industrial
enterprises, involved in the extraction, refinement, and export of minerals, metals, oil, and gas.[34] Like Poland, "extraordinary politics" in Russia was short-lived.
Starting in the summer of 1992, Russia was in the throes of crisis politics. Yeltsin's radical economic policies and conciliatory foreign policies aroused strident
opposition in the legislature, which now acted to reclaim control of the policy
process. Russia's transition was ensnared in a protracted extrication crisis that
included ideological polarization and institutional stalemate. In the political center, executive-legislative relations were paralyzed by a tenacious power struggle
over competing claims on policymaking. Meanwhile, center-regional relations
were thrown into confusion by assertions of sovereignty over policymaking by
provincial governors and legislatures. Yeltsin's attempts to reach a compromise
solution over the institutional and territorial divisions of power were spurned.

In the midst of political crisis, central state actors saw their new revenue
claims subverted by three sets of elites: regional governors, corporate directors,
and private financiers. These actors stood in between the central state and the
revenue sources it claimed in society. To gain access to revenue, the state required
the cooperation of these actors, who became intermediary agents in the revenue
extraction process. The rise of the regional governors was a direct consequence
of the political conflict between Yeltsin's Russia and Gorbachev's Soviet Union.
After the collapse, the territorial division of power in the new Russian state was
formally restructured into a federation. But precisely where the line was drawn
between the center and the regions, particularly concerning revenue claims, was
never clear. Given its weak administrative capacity, the central state relied on
the cooperation of the more prosperous regional governments, the "donor" regions, to collect revenue for the central budget to finance federal programs and to
redistribute it to poorer regions.[35] In his memoirs, Yeltsin spoke openly about his
political dependence on the regional leaders: "Any clash between the president

and the governors would be extremely dangerous for the country.... They are the 100 masters of Russia. Actually, princes, might be a more accurate term."[36]

In the early 1990s, the "donor" regions within Russia challenged the center with tax revolts. The three richest national republics—Tatarstan, Bashkortostan, Sakha-Yakutia—simply stopped sending revenue to the central budget, claiming a special administrative status. Emboldened regional governments threatened to follow suit. Sverdlovsk unilaterally upgraded its territorial-administrative status from oblast to republic, and declared that as the Urals Republic it also was not required to turn over tax receipts to Moscow.[37] Meanwhile, St. Petersburg gave itself a generous 20 percent discount on its federal tax obligations.[38] Finance Minister Boris Federov complained to more than thirty regions about delayed or partial tax payments.[39] Whereas the finance minister aggressively pursued regional governments to fulfill their tax obligations, the president was more inclined toward compromise solutions.

The directors of the large corporations were the second set of revenue intermediaries. They presided over the newly privatized or quasi-private industrial enterprises. Although many firms in the industrial sector languished during the transition, others, particularly energy, metallurgy, and raw materials, quickly became quite profitable. These corporate entities were earmarked as the principal sources of revenue for the new state. The tax reforms introduced at the outset of the transition placed the heaviest burden on these corporations through the VAT, the profits and excise taxes, and export tariffs. Regional governments were even more revenue-dependent on large corporations than the central government. For example, Yukos Oil alone accounted for more than 25 percent of the budgetary income for Samara Oblast.[40] The large corporate sector quickly learned how to use the fractured political system for tax relief, the poorly defined legal system for tax avoidance, and the weak enforcement system for tax evasion.

The third set of revenue intermediaries were the newly arrived financiers who headed Russia's largest commercial banks. Many of these new private banks had originated as the former financial departments of large state-run corporations and economic branch ministries. They had access to enterprise funds and corporate accounts, providing a pool of operating capital. During the high inflation of the early 1990s, commercial banks reaped enormous profits by borrowing from low-interest deposits and providing high-interest loans. This process soon gave rise to a small clique of financiers who proved to be particularly adept at accumulating capital. These financiers then used those profits to expand into other economic sectors.[41] With the support of the government, they formed large vertically structured holding companies, or financial-industrial groups (FIGs), which combined financial services, commodity exports, manufacturing, and mass media. This merger of financiers and corporate directors led to the rise of Russia's big-business billionaire tycoons, the self-proclaimed oligarchs.

As tax resistance from the government's large revenue targets increased, Gaidar insisted that "changes in the tax system were most necessary to assure income to the budget."[42] But the government of free market enthusiasts did not have the chance to revise tax policy. Gaidar's policymaking authority derived personally from the president. Although Russia's path to regime breakdown was elite-driven, Gaidar's team of liberal economists had few connections to the industrial and regional elite. Although they had ties to Russia's democratic movement, this movement never developed into a strong sociopolitical force.[43] Gaidar was dependent on the disposition of the president for political support, which would become apparent when "extraordinary politics" ended.

Making Revenue Bargains: Consensus and Conflict

The tax reforms enacted in Poland and Russia at the outset of their postcommunist transitions helped bring about the end of "extraordinary politics." The political situation in both countries shifted from "low" to "high" contestation. Despite the apparent similarities, the initial conditions that shaped postcommunist tax policy differed notably in these two cases. Concerning the transition in general, Polish elites were able to agree on the broad parameters of economic restructuring and the political regime they wanted. Russian elites, meanwhile, remained bitterly divided throughout the decade over the direction of the transition. Concerning tax policy in particular, Polish tax policy was constrained by self-protective workers, who allied with political parties competing for votes in a parliamentary system. Russian tax policy was constrained by self-enriching elites, who allied with government bureaucrats competing for favor in a presidential system. As the new postcommunist states struggled to locate and claim capital from society, these different political constraints led to different revenue bargains in Poland and Russia.

Poland: Elite Consensus and the State-Labor Revenue Bargain

Poland entered the transition with political institutions designed to sustain a ruling party that by mid-1990 did not exist. This arrangement went bust as society's copious cleavages spilled into view. Competing economic interests and cultural preferences hastened spontaneous political unraveling and realignment.[44] Solidarity was a multifarious movement, not a unified union. The opposition of workers, intellectuals, farmers, and students fragmented into smaller groupings, defined as much by personal rivalry as by political interest. Two loosely organized labor alliances competed for influence—a Solidarity successor confederation and the communist-tainted OPZZ. Unabashed economic liberals and unrepentant cultural secularists set themselves apart from their more populist and conservative former political bedfellows. The communists, meanwhile, splintered into new groupings of varying leftist stripe. Enjoying well-placed access to financial and organizational resources, a contingent of ex-communists found redemption as social democrats and staked out a wide claim on the political left. As the bipolar political structure of the breakdown phase multiplied, Poland lapsed into political crisis.

Poland began 1992 in stalemate: the president tried to grab power from parliament, the prime minister struggled to make policy with a crumbly coalition, while parliament was paralyzed by twenty-eight self-destructive squabbling parties. But the year proved decisive for the Polish transition. In October 1992, rival elites successfully negotiated a provisional division of power, known as the "Little Constitution," a mixed system in which parliament controlled the government and the president possessed limited checking powers.[45] The Little Constitution established the rules of executive-legislature engagement until a new constitution could be enacted. It marked a crucial moment of elite consensus in the Polish transition. At the point at which Poland's transition was imperiled, a bipartisan compromise was reached over an improvised institutional arrangement. It was sustained by a cross-party elite consensus for Western-style democracy. It is not as if Polish politics became less contentious after this time, because it did not. Instead, the elite consensus recognized a set of democratic rules for political competition.

With the political crisis contained, the government was able to focus on state finances. The anti-public-sector bias of Balcerowicz's tax policies provoked protest and noncompliance; in effect, the political and fiscal costs of realizing this tax reform became too great for the economic benefits it was supposed to yield. State-society relations in the Polish transition were not off to a good start. Once the chief shock therapist was removed as finance minister, successor governments tried to soften the social impact of capitalism and lighten the tax burden on public sector workers. The result was an incrementally improvised "state-labor" revenue bargain, which fundamentally revised Balcerowicz's procapitalist postcommunist tax reform in the early to mid-1990s. The revenue bargain benefited three groups—public sector employees, pensioners, and farmers. This study employs the label "state-labor" revenue bargain because the main societal participants in the bargain are employees from state-operated enterprises, public service institutions, and state administrative agencies. In addition, the pensioners also are mostly former public sector employees.

Poland's state-labor revenue bargain entwined three sets of interests—economic, political, and fiscal. First, the groups that most benefited from the revenue bargain were public sector workers, farmers, and pensioners. In the exchange of economic resources, Poland's public sector workers wanted equalization of the tax burden and protection from market capitalism. Second, the political interests of Poland's ex-communists, now reconstituted as a moderate social-democratic left, received an electoral boost, particularly from public sector workers. In alliance with like-minded economic leftists and the Polish People's Party (the peasants' party), supported at the polls by small farmers, the social democrats managed to recapture control of government in 1993. Finally, the fiscal interests of the state was represented by economist-technocrats in the finance ministry, responsible for managing state finances. The state-labor revenue bargain helped to defuse protest politics and legitimated the state's new revenue claims, particularly the personal income tax. Over the longer term, however, the exchange of political and economic resources inherent in the bargain worked against the fiscal interests of the state.

The state-labor revenue bargain was pieced together incrementally under three successively shaky coalition governments. First, the 1991 parliamentary elections brought in the left-leaning government of Jan Oleszewski (December 1991–June 1992). His brief tenure was marked by political conflict and budget crisis that foiled fiscal reform. He did, however, dismiss Balcerowicz as finance minister. As a candidate, Oleszewski railed against the excess wage tax; as prime minister, he relied on the tax as a necessary source of income. Second, the centrist government of Hanna Suchocka (July 1992–October 1993) was also a critic of the *popiwek*. Under this government, the *popiwek* and dividend taxes increasingly became subject of ad hoc negotiation and lax enforcement. Maximum penalty rates decreased from 500 percent in 1991, to 400 percent in 1992, to 300 percent in 1993.[46] In March 1993, state enterprises that expected to make profits and were not in arrears were allowed to haggle for *popiwek* reductions with local tax officials. More than five hundred firms took advantage of this concession by year's end.[47] Even firms operating at a loss that raised worker salaries were permitted to renegotiate their wage tax debts to the state budget. Despite these gestures to ease the burden, many state enterprises still refused to comply with the excess wage and dividend taxes, even though they would not incur any coercive sanction. In autumn 1993, Solidarity pulled its support from the coalition and the Suchocka government failed a vote of confidence in the Sejm.

Third, the social democrat/peasants party coalition government of Waldemar Pawlak (October 1993–March 1995) solidified the exchange of political-economic resources that underlay the revenue bargain. Polish society's resentment of existing tax policy was evident in the 1993 electoral outcome. During the campaign, six parties advocated the outright abolition of the *popiwek*. Four of these parties were among the seven that made it over the 5 percent threshold, including the top vote-getter, the Democratic Left Alliance.[48] The new finance minister, Grzegorz Kolodko, was a veteran of the 1989 Round Table negotiations and every bit the equal to Balcerowicz as economic theorist and policy practitioner. Kolodko was one of the chief policy architects of the state-labor revenue bargain. The social-democratic government made good on its campaign promise to eradicate the unequal tax burden, and the *popiwek* was finally eliminated in 1995. Many state firms, however, were still deep in arrears on wage tax penalties. The social-democratic government canceled most outstanding *popiwek* debts, thereby eliminating any manifestation of a discriminatory tax burden.[49]

The state-labor revenue bargain also involved the redistribution of tax revenue sources to help protect public sector workers from free market capitalism. In the command economy, one's place of work provided not only a job but a host of social benefits. The Balcerowicz Plan intended to shift economic responsibility for social needs from state-managed firms to individual households. After his departure, budgetary resources were increasingly spent on social protection of public sector employees. Indeed, the social-democratic finance minister, Kolodko, did more than just protect state employees; he reinvested capital into the public sector in the expectation that some state enterprises would return to profitability.[50] Fearing the free market's destructive force, public sector workers wanted and now received some assurances about job security, as plans for rapid privatization were delayed.[51] In addition, the social-democratic government vowed to cover the costs of living in a transition economy at least to a minimal extent for those who did leave the workforce by continuing to fund unemployment, retirement, and disability pension programs.

The revenue bargain included labor in the policymaking process. The reemergence of protest politics led to ad hoc and decentralized negotiations concerning wages and the tax obligations of public sector employees. The Suchocka government established the precedent for postcommunist governments of engaging protesting workers in negotiation. This improvised practice quickly evolved into a more formal and centralized process of negotiation. In February 1993, Minister of Labor Jacek Kuron, a trusted Solidarity veteran, proposed a state enterprise pact by which the government and public sector workers could reach a compromise. A centerpiece of Kuron's initiative was the formation of a Tripartite Commission, composed of government, management, and trade union representatives, to consult on economic policymaking. It included subcommittees for state finance, privatization, and financial assistance to the public sector as well as for wage and tax policy. Instead of imposing wage norms and tax demands on public sector workers, the government would engage representatives of the major trade unions in negotiations to come to compromise agreements. In 1994, the social-democratic Pawlak government made the Tripartite Commission a permanent body linking state and labor.

Poland's small farmers were included as well in the state-labor revenue bargain. This required a bit of political bending, since the principal demand of farmers was higher prices for agricultural products, which went against the demand of workers for lower food costs. Farmers did not get higher prices, but they did get other economic benefits, derived mainly from the tax system. As it was, the agricultural sector was not a major source of revenue for the communist state, which nonetheless applied punitively high tax rates to independent small farmers. In the postcommunist state, agriculture provided even less revenue. For most of the 1990s, small farmers paid practically no taxes at all. Farmers were exempted from paying CIT, PIT, and VAT taxes.[52] In addition, farmers secured from successive social-democratic governments low- interest loans, generous discounts on the costs of fuel, and minimal contribution fees to the farmers' social fund.[53]

Next, the revenue bargain entailed a political exchange in the form of electoral support for Poland's reconstituted Left. By providing protective social benefits and personal tax exemptions to individual households, the social-democratic Left managed to redefine itself as a defender of public worker interests. The Democratic Left Alliance (DLA) formed a close relationship with the former communist trade union (OPZZ). In addition, the DLA was supported by the main teachers' union, several small left-wing parties, and a couple dozen social organizations that had been formed under the old regime, such as the Democratic Union of Women and the Pensioners Association.[54] The DLA competed for votes mainly against the Solidarity Alliance. The base of support for social-democratic presidential and parliamentary electoral victories in the 1990s was composed mainly of voters dependent on state financial assistance and tax exemptions: state enterprise managers and workers, public sector employees, uniformed personnel, pensioners, the unemployed, housewives, and students.[55]

Finally, the fiscal interests of the postcommunist state were part of the state-labor revenue bargain. The postcommunist state gave up its discriminatory taxes on the public sector. But even the social-democratic government recognized the fiscal need to tap into household income. As the *popiwek* and dividend taxes were withdrawn, a new personal income tax (PIT) and a social security tax (SST) were put in place. The PIT especially was noteworthy since household income had not previously been a direct revenue source. Initial expectations that the PIT would be accepted by Polish workers and prove to be a reliable revenue source were low. The introduction of the PIT "should be done cautiously," warned one Polish economist. "This new obligation to the state will be a shock to 12 million workers and 7 million pensioners, who for years have not paid taxes, and may create a highly explosive situation, making the British poll tax look like child's play."[56] Such fears were not realized. The PIT went into effect in 1992 without protest. Unlike the *popiwek*, the PIT did not discriminate between private and public employees. It represented an equalization of the tax burden. The government took further steps to ease the burden on households by initially indexing workers' wages both for inflation and for the anticipated salary loss caused by the new tax. Wage indexing became a regular part of the labor bargain.[57] The PIT became the fiscal means by which the postcommunist state was able to gain access to income from individual households. In its first year, the PIT made up 20 percent of all revenues collected, proving to be a more than adequate replacement for the excess wage tax. The next year, 1993, the PIT accounted for nearly 25 percent of state revenues collected.

The Polish revenue bargain had to offer something tangible to workers in exchange for tax compliance. The bargain provided Polish state workers with a fair tax burden, inclusion in the state's policy process when their economic interests were concerned, and protection from the social consequences of market capitalism. In exchange, the Polish state received a respite from protest politics and access to a new revenue source. The state-labor revenue bargain, however, contained an inherent tension between the economic interests of private entrepreneurs and state enterprise workers, which become more apparent later in the decade.

Russia: Elite Conflict and the State-Elite Revenue Bargain

Blowing up parliament, as it turned out, did not encourage elite consensus in Russia. Throughout the 1990s, the Russian transition was plagued by elite conflict. Unlike Poland, there never was agreement among the main political combatants over a general set of rules for the conduct of postcommunist politics and economics; instead, power and wealth were viewed in zero-sum terms, with little regard to rules. In September 1993, elite conflict escalated when the president tried to rein in parliament, and parliament tried to incite popular unrest. The conflict was more boyar brawl than civil war, as no one else seemed to want to get involved. Barricades were erected, street skirmishes ensued, and the parliament was besieged, shelled, and, finally, shut down. Yeltsin pushed through a constitution that favored a strong presidential regime. In December, the new institutional division of power was consecrated through a popular referendum.

Although the constitution resolved the political stalemate, it did not reconcile the political elite with one another. Elite conflict, now waged within the boundaries of the constitution, continued throughout Yeltsin's tenure. Russia's defiant political left wing competed effectively in parliamentary elections. Ensconced in the Duma, the communist-led Left acted not as a loyal opposition but as an anti-system adversary, intent on deposing the president, dismantling the constitutional order, and reversing economic reform. In reaction, Yeltsin built political alliances with regional and economic elites, using generous concessions of economic resources. With a few notable exceptions, Yeltsin was reluctant to employ coercion. Instead, he preferred to engage in a process of discrete bargaining by which the central state ceded its claims on particular resources. Yeltsin's political survival strategy reinforced the fragmentation of state power that had been caused by cadre defection. In place of the unitary framework of the old Soviet state, the postcommunist Russian state in the 1990s resembled a mosaic of competing fiefdoms.

The management of central state finances was skewed by this political situation. The new tax code was modified and manipulated through multiple access points to the policy process. According to the constitution, the president controlled the government and was given powers to circumvent the legislature in the policy process. Decision making on the executive side, however, was not concentrated, but dispersed among the presidential administration, government ministries and agencies, and special commissions. Next, the constitution accorded the legislature formal powers in budgetary and tax policy. Taking full advantage, the Duma came to be known as the "black hole" in the budget process, because of its readiness to grant special tax exemptions and create "offshore" tax havens.[58] Even the state's revenue collection bureaucracies were given discretion over the application of rates and privileges. The customs agency was notorious for granting privileges, while the tax administration earned a reputation for applying higher tax rates.[59] President Yeltsin later conceded that "multiple centers of power" undermined the operation of state finances.[60]

In 1993, Viktor Chernomyrdin replaced Yegor Gaidar as prime minister, with the announcement that economic policy would now entail "less shock and more therapy." Chernomyrdin was the former head of the Soviet gas industry, which was reorganized into a quasi-private monopoly, Gazprom. When it came to tax policy, Chernomyrdin was the consummate backroom negotiator. Under Chernomyrdin, tax resistance to the state's new revenue claims was indulged with the strategy of elite bargaining. Elite bargaining was a hybrid system of revenue extraction that combined the new conditions of the transition economy with practices familiar to the command economy. It rested on a complex web of personal ties stretching across political and economic spheres, and from the center to the regions. The strategy entailed the utilization of informal negotiations, instead of formal mechanisms, to obtain revenue. The bargaining process was ad hoc, idiosyncratic, discrete, and decentralized. Representatives of various industrial and regional groups succeeded in securing concessions on tax rates and other tax privileges. Although a mature capitalist macro-tax-policy existed in principle, it was enforced unevenly and amended repeatedly to reflect the interests of favored regional and business elites.

The central state defused the political challenge of the regional governors by making concessions over the territorial division tax policymaking. First, presidential decrees were issued that formally decentralized tax policy. In December 1993 the regions were granted increased access to revenues collected on their territory and greater autonomy over their budgets.[61] In early 1994, regional and local administrations were allowed to introduce their own taxes without limits on the rates.[62] Also, at this time, the chief nemesis of the regional governors, state-centralizer Boris Fedorov, was removed as finance minister. Second, in early 1994, the center began negotiating special bilateral treaties with the regions, ceding greater political autonomy and special tax privileges. Independent-minded Tatarstan established the precedent. It was allowed to withhold from the center most of its VAT revenues, the principal source of the central state's income.[63] The Kremlin next negotiated a special treaty with Yeltsin's home region, Sverdlovsk, which reduced its total tax burden to the center by nearly 30 percent.[64] Eventually, more than half of Russia's eighty-nine regions struck deals with the center over revenue extraction as part of a bilateral agreement. Third, in the formal division of tax spoils, the regions seized a larger share of the VAT and the profits taxes, which produced the most income. In 1992, the territorial division of the VAT was 80 percent to the center and 20 percent to the regions, but in 1996 the ratio shifted to 75 percent to the center and 25 percent to the regions. In 1992, the profits tax was divided so that 41 percent went to the center and 59 percent remained in the regions, but in 1996 the ratio had become 34 percent to the center and 66 percent to the regions.[65] By such means, the central state effectively recognized the claims of regional governors to a greater share of state revenue sources.

Big business, meanwhile, reduced its tax obligations by lobbying the industry-friendly Chernomyrdin government. Among his first acts as prime minister, Chernomyrdin cut the VAT rate by 8 percent and allowed corporations to defer payment of the profits tax.[66] Deputy Prime Minister Anatoly Chubais intervened in 1994 to force the tax administration to drop its claim to $7 million in disputed taxes from a multinational firm. By 1995, Lukoil had already secured over one trillion rubles in special tax exemptions from the government.[67] In 1996, an ad hoc commission unilaterally cut the vodka excise tax by 5 percent, while the Ministry of Economy declared beer a nonalcoholic beverage, at the bequest of Russia's four largest brewers, in order to exempt beer from a tax hike on spirits.[68] In 1996, the Ministry of Finance amended the VAT rules so that they did not apply to a variety of banking operations, such as purchasing securities or transferring funds.[69] By design, the large corporations in the commodity export sector were meant to supply the bulk of tax revenues. Under Chernomyrdin, firms in the energy sector were given ample opportunity to seek relief from this burden. In exchange, these firms offered to supply valued goods and services to the public sector at little or no cost. Favored firms received special exemptions, rate reductions, payment deferrals, and barter offsets. In some cases, business tycoons were brought into the government, where they could directly award themselves special tax privileges.[70] While acting as first deputy prime minister, Vladimir Potanin granted special tax breaks to his own company, Noril'sk Nikel, in 1996 that saved $100 million for the metals export giant.[71]

Finally, through informal dealings a select group of financiers emerged as the state's preferred private lenders. They orchestrated the "loans for shares" scheme by which they provided low-interest loans to the state in exchange for controlling interest in the most prized enterprises on the privatization block, leading to the rise of powerful financial-industrial groups, which were used to supplement the limited fiscal administrative capabilities of the state. The new state lacked a unified and coherent network of bank accounts for collecting tax revenues and dispensing budgetary outlays, so it relied on new private banks to administer budgetary funds. Thirteen banks were bestowed the status of "empowered agents" of the state budget, which accorded them lucrative contracts to handle multimillion-dollar funds.[72]

In exchange for tax concessions, Yeltsin successfully mobilized economic and regional elites in his ongoing political battles with the communist Left. This relationship was solidified in the 1996 presidential election.[73] In early 1996, Yeltsin's approval ratings were at all-time lows, and he was especially disliked in rural regions and among older voters. According to electoral rules, the winner was determined by raw numbers, which led campaign tacticians to target urban areas and the youth to counter this broad base of discontent. Yeltsin called upon the big bankers, corporate heads, and regional governors to provide the material and organizational resources necessary to get out the vote on his behalf. The business elite underwrote the costs of the president's reelection campaign, including a pop musical festival that toured the major urban areas. And, even more important, they helped pay off overdue wages and social benefits to public sector employees. Yeltsin's political survival was ultimately secured by the voter turnout in the regions that were the chief beneficiaries of the center-elite revenue bargain. In the runoff election, incumbent President Yeltsin prevailed over his communist nemesis, Gennady Zyuganov, with nearly 54 percent of the vote. More than three-quarters of Yeltsin's winning total came from the ten wealthy regions that were the principal beneficiaries of revenue bargaining.[74]

Russia's state-elite revenue bargain grew out of protracted political conflict. The opportunity for ad hoc and discreet negotiating over the tax burden was enhanced by the strong presidential system, which contained multiple points of access to tax policymaking. Whereas particular political and economic elite interests were accommodated by the revenue bargain, the fiscal interests of the Russian state generally suffered. Russia's new tax regime was fundamentally flawed. Unlike Poland, Russia's revenue bargain did not provide incentives to promote societal tax compliance. Elite bargaining produced an entangling web of special favors that ultimately undermined state fiscal capacity. In the second half of the 1990s, this weakness became glaringly apparent when the threat of fiscal crisis loomed once again.

Revenue Bargains as Political Constraints: Failed Tax Reform

The politics of postcommunist tax reform cannot be fully explained without explicit reference to the state-society revenue bargains of the early transition. In Poland, competitive parliamentary elections provided the formal political mechanism from which the state-labor revenue bargain emerged. In the early 1990s, parliamentary elections brought a left-wing social democrat/peasant party coalition to power, which pieced together a revenue bargain that cushioned the impact of the market on public sector workers, farmers, and pensioners. At first, the bargain was not detrimental to state fiscal interests, especially when adding up the income received from PIT-paying, wage-earning households. By the late 1990s, however, state finances showed signs of strain as the revenue bargain expanded welfare rolls, nudged up the budget deficit, tampered with the tax code, and shifted the tax burden onto the private sector.

Meanwhile, in Russia, a protracted executive-legislative power struggle led the constitutionally strong president to adopt a political survival strategy, in which state-managed economic resources were traded for political support from business and regional elite actors. The economic interests of Russia's favored elites came into conflict with the fiscal needs of the postcommunist state. But in a closely contested election, in 1996, presidential politics took precedence over state finances. In the late 1990s, both Poland and Russia were in a political condition of "high contestation," which served to reinforce the political constraints of their respective revenue bargains on policymaking. As a result, efforts in both cases to bolster state finances by enacting tax reform ended in failure.

Poland: Parliamentary Politics and Failed Tax Reform

The Polish state-labor revenue bargain contained an inherent tension between the economic interests of private sector entrepreneurs and public sector workers. The revenue bargain remained intact while social democrats controlled the parliament and the presidency. But the Left eventually lost its leverage in the legislature. New elections in 1997 brought to power an "anti-communist" coalition, forcing the Left into opposition. The new coalition rested on an uneasy alliance of populist Solidarity stalwarts and free-market liberals, who beyond their dislike for the ex-communists had little in common. The alliance sought to reignite the old Solidarity flame, but after seven years of postcommunist change Polish society no longer lined up neatly between Us and Them.

The social-democratic fiscal policy tried to balance economic incentives with social protection. But private business was increasingly subsidizing the public sector. Maintaining the redistribution side of the state-labor revenue bargain required a steady income stream, but Poland's tax system instead was springing leaks.[75] The state's new revenue sources, worker households and small businesses, were compromised by politics. The personal income tax (PIT) was amended more than thirty times. It allowed for 125 different categories of tax relief, ten categories of income deduction, and fourteen categories of tax credits.[76] The most generous PIT exemptions provided relief for basic living costs: housing, education, and childcare. The private business sector also took advantage of tax privileges. The corporate income tax (CIT) was amended almost as many times as the PIT. By 1997, businesses could reduce their tax bill by way of forty investment deductions, sixty-three depreciation allowances, and seventeen special tax zones. New private ventures and foreign firms continued to enjoy CIT tax holidays that lasted from five to ten years.[77] Meanwhile, public sector enterprises were especially successful in securing special treatment from tax collectors under the social-democratic government. By 1998, tax arrears reached 3 percent of GDP, with state-managed railroads, coal mines, and steelworks topping the list of largest debtors to the state budget. State firms accounted for nearly 75 percent of tax arrears on social security contributions, the main source of revenue for pension programs.[78]

The rising costs of public welfare prompted calls for tax reform from the political Right *and* Left. On the right: by the mid-1990s, private business groups were particularly resentful of the politically privileged state enterprises, which they believed should be paying more. On the left: populist-inclined participants in the social-democratic government wanted to revise the rate brackets for the PIT, forcing the wealthy to pay more.[79] The 1997 parliamentary elections provided a forum for the reconsideration of the state-labor revenue bargain. Competing tax policy preferences once again were prominent during the campaign. With a 5 percent vote threshold to clear, the elections sent five party blocs into the Sejm, representing nearly 90 percent of all ballots cast. Of the five party blocs that made the Sejm, four promoted fiscally populist tax reforms; these included (with their share of the vote): Solidarity Electoral Action (33.8%), Democratic Left Alliance (27.1%), Polish People's Party (7.3%), and Movement for Reconstruction of Poland (5.6%). Only Balcerowicz's promarket Freedom Union (13.4%) was explicitly against the state-labor revenue bargain.[80]

The big winner with more than one third of the vote was Solidarity Electoral Action (AWS), an umbrella organization that brought together the tattered remnants of communist-era Solidarity. A visit by John Paul II to Poland on the eve of the elections gave the AWS a papal bounce in the polls. The AWS included over thirty small political parties, mostly socially conservative Catholics and anti-social-democrat trade unionists. The AWS delivered a loud "family values" message that resonated with voters. On tax reform, however, the AWS was explicitly murky, promising to maintain a profamily tax policy bias and to reduce the state's role in revenue redistribution.[81] Balcerowicz's liberal party, the Freedom Union, formed in 1994, was the only bloc that was explicitly against the revenue bargain. The Democratic Left Alliance gained a larger percentage of the vote than in 1993, but it was only good enough for second. In autumn 1997, an "anti-communist" coalition was formed between the ex-Solidarity (AWS) bloc and the Freedom Union (UW), sending the social democrats to the political sidelines. The senior partner Solidarity bloc chose a former chemistry professor and trade unionist, Jerzy Buzek, to serve as prime minister. In his first major public address, the new prime minister stressed the need to "heal the state through moral purification" and to put "the state in service to the family."[82] Buzek confirmed that the coalition was committed to tax reform, but he did not offer details. The political situation, however, was complicated by the continued presence of a popular social-democratic president, Alexander Kwasniewski. Political cohabitation Polish-style had begun.

In the division of ministerial portfolios, the Freedom Union's economic liberals claimed state finance, and returned Leszek Balcerowicz to office as deputy prime minister and finance minister. He replaced the social-democratic team at the Ministry of Finance (MinFin) with a cohort of promarket economists.[83] In place of the state-labor revenue bargain, Balcerowicz vowed to enact an "Entrepreneurs Constitution," which would encourage private sector growth, eliminate public sector profligacy, balance the budget, and jump-start the stalled privatization process.[84] The first steps were easy. Balcerowicz pulled tight on the purse strings of the fisc. MinFin simply ceased supplying credit advances and tax exemptions to unprofitable public sector enterprises. MinFin also devolved responsibility for health care costs to local governments, and introduced means testing and spending caps for pensioners.[85] Finally, Balcerowicz promised a tax reform that would benefit private entrepreneurs and reduce the burden on the economy as a whole. In early 1998, MinFin distributed a *White Paper on Taxes* to legislators, the media, and business groups that laid out the case for radical tax reform.

When the Sejm reconvened from summer break to take up the budget, Balcerowicz submitted his long-awaited tax reform. It lived up to the Hayekian hype, and directly challenged the state-labor revenue bargain. First, PIT: almost all exemptions and deductions were scheduled for termination, while the three-tiered rate structure was to be replaced with two tiers, set at reduced rates of 22 percent and 32 percent. But it did not end there: it promised a single 22 percent rate for PIT by 2002, flattening any progressive pretenses out of the personal income tax structure. Next, CIT: corporate income rates were to be lowered from 36 percent to 32 percent, with the understanding that successive rate cuts would follow, eventually reaching 22 percent as well by 2002. Finally, VAT: the reformers expected to expunge almost all existing VAT exemptions for basic living goods and housing allowances. The VAT reform was supposed to make up for revenue lost from lower PIT and CIT rates. Balcerowicz's tax reform caused a clash between free markets and family values, exposing the ideological rift in the ruling coalition. According to the *Warsaw Voice*, the reform had "few friends outside the business community and the plan's own author."[86] The Solidarity bloc (AWS) was dismayed by the reform's disregard for families, children, and the poor. In press statements, the AWS and the prime minister disassociated themselves from the proposal, saying, "this is Balcerowicz's plan, not the government's."[87] Coalition partners squabbled over taxation throughout the fall. In the end, Balcerowicz's ambitious tax reform never made it out of the Sejm.

In 1999, Balcerowicz tried again. The determined finance minister announced right off that if the government did not back him fully, then he and his sixty liberal seats would quit the coalition. Nonetheless, intracoalition conflict once more rattled the reform. In October, Warsaw's streets were clogged with tens of thousands of public sector protesters, who railed against the proposed reform. The Solidarity bloc submitted its own counter tax reform. With the legislative season winding down, the prime minister and the finance minister were compelled to come up with a compromise. The free-market liberals accepted a few "profamily" modifications: a progressive PIT rate structure, more gradual CIT rate reductions, and special tax breaks for large families. "If this accord is not implemented," Balcerowicz announced, "then I do not see a place for me in this government."[88] Somehow the cranky coalition held together. In late November, the Sejm finally passed a tax reform bill and sent it to the desk of the president, who vetoed it. Tax reform was thrown into turmoil. President Kwasniewski derided the government for violating the norms of social justice.[89] With the social-democratic president now part of the process, tax reform was further watered down. The CIT would be lowered, but over five years. The reform of VAT and PIT social exemptions was postponed.[90] Given the constraints of coalition politics, it was the best Balcerowicz could do.

From potatoes to pornography, the Freedom Union and the Solidarity bloc continued to quarrel over nearly every piece of legislation that came along. When the budget season got under way the next year, a group of back bench Solidarity deputies bolted the majority and blocked Balcerowicz's attempt to impose a 3 percent VAT on agricultural products. Until then, Poland's hard-up farm sector had been exempt from such taxes. Balcerowicz readied yet another resignation letter. This time Buzek accepted and the Freedom Union also withdrew from the governing coalition. Upon exiting the coalition, one relieved Freedom Union deputy remarked: "I feel like I've moved out of my terrible mother-in-law's place."[91] In 2001, new parliamentary elections left the pro-business, tax-cutting Freedom Union with a mere 3 percent of the popular vote, 10 percent less than in 1997. In a condition of high political contestation, the party that supported promarket tax reform was tossed out of parliament. The state-labor revenue bargain prevailed.

Russia: Presidential Politics and Failed Tax Reform

As early as 1993 the need to mend the Russian state's faulty tax system was clear, at least to those who ran the Finance Ministry. Finance Minister Boris Fedorov created an ad hoc committee to study a tax reform that would broaden the revenue base, lower the tax burden, and simplify the collection process.[92] But Fedorov's commission never completed its task. In 1994, he was dismissed from his post by the new prime minister, Viktor Chernomyrdin. Fedorov's tax committee was disbanded when his replacement declared that the system did not need reform.[93] With corporate and regional elites entrenched in the policy process, the issue of tax reform was relegated to a small MinFin discussion circle. The rancorous relationship between the executive and the legislature made prospects for tax reform more unlikely than Rasputin rising from the Neva. Chernomyrdin chose not to spend his political capital on such a dubious legislative venture.

In 1995, MinFin submitted a tax reform proposal. This time, St. Petersburg mathematician Sergei Shatalov was put in charge. As deputy finance minister, Shatalov would be the principal architect of tax reform for the next decade.[94] His aggressive advocacy of promarket tax reforms endeared him to the international financial community and estranged him from domestic political elites. Shatalov promised to address the dual needs of improving tax collections for the state budget and aligning tax policy with international standards.[95] Shatalov's team produced a comprehensive reform that proposed condensing the tax code from two hundred to thirty taxes, lowering rates as an incentive for businesses to come out of the shadow economy, shifting the burden away from the largest corporations and broadening the tax base, and eliminating tax exemptions that facilitated tax evasion.[96] The draft reform circulated around the Council of Ministers for several months, without garnering political support. Chernomyrdin's government simply did not care to make tax reform a legislative priority.

A dramatic drop in revenue in 1996 finally brought together a loose coalition in favor of tax reform. The advocates were united by a disdain for elite revenue bargaining. The coalition was led by Shatalov and his technocratic team in the Finance Ministry. Also on the executive side, the State Tax Service, whose beleaguered and bewildered inspectors were left to sort out the vagaries and contradictions of the existing tax code, publicly endorsed tax policy reform. The tax administration journal was a frequent critic of the government's penchant for elite bargaining: "Tax policy has turned into a system of special assistance. It is better to have lower rates and fewer privileges, than higher rates and many privileges."[97] They were joined in the Duma by the centrist Yabloko Party, led by economist Grigory Yavlinsky, who was an influential voice on state finances. Yabloko initiated the first legislative proposal for a flat-rate income tax reform. The cause of these domestic actors was given a boost by a foreign actor, the International Monetary Fund (IMF), whose managing director Michel Camdessus stated bluntly that "Russia has allowed a culture of tax evasion to develop and must fight this."[98] IMF negotiators explicitly linked the issue of tax reform to the approval of a $10 billion loan, one-third of which had already been counted by Chernomyrdin's government as a source of income for the 1996 budget. Encouraged by this newfound support, MinFin resubmitted its tax reform plan at the start of the new legislative season.

But 1996 was a presidential election year, and political survival trumped fiscal stability. Tax reform and campaign politics came into conflict. A Communist Party member declared in the Duma that "entrepreneurs who deceive or avoid taxes are, in fact, Russian patriots who should not fear the communists coming to power."[99] Instead of fiscal discipline, all available means were mobilized to mollify the angry electorate. Big enterprises paid their workers, but not their taxes. Regional governors doled out the political pork, helping themselves to a larger share of locally generated tax revenues. The capital-starved public sector was awash in new funding. The managers of military-industrial firms presented Yeltsin with a billion dollar "wish list" of investment projects in exchange for their endorsement.[100] This budget-busting bonanza was paid for with credit, not cash. The fear of Russia's unrepentant Communists taking charge prompted newfound generosity. The IMF suspended its calls for tax reform, and instead rushed through a three-year $10 billion loan, making more than a billion dollars immediately available.[101] When it was over, Shatalov conceded there would be no tax reform for at least another year.

The political red scare now gave way to a fiscal red scare. The IMF began to pester the Russian government anew about tax reform. Feeling ignored, Camdessus temporarily halted the transfer of the first $330 million loan tranche to the Russian Central Bank. Yeltsin took note. In his 1997 state of the union message, the president announced that tax reform was a policy priority and ordered the government to submit a new tax code to the Duma. He delegated the unenviable task to Anatoly Chubais, newly returned to the government as deputy prime minister and finance minister. Chubais wasted no time, rushing Shatalov's long-neglected draft to the Duma. The Duma was slow to react. Duma speaker and Communist Party member Gennady Seleznev at first refused to schedule a reading. Just before the summer recess, the Duma passed the reformed tax code—subject to amendment in the fall session. Over the break, the draft reform made the rounds through the lower house, the upper house, the council of ministers, regional governments, political parties, and corporate lobbies. By the time Duma deputies reconvened to discuss tax reform, more than four thousand amendments had been proposed. In the meantime, the reform drive was decapitated when scandal-plagued Chubais was sacked and worn-out Shatalov resigned.[102] The draft tax code and the pile of amendments were exiled to the Duma's budget committee. The urgency for reform subsided, and the project was abandoned for another year.

In the spring of 1998, Russia's fiscal crisis arrived. Revenue was no longer sufficient to cover budgetary expenses and outstanding debts. In desperation, Yeltsin dismissed Chernomyrdin and replaced him with a political novice, Sergei Kirienko. The Russian government was now fully in the hands of promarket reformers, who displayed a heightened commitment to tax reform. In Shatalov's absence, tax policy was entrusted to two Yabloko members from the Duma Committee on Budget, Taxes, and Finance: Mikhail Zadornov, the new finance minister, and Mikhail Motorin, the new deputy minister in charge of tax policy. In addition, feisty Boris Fedorov returned to the government as head of the tax administration. Fedorov was enthusiastic about using coercion to intimidate privileged elites into paying their debts. "The hands of the tax administration will not be empty for long," he vowed. "We'll arrest you, take your property and make you bankrupt. I will be like a tank."[103] The new team submitted a tax reform plan to the Duma, which again tried to delay and amend it to death.

With Yeltsin threatening to dismiss the Duma and call new elections, the Duma eventually passed part of a reformed tax code. But it was too little, too late. Legislative consideration of the more contentious second part of the new tax code was put off until the autumn session. The debate never occurred, as the state tumbled into fiscal abyss. In August, the government reneged on its outstanding debts and unilaterally devalued its currency. The well-intentioned

Kirienko government was forced to resign. The 1998 fiscal collapse laid bare the enduring political constraints of the state-elite revenue bargain. In a condition of high contestation, the Russian government failed to enact a tax reform, even when the state was on the brink of fiscal collapse.

Remaking Revenue Bargains and the Eastern European Tax Revolution

In the 2000s, postcommunist Eastern Europe experienced a second wave of tax reform that fundamentally revised the mature capitalist tax model. These reforms sought to adjust tax policy to better fit a transition economy. The mature capitalist tax model came with multilevel progressive rate schemes, made more elaborate by ever-changing lists of special allowances, and rested on relatively high levels of compliance. This policy design overwhelmed the monitoring capabilities of the postcommunist states, which struggled to build public trust to legitimate revenue claims.[104] In response, the second wave of tax reform streamlined tax codes and simplified tax compliance. It consolidated and lowered tax rates to an extreme level, culminating in the widespread adoption of flat taxes. Not all postcommunist states, however, followed the second wave. The likelihood of joining Eastern Europe's "flat-tax revolution" was directly influenced by political conditions. Those cases exhibiting "low contestation" were more likely to enact reform, while those cases exhibiting "high contestation" were less likely.[105]

By the early 2000s forces from without and within targeted Poland's state-labor revenue bargain. From without, the desire to be part of "Europe" and a member of the European Union was yet another issue on which the Polish transition displayed elite consensus. The prospects of joining the EU encouraged a temporary alliance of political foes who favored accommodating to EU accession demands. Their shared goal facilitated a brief ad hoc condition of "low contestation" concerning several tax policy reforms. As a result, Poland enacted a partial tax reform that eliminated some tax subsidies and exemptions from indirect taxes, which had been benefiting public sector workers and farmers. From within, the social democrat/peasant party coalition of the 1990s finally came undone, enabling market liberals to reclaim control of state finances. Their goal of enacting more radical tax reforms, however, beyond those necessary for EU accession encountered the political conditions of "high contestation." In particular, the repeated attempts of liberal finance ministers to join Eastern Europe's flat-tax revolution were dashed by the enduring political constraint of the state-labor revenue bargain.

The 1998 financial collapse upset Russia's precarious balance of power. Elite conflict raged anew in a scramble to seize power resources from the bankrupt state center. Political uncertainty encouraged both elite and state actors to revise the revenue bargain to their own advantage. The crisis hastened the departure of President Yeltsin. His successor, Vladimir Putin, brought an end to elite conflict by a combination of political maneuver and coercive muscle. As a result, Russia in the early 2000s moved decidedly away from the condition of "high" to "low" contestation, as the regime was transformed from a flawed democracy into a façade democracy. The 1998 financial crash showed state-elite revenue bargaining to be a fiscal failure. President Putin was determined to reassert the interests of the central state against big business and regional elites. The political constraints of the state-elite revenue bargain were finally broken, and Russia became one of the leaders in Eastern Europe's second wave of tax reform.

Poland: Adjusting Political Constraints and Partial Tax Reform

"The main goal of Polish foreign policy over the next few years is to become a fully integrated member of the European Union," pronounced Foreign Minister Bronislaw Geremek in his May 2000 report to the Sejm. At that moment intracoalition conflict was reaching a splitting crescendo: in a fortnight Geremek's Freedom Union would strand the Solidarity bloc in a minority position, while the social-democratic Left was poised to pounce. Animosity and intrigue abounded, and any day the government might be up for grabs. In the midst of all this, the Sejm voted to approve Geremek's goal of Polish membership in the European Union by an overwhelming 379–8 margin.[106] Now that's consensus.

In 1997, Poland was one of eight postcommunist states that were invited to apply for EU membership.[107] The European Commission monitored the intensely bureaucratic accession process, which covered twenty-nine separate policy areas—one of which was taxation. The Commission had three particular tax concerns: (1) tax rates, (2) special privileges, and (3) tax administration.[108] First, getting tax rates in line was a policy priority for the Commission. The EU had a direct mandate over indirect taxes (transaction and excise taxes) and an indirect influence on direct taxes (PIT and CIT). The VAT was the principal form of cross-border revenue extraction in the EU, accounting for more than one quarter of the total revenue take in EU states. Poland's VAT regime violated EU standards with its many reduced rates and exemptions, rooted in the state-labor revenue bargain.[109] Second, the Commission was concerned about "harmful tax practices" that conferred special privileges and skewed competition in favor of local businesses or foreign investors.[110] Again, Poland was guilty. Reduced VAT rates, raised import tariffs, and special tax breaks were prevalent. The Commission also identified tax exemptions and lax enforcement for state industry and agriculture as obstacles to admission.[111] Third, EU member states feared losing revenue through Poland's leaky tax administration.[112] To bring things up to standard, the Commission demanded that Poland retool and retrain its customs service, become integrated into a Europe-wide high-tech accounting system, and set up special tax warehouses for inspection and certification of a long list of tradable goods.

The Polish government did not rush to accommodate Brussels. The main obstacle first came from within the Solidarity bloc, where a narrow but noisy contingent of protectionists and nationalists resided. The Buzek government initially startled its accession interlocutors with a quarrelsome negotiating stance.[113] Meanwhile, Balcerowicz's attempt to align Poland's indirect tax rates with EU standards was frustrated by his own coalition partners. The European Commission's 1998 progress report was explicitly critical of the government's efforts in tax reform, threatening Poland's membership application.[114]

Once again, Poland's postcommunist transition displayed elite consensus, this time in the form of a temporary tactical alliance between social democrats and liberals. Working together, they sorted out the details of a tax reform that would *both* meet the EU's membership preconditions and preserve as much of the revenue bargain as possible. In December 2000 the social democratic president won a second term in a first-round rout. In his inaugural address to the Sejm, President Kwasniewski stressed that the main goal of his second term would be the "historical task of leading Poland into the European Union." Kwasniewski set up a new position, Office for European Integration, which would coordinate policy among different ministries and branches of government, keep the public informed about policy changes, and report directly to the president.[115] These bureaucratic innovations were established explicitly to depoliticize the policy process in order to expedite the enactment of EU-dictated legislation. In 2001, new parliamentary elections were held in which the Democratic Left Alliance trounced the Solidarity bloc and the Freedom Union. The social democrats were strongly pro-Europe and ready to negotiate on accession demands. The new government, with Leszek Miller as prime minister and Marek Belka as finance minister, began to work through a hastily improvised "Europe" committee in the Sejm. In the final months of negotiation, Grzegorz Kolodko returned as finance minister in the social democratic government. One of the main architects of the state-labor revenue bargain, Kolodko now spoke of the need to allay the Commission's concerns and enact partial tax reform.[116]

The Treaty of Accession was signed in April 2003, conferring European Union membership on Poland. The European Commission's final report concluded that

Poland had "essentially met the commitments and requirements" for taxation.[117] The fine print, however, told a different tale. Concerning the alignment of tax rates, the report noted that "in the areas of VAT and excise duties, Poland was only partially meeting its commitments."[118] Poland was still using unequal VAT rates to protect local products from foreign imports. Although excise rates on tobacco and alcohol were raised closer to the EU standard, "full alignment has not been achieved." Regarding special privileges, the EU got the government to eliminate many tax deals for businesses, which the government then gave back in the form of lower corporate income tax rates. Besides that, the report noted that "all other special tax deductions have been maintained." And, on Poland's passive tax administration practices, it was stressed that "priority still is needed to be given to improving the efficiency of tax collection and fiscal control."[119]

Once membership was secured, Poland deployed a new tactic to preserve tax policies that supported the state-labor revenue bargain. Because EU fiscal policy required unanimous consent of the member countries, Poland threatened to exercise its newly acquired *liberum veto* to frustrate Europe-wide tax policy.[120] In January 2006, the French and Dutch governments sought to extend special VAT tax breaks for certain small businesses, including hair stylists and bicycle repairmen. Poland seized the opportunity to threaten a veto unless it secured its own extensions of lower VAT rates.[121] In February 2006, Poland finally agreed to the special VAT exemptions for France and Holland in exchange for the continuation of its own special VAT rates, benefitting working families.[122] Despite accession-driven external pressures, Poland enacted only partial tax reform and the state-labor revenue bargain endured.

Even after Balcerowicz and the liberals were voted out of parliament in 2001, the issue of direct tax reform did not go away. The 2001 parliamentary election results suggested that the tax burden on the economy as a whole was a cause for concern across the political spectrum. The total tax bill for the Polish economy remained nearly as high as it was in communist days—over 40 percent of GDP.[123] It gorged on entrepreneur profits as well as worker paychecks. All the political parties that won election to the Sejm in 2001 agreed that the tax burden on the corporate sector was too high, although they disagreed over the details of corporate tax reform.[124] From this time, Poland's corporate income tax rates were significantly reduced by both liberal and social democratic finance ministers. It began with Balcerowicz in the late 1990s, and continued with Kolodko in the early 2000s. In 1995, the CIT rate was 40 percent; in 2000, it was 30 percent; and, in 2005, it was 19 percent.[125] These cuts were consistent with wider trends in postcommunist Eastern Europe, related to the fiscal preconditions for EU membership. After being forced to eliminate numerous VAT exemptions, Eastern European governments responded by significantly lowering corporate tax rates.

The centerpiece of Eastern Europe's second-wave tax revolution, however, was low-rate flat taxes on personal income. Poland did not follow this trend, because it remained in a condition of high contestation. In the early 2000s, the Polish state was increasingly strained by its financial commitment to the state-labor revenue bargain. Even Kolodko, in his second stint as finance minister, endorsed a tax reform that would institute at least a moderate revision of the revenue bargain.[126] But Poland's social democrats had their political and ideological limits, and insisted on maintaining the progressive character of the personal income tax. The social democratic head of MinFin's fiscal administration gave assurances that "the pro-social character of the Polish tax system will be maintained."[127] And former prime minister Marek Belka, in his second turn in charge of MinFin, turned the tables on Balcerowicz's flat-tax proposal by introducing an alternative PIT reform that would increase the number of people in the "0 percent" bracket as well as increase the number of people in the highest "40 percent" bracket. "In a situation where there is danger of social unrest," Belka said, "we have to respond by shifting the tax burden to the better off."[128]

The return of the social democrats to the government, however, was short-lived. As economic conditions worsened, popular enmity spread for the scandal-wracked social democrats. The budget deficit reached more than 5 percent of GDP, its highest level since the fiscal crisis of the early transition. Before the next round of parliamentary elections, the existing political blocs went through a splintering of parties and a reshuffling of personalities. As a result, in 2004 the new liberal party, the Civic Platform, emerged as part of a tenuous centrist coalition government, with promarket Miroslaw Gronicki acting as finance minister. Radical tax reform was back on the menu. In 2005, Gronicki proposed an across-the-board flat tax of 18 percent for PIT, CIT, and VAT, in 2005, but a new round of parliamentary elections delayed action on the reform. The Civic Platform was heavily favored to win the popular vote. On the campaign trail, market liberals promised an even more radical tax reform, the "3x15 percent" tax policy—a flat 15 percent rate for PIT, CIT, and VAT.[129] But the Civic Platform was upset in the popular vote, and subsequently excluded from the next government. The new coalition, formed in 2005, consisted of socially conservative fiscal populists: the senior Law and Justice Party, which campaigned for a two-bracket progressive PIT rates, and the junior Self-Defense of the Polish Republic, which campaigned for giving lower-income households a PIT exemption and raising to 50 percent the top PIT bracket for high-income households.

The Civic Platform's flat-tax proposal was pitched to workers as a form of tax relief. Poland's public sector workers, however, were skeptical. From the time that Balcerowicz first suggested a flat tax, in 1998, the Polish public consistently expressed opposition. A public opinion survey at that time showed nearly twice as many respondents saying that a progressive PIT was "more fair" than a flat-rate PIT.[130] The opposition to the flat tax was infused with a sense of social injustice. Even in the second half of the 2000s, when support for the social democrats declined, the advocacy of tax policies that upheld the state-labor revenue bargain still made for good politics. In the end, a political condition of "high contestation" prevented Poland from joining the flat-tax revolution.

Russia: Pulverizing Political Constraints and Fundamental Tax Reform

The transfer of the presidential throne from Boris Yeltsin to Vladimir Putin changed the conditions of contestation. President Putin proved adept at making the parliament a political appendage of executive rule, rather than the institutional home of a disloyal opposition. Moreover, Putin was far less inhibited than was his predecessor in deploying the coercive resources attached to the presidential office. In so doing, he significantly lowered the level of contestation in Russian politics. Whereas Polish state actors moderately adjusted the constraints of the state-labor revenue bargain, allowing for partial tax reform, Russian state actors pulverized the constraints of the state-elite revenue bargain, making fundamental tax reform possible.

For Russia's new economic elite, the 1998 financial crisis was seen as an opportunity to fortify the boundary line between the state and their economic holdings. Russia's business tycoons offered a grand bargain to the state by which they would cooperate in fulfilling their tax obligations in exchange for the formalization of their claims over the economic concessions they had acquired. In the early 1990s, Russia's tycoons were accustomed to act individually. They thrived in the idiosyncratic system of elite bargaining by which they reduced tax obligations. But the 1998 fiscal crisis forced the business elite to put aside personal rivalries, at least temporarily, to preserve their gains. They appealed to the new prime minister, Yevgeny Primakov, who offered the compromise.[131] But the deal was rejected by Yeltsin. After leaving the government, Primakov was appointed head of the Russian Chamber of Commerce and Industry. When Putin came to power, Primakov again attempted to broker a deal between the tycoons and the state, proposing a pact in which big business would stop avoiding taxes if the state would grant an amnesty on the redistribution of wealth.[132] Again, the proposal was rejected.

In his midnight diary, Yeltsin said that he chose the little-known Putin as his successor because of his conscientious service to the national interest.[133] There is likely more to the story. One thing was certain: Putin's firm and steady leadership style differed markedly from Yeltsin's. Putin was neither a polarizing personality nor an unconvincing patriot. In his first political test, the 1999 Duma elections, Putin's hastily organized Unity Party directly opposed Fatherland All-Russia, a formidable political bloc of business and regional elites led by Primakov, who had recently been dismissed as prime minister, and Moscow mayor Yury Luzhkov. In a close vote, Unity bested Fatherland by nine seats.[134] The election result meant that Putin would not be compelled to maintain the same political alliances or policy commitments that Yeltsin had in his tumultuous reign. Putin adroitly added to his advantage: manipulating legislative coalitions, managing electoral competition, building political machines, and engineering constitutional change. But it wasn't all political prowess; Putin's nimble political hand was complemented by an iron coercive fist.

In the Russian transition, the coercive resources inherited from the old regime were neither dismantled nor constrained. Instead, a more personalistic check was devised: the police were subordinated to the president. In the 1990s, the state's coercive organs acted with restraint, their postcommunist mandate still ambiguous. Here is where Putin's style differed most notably from Yeltsin's. The former secret policeman was much more willing than the former construction boss to deploy the coercive resources attached to the office. Under Putin, the state's coercive apparatus became an instrument of intimidation against the postcommunist elite.[135] The use of coercion to redefine postcommunist state-elite relations culminated in 2003 in the Yukos Affair. The case against Yukos involved several core allegations: defrauding the state of privatization revenues, setting up an illegal offshore company to hide oil profits, evading corporate and personal income taxes, and stiffing the pension fund. When it was done, Yukos chief Mikhail Khodorkovsky was sent into Siberian exile, while the company's assets were plundered and redistributed between the state and more politically compliant tycoons. More than any other act, the Yukos Affair enabled central state actors to smash the constraints of the state-elite revenue bargain by demonstrating the capability and willingness of the central state to use unbridled coercion against the elite.

By breaking the political constraints, Putin succeeded in reshaping tax policy. First, the success of Unity, the progovernment political party, in the 1999 and 2003 Duma elections finally created the opportunity for executive-legislative cooperation over tax reform. Second, in alliance with the Duma, the president pushed through constitutional changes that removed regional governors from the upper house of parliament and the president acquired the right to fire governors who violated federal law. Putin refused to extend the bilateral treaties, containing special revenue deals, which particular regions had negotiated with Yeltsin.[136] The central state then reclaimed a greater share of tax revenue from the regions. Finally, in Putin's first term bargaining over tax policy between the state and big business became more routinized. Business interests were not removed from the policy process, but the manner of interest articulation was organized more collectively, rather than individually.[137] In the profitable energy sector, oil and gas duties were regularly discussed and revised by government commissions in consultation with industry representatives.[138] However, the bargaining process was now tipped in favor of the state. Collective business interests were given a voice, but the state was not compelled to listen.

Putin assembled a formidable team of tax reformers, led by the new finance minister, Alexei Kudrin. When Kudrin had headed the St. Petersburg financial department during the mid-1990s, his solution to the second city's chronic budget deficit was simple: "Do not raise taxes, lower taxes. Everything else is secondary."[139] As Russian finance minister, Kudrin succeeded where others had failed, by bringing fiscal stability to the postcommunist state. Obviously his long tenure benefited from the coincidental boom in world energy prices, but his steady temperament and sound policies mattered too. The new finance minister was a cautious capitalist and a staunch fiscal conservative. The tax team also included Sergei Shatalov, who returned to the government as first deputy finance minister with responsibility for overseeing state finances. Mikhail Motorin, meanwhile, continued to work out the details of tax policy. The new head of the tax administration, Gennadi Bukaev, was also on record in support of tax reform.[140] Between 2000 and 2005, this team designed and implemented a comprehensive set of fiscal reforms, that became known as the "Russian Tax Revolution."[141]

"The goal of tax reform," explained Shatalov, "has changed little since Adam Smith—the tax system must be as fair and simple as possible."[142] To make Russia's convoluted tax system "fair and simple," the reformers pursued three policy tactics: streamline the tax code, reduce tax rates, and make tax enforcement uniform. First, by the end of the 1990s the tax code included more than two hundred different taxes, which were claimed by central, regional, and local state authorities. So many taxes had perverse fiscal effects on tax collection by encouraging competition among the different levels of government for the same revenue source, causing confusion for tax administration officials and imposing an excessive burden on taxpayers. In 2001, the reformers took shears to the Medusa-like tax code. Five payroll and social security taxes were consolidated into one new Unified Social Tax. By 2002, the total number of taxes was reduced to fifty-four, a decrease of three-quarters of all existing taxes. The pruning continued as road use fees, foreign currency fees, turnover taxes, and sales taxes were abolished. By 2005, the number of taxes contained in the tax code had been cut even further to a total of nineteen among all levels of government.[143]

Second, the reformers cut tax rates, lowering the overall tax burden on the economy. The centerpiece was the 2001 personal income tax (PIT) reform. The new 13 percent flat rate was among the lowest PIT rates in the world, and re-placed a progressive rate scale of six categories ranging from 12 percent to 45 per-cent.[144] Business taxes were also reduced, but in a less radical manner. The 2002 corporate income tax (CIT) reform reduced business taxes from 35 percent for industrial and retail firms and 43 percent for financial firms to a flat 24 percent rate. Reducing VAT rates proved to be more contentious, however. Finance Min-ister Kudrin took a cautious approach to cutting the main source of income for the state budget, despite near constant pressure from corporate lobbies and rival government ministries. In 2004, the VAT was finally reduced from 20 percent to 18 percent, with promises of future cuts depending on world energy prices.[145] In 2003, a new tax arrangement was created to encourage small-business activity, by establishing a consolidated 15 percent rate for small businesses. Continuing the trend, in 2005 the Unified Social Tax rate was cut from 36.5 percent to 26 percent.

Finally, the reformers sought to impose more uniform enforcement of tax regulations. This component of tax reform directly challenged the elite revenue bargain, which contained so many special exemptions and privileges. By stream-lining the tax code and reducing tax rates, the reformers ran the risk of under-cutting budgetary income unless the new polices were applied consistently to all taxpayers. The trade-off for fewer taxes and lower rates was fewer exceptions. For example, millions of public employees had been exempted from paying personal income tax, including the military, police, prosecutors, and judges. But these oc-cupational exemptions were removed as part of the flat-rate PIT reform. To ease the burden, previously exempted public employees received an increase in salary as compensation.[146] Likewise, the CIT reform entailed the elimination of nu-merous special corporate tax privileges and concessions. In 2004, new restrictive legislation effectively curtailed tax avoidance practices by closing down regional tax havens and outlawing corporate tax shelters. Russia's radical tax reforms sig-nificantly lowered tax rates while eliminating special exemptions; as a result, the central state actually increased its revenue take at the expense of big business and wealthy regions. Tax policy reform was possible because the state-elite bargain was forcibly broken, creating a condition of "low contestation."

What explains the variant responses among postcommunist states to the first and second waves of tax reform in Eastern Europe? The new tax systems that were built for the transition economy were shaped as much by political as by economic constraints. Because of "extraordinary politics," a temporary political condition of low contestation, fiscal architects successfully implemented a fun-damental tax reform, based on a macropolicy design of the advanced capitalist states. Since Poland lacked concentrated lucrative revenue sources, it targeted wage-earner households to raise capital to climb out of fiscal crisis; by contrast,

Russia contained rich concentrated revenue sources, which were targeted as the state's principal sources of income during the difficult first years of economic restructuring. But both the Polish and Russian states soon faced societal opposition to new revenue claims. In Poland, public sector workers mobilized collective protests against the state's tax policies, while in Russia strategic economic and regional elites used their control over valuable economic assets to abscond with the state's tax base. These tax revolts were resolved through the making of revenue bargains, by which a particular set of societal actors were allowed to keep a greater portion of the revenue claimed by the state, in exchange for the political support of a particular set of state actors who were competing for control over the policy process.

But revenue bargains, unlike diamonds, are not forever. In both cases, the political constraints of the revenue bargains were redefined enough to enact tax reform. In Poland, the prospect of joining the European Union prompted a pro-Europe alliance of social democrats and market liberals, creating a temporary political condition of low contestation. The result was a partial tax reform that at the behest of EU overseers eliminated many tax subsidies for the public sector and farmers. The social democrat/peasant party coalition was undone, and the social democrats lost control of parliament. But even with market liberals in charge of state finances, Poland only partially followed the Eastern European tax revolution of radical rate cuts and flat taxes. The state-labor revenue bargain, in modified form, still acted as a political constraint on tax reform. In Russia, the political constraints of the state-elite revenue bargain were smashed when a new president took office. By the suppression of executive-legislative conflict and the demonstration of coercive force, a political condition of low contestation was reestablished. The state-elite revenue bargain was unilaterally redefined to the advantage of the state center. As a result, the government successfully enacted radical tax reform, making Russia a leader in the second wave of postcommunist tax reform, the Eastern European flat-tax revolution. The state-society revenue bargains provided the political foundation upon which postcommunism's transitional tax regimes were built.

STATE MEETS SOCIETY IN THE TRANSITIONAL TAX REGIME

Why do people pay taxes? Revenue-maximizing rulers have asked this question for centuries. The first examples of human writing were cuneiform ledgers of the tax payments received and debts outstanding to Mesopotamian kings. And the reason Jesus of Galilee was born a hundred miles away in Judea was because that was where the head of his household was obliged to register for an imperial census, so that Caesar could have a reliable record of his renderings. The most ancient texts confirm that a revenue-maximizing impulse long prompted rulers to create ever more complex systems of fiscal accounting and information gathering, in order that the state can better see society, or rather, society's wealth. But for revenue-hungry states, knowing what is out there to tax is only half the task. When power finds wealth, wealth tends to move, if it can. States must give those who create wealth a reason, or two, to stay in place and be counted. The threat of punishment is one reason, but it is not nearly as profitable as more positive enticements, such as delivery of valued goods or promotion of normative appeals. So, in order to make good on revenue claims, states must devise *both* means of extraction and incentives for compliance.

Getting people to pay taxes was among the most daunting challenges for postcommunist states. It was one thing to enact tax reform, and quite another to fill state coffers with tax income. In dealing with the challenge, postcommunist states gave rise to different types of "transitional tax regimes." Transitional tax regimes were more than just formal tax codes and informal revenue bargains; they also included the means of state extraction and patterns of societal compliance. They were transitional in that they were the product of hastily improvised and readily compromised designs of early postcommunist state builders, who were desperately seeking capital from rapidly transforming transition economies. Transitional tax regimes were distinguishable among postcommunist states based on variation in the means of extraction and patterns of compliance. In the 1990s, transitional tax regimes were one of the main determinants of the institutional reconfiguration of power and wealth across the postcommunist realm.

The postcommunist transitions gave rise to two ideal-typical tax regimes. First, coercion-based tax regimes inclined toward "taking" wealth. Taking is simply that; it is the impulse to take something from someone else because you can. It implies a preponderance of power resources, which enables one to gain access to wealth without having to haggle. The most recognizable forms of taking are plunder and tribute, as conceptualized in Tilly's protection racket model of early modern state building. The main incentive for giving up at least part of one's wealth is that to do otherwise incurs risks to person or property. Second, consent-based tax regimes inclined toward "trading" for wealth. It is possible that taking comes instinctually, but not so of trading, which has to be learned. Trading is an alternative means of gaining access to wealth, which becomes a more attractive option when the distribution of power resources are more evenly balanced, the costs of using power resources are higher than the economic resources returned, and/or economic resources are more widely and thinly dispersed. Power still gets wealth, but not on its own terms. Wealth is given up as part of an exchange with power for something in return—public goods, social status, economic entitlement, political rights.

Poland and Russia provide a nice contrast of different types of tax regimes. Poland developed a tax regime characterized by "legalistic consent," a trading-based extraction relationship. The means of extraction were "legalistic," meaning that state agents were constrained by administrative rules and legal checks in dealings with societal actors. The pattern of compliance was "consent" based, meaning that the state collected a significant portion of revenue without resort to coercive threats. "Legalistic consent" was a minimalist form of quasi-voluntary compliance. Meanwhile, the Russian tax regime came to be defined by "bureaucratic coercion," a taking-based extraction relationship. The means of extraction were "bureaucratic," meaning that state agents were not fully constrained by administrative or legal checks in dealings with society. The pattern of compliance was "coercion" based, meaning that the state relied heavily on coercive threats to compel society to give up its wealth.

This chapter shows how these two types of transitional tax regimes were consolidated in Poland and Russia, focusing first on the actions of the state and then on the reactions of society. From above, postcommunist states were forced to devise the means of revenue extraction from the institutional inheritance of the old regime. This process entailed building a new fiscal-administrative apparatus that was suitable, including monitoring and enforcement, for a transition economy. From below, postcommunist societies were released from the rigid constraints of the command economy to become autonomous economic actors, and legally anointed taxpayers. Society responded to the state's new revenue claims with compliance and noncompliance, varying in extent and form. The cumulative actions of the state and reactions of society reveal distinctive tendencies that delineate the two types of transitional tax regimes.

The State Acts: Devising the Means of Extraction

Postcommunist states were hard-pressed to devise means of extraction to collect taxes from the transition economy. The state's means of extraction entail the formal features of the tax regime—fiscal policymakers, tax administration, and tax enforcement. The organization of the means of extraction in Poland and Russia are distinguishable by two types: legalistic and bureaucratic. The distinction is based on observable variation along a set of organizational traits. Poland's "*legalistic*" state apparatus was *coherent* in the division of authority, *coordinated* in its internal operations, *checked* by legal-institutional mechanisms, and *rule-governed* in the conduct of its affairs. Russia's "*bureaucratic*" state apparatus was *incoherent* in the division of authority, *uncoordinated* in its internal operations, *unchecked* by legal-institutional mechanisms, and *politics-governed* in the conduct of its affairs.

The tendency toward variant types of means of extraction in Poland and Russia was a direct consequence of their divergent paths to regime breakdown. The fall of communism in Poland was a negotiated process in which counterelites eventually assumed control of the government from communist elites. When counterelites came to power, they inherited a state apparatus more or less intact. In Russia, regime breakdown was prompted by defecting cadres, or old regime elites, making claims to the economic, coercive, and bureaucratic resources of the state. The process led to a fragmented state apparatus. The restraints placed on law enforcement in Poland reflected an elite consensus to depoliticize the security forces and subordinate them to civilian control. In Russia, the protracted elite conflict reinforced the autonomous status of security forces, which were subordinated to the personal discretion of the president. This section focuses on three essential features of the means of extraction: organization of state finances, capacity and culture of the tax administration, and role of tax enforcement.

Poland: Building the Means of Extraction

ORGANIZATION OF STATE FINANCES, 1989–98

Poland's first postcommunist government may have fantasized about binding the state and freeing the market, but once in power it was still dependent on the old regime's administrative apparatus. In the area of state finances, there was no attempt to dismantle the existing fiscal-administrative structure. Postcommunist Poland inherited a system of state finance that was coherent, coordinated, rule-governed, and checked. The Sejm was responsible for enacting tax laws, the Finance Ministry was responsible for working out the details of tax policy and overseeing its execution, and the tax administration was responsible for implementing tax policy. The separation of powers and roles was overseen by several independent legal-administrative mechanisms. Overall, the component parts of state finance were in sync.[1]

The Ministry of Finance's dominance over state finances was reinforced by a succession of ambitious and savvy finance ministers—Balcerowicz, Kolodko, Belka. MinFin was responsible for building a new system of revenue extraction. Tax policy, tax administration, the customs agency, fiscal control, and the state treasury were subordinated to the ministry.[2] Bureaucratic competition occurred among the departments but the all-inclusive organizational scheme kept interagency rivalry from causing fiscal dysfunction. The delineation of bureaucratic jurisdictions was clearly recognized and rarely challenged. In general, the government refrained from creating special committees to circumvent established fiscal organs.[3] Within MinFin, revenue extraction was a priority sector, as indicated by the "vice minister" status routinely accorded to the undersecretaries for tax collection and fiscal control. State tax collection benefited from the continuity of leading organizational personnel, especially in the formative years under social democrats from 1992 to 1998.[4]

Not only did the authority of MinFin extend horizontally across the central state but also vertically down the territorial-administrative chain. MinFin oversaw forty-nine provincial fiscal chambers, which coordinated policy implementation while remaining dependent on and accountable to the center. Only at the local level, which included almost twenty-four hundred administrative units, was there limited fiscal autonomy. Most revenues extracted by the Polish state went directly to the central coffers, leaving less than 10 percent to the discretion of local administration.[5] There was not much leeway for local actors to tinker with policy or divert revenue flows. Local government was revenue dependent on a small cut from PIT and CIT, and centrally-allocated subsidies.[6] This structure enabled the state center to make revenue claims and enact fiscal policy, without competition from regional and local officialdom.

The tax administration was the main forum where state met society. It was supposed to identify taxpayers, determine income levels, and collect revenue. The capitalist shock brigade that introduced neoliberal reforms, however, was neglectful of the administration of tax collection. The new system was, in the words of one of Poland's largest retailers, "a little monster dreamed up by Balcerowicz over one weekend."[7] Poland's first postcommunist government left the tax administration understaffed, underfinanced, and underequipped. Meanwhile, the formal powers of the tax administration vis-à-vis taxpayers were tightly constrained. Taxpayers, for example, had a right to unlimited appeals against the tax administration, causing long delays in the resolution of investigations. The head of MinFin's tax department complained that "agents spent more time writing replies to appeals, than calculating taxes and conducting inspections."[8] In 1992, Balcerowicz's replacement as finance minister, Jerzy Osiatynski, described the tax administration's problems as "the typical poor man's plight—overworked and underpaid."[9]

At the transition's outset, the tax administration was staffed by roughly forty thousand employees, thinly spread across forty-nine regional fiscal chambers and 352 local tax offices, with just 125 officials employed in the center. The territorial distribution of the workforce did not correspond with the territorial distribution of wealth. Moreover, it lost out annually in the bureaucratic battle for resources, accounting for less than 1 percent of the state budget.[10] In the command economy, tax administration was a low-skill, low-paying job that was filled mostly by female accountants. The lingering culture of socialism's occupational patriarchy reinforced the low professional status of tax inspectors.

Polish revenue agents were overwhelmed by the rapidly changing transition economy. In 1991, a group of tax inspectors from Krakow and Novy Sacz confided to an interviewer just how difficult their job was.[11] "Old habits die hard," lamented one inspector, referring to communist-era tricks, such as double bookkeeping, that were used to cheat the postcommunist state. Another inspector expressed frustration with the new small businesses, saying that "even if every tax inspector in Poland was reassigned to the central market in Warsaw, it would not be enough manpower." The Krakow city office had only twenty inspectors, who said it was not worth the effort to go after flagrant tax-evading small entrepreneurs because of their meager returns. Instead, they targeted larger firms, but without great success. Large private firms were "protected by good lawyers, who easily beat the tax administration in court." Meanwhile, the tax inspectors expressed more sympathy than antagonism toward tax-delinquent public sector firms. One Novy Sacz inspector said that the refusal of the state sector to pay the excess wage tax, the *popiwek*, was "not really premeditated evasion, but a desperate attempt to stave off bankruptcy."[12]

The tax administration simply could not "see like a state" in the transition economy. It was supposed to be fitted with a high-tech information-gathering system called Poltax. But it was not until 1993, more than three years after the introduction of radical economic reform, that a network of French-provided computers began to be installed.[13] And it was not until the following year that MinFin began to assign tax identification numbers to the country's nearly twenty-five million taxpayers.[14] Meanwhile, MinFin was slow to create a cadastre, or property registry, one of the main sources of information for the proposed Poltax database.[15] Neither the Poltax system nor the cadastre were fully up and running until the final push to join the EU in the early 2000s. Thus, tax collection suffered from bureaucratic blind spots.[16]

The tax administration was further constrained by its narrow powers of investigation and enforcement. Taxpayer bank accounts were off limits to inspectors. This information could only be obtained by special permission from the Inspector General's office, which itself could not be obtained unless a tax law was clearly violated. But without access to complete financial records, tax inspectors could not easily determine violations. In order to establish wrongdoing, the onus was on the tax administration to prove *intentional* fraud. Moreover, tax inspectors could not declare that fraud had been committed or issue fines; these were matters that only the courts could decide. The director of MinFin's tax department, Andrzeij Zelechowski, complained that the courts were too slow and too lenient in dealing with tax cheats.[17] The tax inspector was anything but an imposing figure. It was not unusual for tax inspectors to be refused access to records and shown the door at businesses they came to audit, nor was it uncommon for tax inspectors and their families to receive threats. A Poznan inspector handling a high-stakes fraud case was badly beaten on a city sidewalk in the middle of the day and robbed of his briefcase, which was filled with audit documents. MinFin appealed to the prosecutor general to do something to protect its tax agents, but the prosecutor's office declined to get involved.[18]

As early as 1993, the Finance Ministry urged the Sejm to bolster the authority of tax inspectors, but it took three years before ministerial urge became legislative proposal.[19] MinFin sought to expand the information-gathering powers of inspectors, to allow inspectors to enter the homes of suspected evaders, to limit the number of taxpayer appeals against the claims of the tax administration, and to relieve the tax administration of having to prove premeditated evasion in court cases. In 1996, the Sejm finally enhanced the powers of the tax administration. But the reform immediately aroused indignation among taxpayer groups, the mass media, the National Bank, and even the Helsinki Commission. The opposition was especially determined not to allow inspectors access to bank records. A public opinion survey, conducted in 1998, showed 60 percent of respondents

opposed to allowing the state to access private bank accounts.[20] The Ombudsman's office, an official constitutional watchdog, said that this measure violated
the right to privacy. The Constitutional Tribunal agreed, and the provision was
struck down. This would become a recurring scenario regarding the government's attempts to enhance the powers of the tax administration.

The most significant fact about the means of extraction in Poland was the in-
significance of coercion. As the postcommunist state struggled to realize its new
revenue claims, the need for more vigorous tax enforcement was frequently recognized, but rarely acted on. In 1991, the Sejm rejected a proposal for an autonomous six-hundred-person economic police force to combat organized crime,
corruption, and tax evasion.[21] Instead, MinFin asked for its own enforcement
agency, which it got. In February 1992, the Sejm authorized a Department of Fiscal Control "to fight tax evasion and the misuse of budgetary funds."[22] Fiscal Control was supposed to be an elite force of treasury agents, but its powers were weak.
Originally staffed by 1,524 university-trained tax inspectors, in its first month in
operation it lost twenty agents to the companies they were sent to investigate.[23]

Fiscal Control was sometimes referred to as Poland's "tax police," but they were
more like a "paper tiger."[24] They were not permitted to carry firearms until 1998,
and even then only sixty special "enforcer" agents were entrusted with weapons.[25]
Fiscal Control was allowed to conduct raids on suspected tax evaders—as long as
it notified the business in writing ahead of time. Instead of coercive resources, Fiscal Control was given economic resources to combat evasion. The department was
allocated a small slush fund to reward the civic-minded and personally resentful
who came forward to rat out tax-evading neighbors. The use of citizen informers,
a long despised communist practice, was controversial, but apparently successful.
The Warsaw office claimed to receive on average of twenty denunciations a week.[26]

The Polish state simply did not pose a credible coercive threat. In 1998, the
government cancelled over 630 million zloty worth of outstanding tax debts,
more than the entire budget for the police.[27] To be investigated by Fiscal Control
was exceptional. Of approximately forty million tax returns filed each year, about
twenty-five thousand were sent to fiscal control on suspicion of tax evasion, a
ratio of roughly one in sixteen hundred returns.[28] By decade's end, Fiscal Control
included twenty-five hundred agents responsible for audits, but only 150 agents
were assigned to criminal investigations.[29] The Warsaw office had seventy-four
agents to sift through more than one million tax returns.[30] Like the tax administration, the state's main organ for revenue enforcement was overwhelmed.

CONSOLIDATION OF THE MEANS OF EXTRACTION, 1999–2008

In January 1998, a conference was held in the old town of Torun to commemorate the eightieth anniversary of the tax administration, whose existence dated

back to Poland's return to statehood. The celebration was short-lived. Leszek Balcerowicz, who had been reinstalled as finance minister after recent parliamentary elections, used the occasion to assail social-democratic tax policy in general and tax administration in particular.[31] He warned that the current status of revenue extraction would surely imperil Poland's EU membership application. Fiscal administrative reform was about to pick up pace. By the time Poland was officially welcomed into the European Union six years later, the state's means of extraction were modified: fiscal policy was decentralized, administrative capacity was strengthened, and enforcement was enhanced.

In the 2000s, Polish state finances continued to exhibit institutional coherence, with the Finance Ministry acting as bureaucratic centerpiece. Although control of MinFin changed hands among market liberals, social democrats, and conservative populists, state fiscal policy did not deviate significantly from the initial compromises that produced the state-labor revenue bargain. State finances, however, did undergo one significant organizational change, the decentralization of fiscal administration.[32]

By this time, frustrated regional actors were clamoring for more fiscal authority, which beleaguered central actors gladly conceded. The resulting 1999 territorial-administrative reform consolidated Poland's forty-nine small provinces into sixteen regions, which in turn presided over 373 cities and rural districts and almost twenty-five hundred local administrations.[33] As part of the reform, sixteen new regional fiscal boards were created to supervise and coordinate the local organs of state finance.[34] Although MinFin was happy to shed its responsibility for public services to local officialdom, it was hesitant to share revenue. By 1999 local administrations depended on central subsidies for roughly half of their total income[35] This arrangement was derisively dubbed "representation without taxation." In early 2003, with social democrat Kolodko back in charge at MinFin, center-regional fiscal relations were finally redefined. The state center reduced the budgetary fund for local subsidies and, in exchange, allowed local administrations to increase their revenue share.[36] The percentage of locally collected PIT remaining in the region was raised from 27 to 41 percent; while the percentage of CIT was raised from 0.5 to 18 percent.[37] The reform devolved particular details of fiscal policy, but it did not represent a fundamental devolution of state finances, which were still coordinated by MinFin from above.

The main impetus for tax administration reform came from Poland's bid to join the European Union. Western Europe's rich member states feared losing revenue through Eastern Europe's poor tax administrations. The European Commission helped with infrastructural upgrading and personnel retraining. In October 1999 the Commission issued a highly critical report on the internal operations of the Polish tax administration. In November 2000 the Commission again declared that "substantial improvements were still needed regarding tax administration."[38] To make matters worse, the World Bank issued a report in 2000 stating that tax collection was plagued by inefficiency and corruption. The Polish government's own checking body, the Supreme Audit Chamber, piled on with a report that nearly a billion dollars in revenue was left uncollected each year by local tax inspectors because of compromise settlements with taxpayers.[39]

In reaction, MinFin devised a comprehensive plan to raise professional standards in the tax administration and make a more determined stand against tax evasion.[40] Hoping to impress EU observers, the Council of Ministers adopted without fuss an ambitious reform package, the "Tax Administration Modernization Strategy."[41] A main feature of the reform led to the redeployment of tax collectors. By the mid-2000s the ranks of the tax administration were fortified with new recruits, increasing the staff to more than fifty thousand employees. In the center, twenty specialized offices were created for large corporate taxpayers.[42] In the regional apparatus, instead of the widely dispersed force, personnel were relocated to where they were most needed. Tax inspectors were concentrated in the larger and richer urban areas. In 2001, for example, one hundred inspectors were added to the Warsaw city tax office, nearly doubling its force. According to Finance Minister Jaroslaw Bauc, the capital city was notorious for tax evasion. Bauc ordered inspectors to focus attention on large taxpayers and to avoid time-consuming contentious revenue claims.[43] In addition, local inspectors were forbidden to make ad hoc deals with local businesses. In the first year, the refortified Warsaw office brought in an additional 120 million zloty. By the end of 2003 MinFin had made enough progress to satisfy the European Commission, who approved Poland's membership application.[44]

In the late 2000s, the electoral success of conservative populists brought a new attack on the tax administration. It was accused of complicity in the financially murky relationship between social-democratic governments and state sector firms, which a Sejm investigative committee referred to as a "moral swamp."[45] Indeed, an anonymous survey of MinFin employees revealed that more than half on at least one occasion felt pressured to act in violation of the law.[46] In 2006, the newly installed finance minister, Zyla Gilowska, a member of the Law and Justice Party, proposed the creation of a National Fiscal Administration, consolidating over four hundred local tax administration and customs offices into one suprastreamlined extractive bureaucracy. Further, Gilowska imposed a wage freeze on tax administration employees, causing many tax inspectors to move to the private sector or take early retirement. The Warsaw staff of 217 tax officers was reduced by forty retirements in the six months following Gilowska's announcement. In 2008, roughly 10 percent of the tax administration resigned. Those who remained petitioned the government for better working conditions and higher salaries; when their demands were ignored, tax inspectors went on strike. In spring 2008, tax inspectors and customs agents staged various work protests, demanding higher wages and better working conditions, including a three-day strike that coincided with the tax filing deadline.[47] A change in government restored stability to the bureaucracy, but the tax inspector remained a low-status occupation.

In the early transition, state fiscal managers were satisfied just getting post-communist society to accept the status of taxpayer. They were reluctant to use force, tolerating some cheating around the edges. But in the 2000s, tax evasion took bigger bites from the budget. Tax collectors were overmatched by ever more inventive and brazen taxpayers. Finance Minister Miroslaw Gronicki showed off the government's get-tough demeanor: "We need to make the system friendly for sincere taxpayers, but relentless against tax dodgers. Al Capone did not go to jail for being a gangster, but for not paying his taxes."[48] It was time to get tough with tax cheats; it was time to call the police.

In December 2000, a special interministerial team headed by Interior Minister Marek Biernacki was formed to fight economic crime.[49] Biernacki lobbied for expanded police powers to pursue tax crimes and for jointly conducted police-tax administration investigations. "It is a sad situation," the top cop said, "that the tax administration cannot uncover the money which allows so many distinctively well-dressed young people to drive around in the best cars."[50] Finance Minister Bauc directed the police toward the business community in general, and to VAT evaders in particular. Tax inspectors simply could not keep up with the high volume of VAT receipts, genuine and fraudulent, without additional support.[51] The long list of special VAT discounts caused endless confusion for tax inspectors, who were more inclined to let things slide rather than fight taxpayer claims that the tax inspectors themselves were not sure were illegal. New legislation was supposed to impress taxpayers with more severe penalties for evasion, including prison terms, but not much changed.[52] The penal fiscal code explicitly stated that tax evaders should be given ample opportunity to repent and repay voluntarily; punishment was a last resort.[53] The code recommended that when evidence of evasion is discovered, tax authorities should first send a note and give the taxpayer the chance to come clean.[54]

In 2002, Fiscal Control was endowed with new powers to access financial information and to seize property, with prior court permission.[55] The Interior Ministry was allowed to revoke the passport of individuals with large tax liabilities.[56] And the police were actively assisting tax inspectors with investigations of suspected evaders. More revisions in 2005 made corporate tax advisers personally liable for their clients' returns.[57] The state's new get-tough approach appeared to be working when Fiscal Control, the police, and the tax administration together cracked the notorious "fuel mafia," a network of private businessmen, public organizations, local officials, and the fishing fleet who were reaping huge profits from the resale of subsidized fuel, and evading taxes on it all.[58] But almost as soon as the state made a show of force, society organized resistance.

The Polish Confederation of Private Employers lodged an appeal to the Constitutional Tribunal, opposing the use of police powers to collect taxes.[59] In 2005, the Tribunal agreed, stripping Fiscal Control and tax administration of their new powers, and forbidding the police from participating in tax investigations. Meanwhile, the courts continued to place the burden of proving criminal intent on tax inspectors instead of taxpayers. Despite the bluster about harsher penalties, the courts still treated tax evaders leniently. In 2002, tax authorities initiated twenty-eight thousand investigations of taxpayers suspected of fraud, of which more than ten thousand were prosecuted in court. Once in court, about two-thirds were found guilty and fined small sums, while just twelve people were actually sent to jail for tax evasion. The courts issued fines to sixty-seven hundred taxpayers: those found guilty of "petty fiscal offense" paid on average of 738 zloty ($185), while those found guilty of larger "fiscal offense," punishable by jail, instead remained free and paid fines on average of 1,958 zloty ($490). Only 40 percent of the outstanding tax debts identified in these cases was returned to the state budget.[60]

Following the Constitutional Tribunal's 2005 ruling, MinFin tried again to make the most of its limited enforcement mandate.[61] Tax inspectors were given expanded power to acquire financial information from taxpayers, including the right to search private homes and to stop "fleeing vehicles."[62] Automatic fines were issued to businesses that refused entry to tax inspectors.[63] The time allowed for the state to establish guilt in a tax evasion investigation was extended from six months to one year, with interest accrued on the disputed amount.[64] Another legislative initiative again made it legal for tax inspectors to use information collected by the police.[65] MinFin promised that investigations would not intrude into private lives and that personal information would remain classified.[66] Predictably, these acts were challenged by business associations, and the new business-friendly government placed a new set of restrictions on tax enforcement.[67]

Instead of coercion, the Polish state began to practice revenue extraction with a human face. In the 2000s, state fiscal leaders promoted a nonantagonistic service culture in the tax administration, which, it was hoped, would increase consent-based compliance. In 2004, the Finance Ministry described the EU-influenced plan for tax administration: "The new approach combines service and audit functions, and treating the taxpayer as a client. Voluntary compliance should be encouraged to the maximum extent." Accordingly, the tax administration was revamped to include public service centers in all regional and local branch offices; private consultation rooms for more complex cases, and a nationwide telephone information service system.[68] By 2005, state revenue extraction employed more trained public service advisers (3,200) than fiscal control investigators (2,500). The tax administration began rewarding employees for public service. It boasted that in the first two years (2002 and 2003) of a government-initiated competition for "friendliest civil administration office," involving a dozen different state agencies, local tax offices in Plonsk and Sierpc had taken first place.[69]

Russia: Building the Means of Extraction

ORGANIZATION OF STATE FINANCES, 1992–1998

In contrast to Poland, state finances in the early Russian transition were plagued by institutional incoherence. This was the product of Russia's alternative path to regime breakdown. The Soviet regime collapsed via cadre defection, which led to the fragmentation of the state apparatus. The Polish state made it through the breakdown phase with the state apparatus still intact. In the Soviet command economy, state finance was conducted through an ostensibly centralized bureaucratic system. By the late communist period, however, rival intraparty patronage networks gained informal control over component pieces of state finance. After the communist collapse, an open competition unfolded among rival postcommunist elites to claim formal control of state finance.

Early in the transition, Finance Minister Boris Fedorov sought to restore a semblance of political coherence to state finances. An ardent defender of central state prerogatives, Fedorov was one of the most talented and energetic personalities to hold the post. He proposed that the Finance Ministry serve as command center with exclusive authority over the fiscal-administrative apparatus, supported by a well-trained cadre of tax inspectors with strong enforcement powers.[70] But Fedorov's tenure at MinFin was cut short. Unlike Poland, Russian finance ministers in the 1990s were not dominant political actors, but rather just one of many competing players trying to influence state fiscal policy. Between Fedorov's dismissal in December 1990 and Putin's appointment of Aleksei Kudrin in May 2000, the government went through eleven finance ministers, none of whom served as long as two years.

The administration of Russian state finance was a patchwork of mini fiscal fiefdoms. In the center, revenue extraction was divided among more than a half dozen agencies, including the tax administration, the customs agency, special off-budgetary funds, and the state property committee. Even the coercive arm of the tax administration was spun off into an independent tax police, which became yet another bureaucratic competitor for tax revenue.[71] The tax administration and tax police for several years filed income statements for the same revenue sources, which were both entered into the ledger as budgetary receipts.[72] And no one in central state finance knew how much income existed in the special off-budget accounts of the power ministries. The military, for example, consumed roughly 25 percent of budgetary expenditures, yet it was unaccountable to the Finance Ministry.[73]

Institutional incoherence was exacerbated by the decentralization of state revenue flows. Regional and local administrations had their own teams of tax collectors, which competed with one another and together against the center. The central state could not track budgetary income and expenses. In 1992, MinFin sought to impose order over this system by creating a new Treasury to coordinate the flow of revenues in and out of the state budget.[74] But two years later, treasury offices existed in only seventeen of the federation's eighty-nine regions.[75] Those regions that secured special revenue deals with the center avoided having the Treasury involved in the handling of locally collected revenue.

As an alternative to the Treasury, the government authorized selected commercial banks to collect and distribute budgetary funds. This practice was copied in the regions, where private bankers subverted the Treasury.[76] Tax receipts were channeled through a three-tiered banking hierarchy. At the top was the central bank, which received taxes and deposited the income into central accounts. In the middle were the regional branch offices of the central bank, which passed upward the revenue funds they received in the form of transfers from individual taxpayer accounts. At the lower level, where individual taxpayer accounts were kept, were other state-affiliated banks and private commercial banks. The state used these lower-level banks to supplement its underdeveloped treasury system. But there was a conflict of fiscal interest. In the mid-1990s, over one thousand commercial banks were formed, few of which were financially independent. Instead, they were "pocket" banks, meaning that they were instruments of corporate enterprises or regional governments, the main competitors to the central state for capital.[77] These lower-level banks frequently hid information from the center and delayed or sometimes neglected to transfer revenues into the central banking system.[78] By early 1997, tax officials estimated that commercial banks deliberately did not turn over as many as forty thousand tax payments per month.[79]

In early 1997, Chernomyrdin announced that only the Treasury would be involved with the implementation of the federal budget. Taxpayer accounts and budgetary funds handled by commercial banks would have to be transferred to Central Bank branches or Sberbank, the country's largest savings bank, also owned by the Central Bank. Firms were told to pay taxes directly to these accounts.[80] But implementation of the prime minister's order was postponed, compromised, or in some regions simply ignored. By the second half of the 1990s, the few and feeble efforts to recentralize state finances were obstructed by regional and financial elite actors, whose political influence secured revenue bargains that continued to give them direct access to the economic resources of the state.

In 1991, by presidential decree, a new tax administration was cobbled together from institutional remnants of the old regime.[81] The Soviet tax administration was never organized as a professionally autonomous bureaucracy. Instead, tax administration was a subordinate department within MinFin, and tax collection was just another form of interenterprise resource reallocation. In this system, tax inspectors were regionally based employees who monitored the finances of local enterprises. By the late Soviet period, enterprise profits were no longer automatically given up entirely to the center, and tax administrators held discretionary powers to negotiate the tax bill with enterprise managers. This policy was meant to offer some material incentive to encourage economic efficiency; in practice, it made for individualized and unsupervised relations between managers and inspectors.

Yeltsin's decree merely reclassified the old regime's territorial-based revenue departments into a hastily improvised tax administration. Like Poland, the far-flung territorial dispersion of staff in more than twenty-six hundred local offices made for an inefficient allocation of human resources.[82] The tax administration covered all corners of the country, but it lacked sufficient staffing where economic activity was most heavily concentrated. Moreover, organization and practice varied from one region to next, making it difficult to coordinate activities and process information.[83] In 1995, the central office of 710 employees directed a workforce of more than 160,000 employees.[84] Tax inspectors were dependent on regional leaders for administrative assistance and financial support. As a result, revenue agents had to balance conflicting professional and political demands. Regional leaders took advantage of this situation by protecting favored local corporations and preventing regional revenues from being transferred to central coffers. It did not help that tax inspectors were so poorly compensated, and sometimes forced to wait for their wages. The situation was so bad that in Yaroslavl local tax collectors went on strike in 1997 to protest unpaid salaries.[85]

The personnel of the tax administration lacked the expertise and resources to locate and claim revenue from the transition economy.[86] Meanwhile, the tax administration lacked information on the income and property of individual households. Even its ability to monitor the large corporations waned as the former socialist enterprises were privatized and restructured, and their financial accounts were transferred to commercial banks. Beyond the industrial sector it would take nearly a decade before state revenue agents could routinely track transactions and income flows in the private sector and in individual households. And even then they were not very good at it. Underdeveloped fiscal-administrative capacity caused Russian state actors to lean more heavily on coercion to compel society to comply with new revenue claims.

In March 1992, coercion became a principal feature of revenue extraction. By presidential decree a new bureaucracy, the Main Administration of Tax Investigation, was created to serve as a coercive complement to the tax administration. The agency was inspired by the Financial Guard in Italy, and it soon was known as the Russian Tax Police. It was charged with securing the physical defense of tax inspectors. According to the official history of the tax police, "In these complex conditions, the tax inspectorates, in which 80 percent of the employees were women, could not oppose the new forms of tax criminality. The work of the tax inspectors had become a risky and dangerous business."[87] The new agency was authorized to carry weapons, use physical force, and employ "special" means to enforce state revenue claims.[88]

In the competition for economic resources in the tax regime, coercion was not only directed from state to society but also from society toward the state. Private wealth went hand in hand with private coercion in the form of incorporated security firms and organized criminal gangs, who tangled with tax collectors. The number of officially recorded attacks increased at an alarming rate. In 1992, the tax administration listed one murder, fifty-two murder threats, and four arson attacks against its inspectors.[89] In 1996, the tax administration listed twenty-six tax collectors as killed in the line of duty, seventy-four inspectors had received serious bodily injury, six inspectors were kidnapped, and forty-nine inspectors had their homes firebombed.[90] Yet, when I once asked whether tax collection was a risky business, an ex-KGB tax police major pointed to his chest and defiantly answered, "We're the dangerous ones."[91]

The tax police was initially subordinated to the tax administration. But in 1993 a presidential decree made the tax police an autonomous hybrid fiscal-coercive agency. Its agents were mostly recruited from the old KGB. As a tax police colonel remarked on the agency's security origins, "it is not something that we merely recall, but it is the root of who we are."[92] The tax police quickly became a force in tax collection, with its contribution to the overall revenue take increasing from just over 1 percent in 1993 to more than 6.5 percent in 1998.[93] The tax police raised the coercive threat for taxpayers: the number of criminal cases initiated by the agency increased from six hundred in 1993, to twenty-five hundred in 1994, to sixty-one hundred in 1998.[94] The tax police started out with a limited mandate and a twelve-thousand- strong workforce. But as tax evasion became more prevalent, its powers of criminal investigation widened and its staff increased to more than fifty thousand employees. Combined with the tax administration, this meant that roughly one of every four tax collectors in Russia was an enforcement officer. In December 1994, the Institute for the Tax Police was founded in St. Petersburg to cultivate an elite corps of expertly trained cadres. In June 1998, the Institute's first class of forty-seven students graduated, receiving a degree in finance and the rank of lieutenant.[95]

A defining feature of the tax police was the display of force. The agency employed a corps of coercion specialists, who, when called, arrived at the scene wearing black masks and wielding automatic rifles. The "mask show" was performed by former members of the KGB's elite "Alfa" force, who worked for the tax police in teams of five to seven "*fiziki*" (agents empowered to use force).[96] This spectacle of intimidation was used in roughly one-third of tax police investigations. It was meant to instill fear in taxpayers under audit to assure their cooperation. As one tax policeman explained: "When we arrive we say 'tax police, everyone stay in your place, prepare documents, do not move, because if just one small paper is destroyed, the entire audit may be invalidated.' But this first phase is always ignored by everybody. People do not stop moving, instead they start arguing."[97]

The tax police were the institutional embodiment of "bureaucratic coercion." The agency represented an institutional adaptation of the coercive capacities of the communist regime to the dynamic circumstances of the transition economy. It was infused with the bureaucratic culture and operational conduct of the old regime's security elite. Its agents viewed the relationship between state and society as inherently antagonistic, which influenced the emergence of coercion-based compliance in the Russian state. But it would not be until the fiscal crisis later in the decade that the coercive powers of the tax police were fully unleashed on society. Until then, the state-elite revenue bargain provided political protection for business and regional elites against the coercive threats of the central state.

CONSOLIDATING THE MEANS OF EXTRACTION, 1999–2008

The 1998 fiscal crisis provided the political opportunity to restructure state finances. Russia's second president, Vladimir Putin, vowed to restore the "vertical power" of the state to assure that the central executive's policies were implemented, its laws obeyed, its taxes collected. Unlike the 1990s, the Russian central state in the 2000s displayed a willfulness of purpose, which was most evident in tax collection. The state's means of revenue extraction displayed more capable administrative practices and less restrained coercive impulses.

To begin, the central state finally imposed greater coherence over the fragmented fiscal-administrative process. In the formal command chain, the Finance Ministry emerged as the state's principal fiscal-administrative organ. Much of the reason for this was due largely to the appointment of Alexei Kudrin, whose decade-long tenure brought stability and prudence to state finances. What Kudrin lacked in charisma and outward ambition, he made up in competence and inside influence. Most important, he had the strong support of President Putin, with whom he shared a common past in the St. Petersburg city administration. Under Kudrin, MinFin reasserted the center's fiscal interests, penetrating ministerial and regional fiefdoms across the state. MinFin subordinated the once-independent tax administration in 2004, and pried the customs service free from its rival, the Economics Ministry, in 2006.[98] Even the opaque windows of military finances were cracked open by the unprecedented appointment of civilian fiscal administrators to the high command of the military bureaucracy[99] Through the Kremlin's informal command chain, MinFin's newfound assertiveness was bolstered by the presidential administration, where former St. Petersburg secret policeman Viktor Ivanov guarded central state interests in revenue extraction.

The central state imposed greater control over fiscal affairs in the regions. This task was enabled by the creation of a new territorial-administrative layer, the federal district, which reestablished the role of centrally empowered viceroys to oversee local affairs. The president's viceroys were recruited mainly from the security forces and were charged first with recentralizing coercive resources.[100] Soon after, an array of fiscal bureaucracies—tax inspectorates, customs agencies, and central bank branches—were consolidated into a new regional administrative scheme, creating a more concentrated deployment of labor and resources.[101] Fiscal-administrative capacity was further strengthened by the consolidation of revenue flows. In March 2001, the Treasury finally established a branch office on the territory of Tatarstan, the last region without one.[102] By the early 2000s, MinFin started to intervene directly in the finances of the previously politically privileged and economically semiautonomous donor regions.[103] Regional and local governments could no longer issue debt bonds without MinFin's explicit approval. All forms of local script were declared void as legal tender. MinFin also centralized the process of dealing with the large revenue-rich corporations in the regions that ran up huge tax debts. And, it created a single department to deal with outstanding debts, instead of four separate departments, and curbed the power of regional tax inspectors to negotiate settlements.[104]

In the 2000s, the tax administration underwent several reorganizations, which refocused the resources of the agency on the richest income sources in society. The most effective organizational innovation was the creation of sector-based, interregional departments, which enabled the tax inspectorate to monitor more closely the economic activities of large taxpayers. These special departments set up offices on the premises of the big corporations, from which teams of inspectors monitored transactions on a daily basis.[105] In 2001, the tax administration created three special interregional departments: oil, natural gas, and alcohol and tobacco. Interregional Department No. 1 included three oil producers, Lukoil, Rosneft, and Slavneft, as clients/targets, while Interregional Department No. 2

focused on Gazprom. According to the head of the Federal Tax Service, after the formation of Interregional Department No. 2, tax receipts from Gazprom to the state budget increased by more than 13 percent. In 2003, four additional interregional departments were established: electricity and energy, metallurgy, transportation, and telecommunications. This trend not only focused on large corporations but also extended to personal income under the leadership of Anatoly Serdiukov, a former furniture store businessman and political protégé of the St. Petersburg secret police. As a matter of routine, tax inspectors were instructed to focus attention on company directors and managers, and to assume that the highest-paid individuals were evading taxes.[106]

Beyond big targets, the tax administration improved its ability to gather information from small businesses and households. To make it more difficult for small businesses to hide, the tax administration was entrusted with responsibility for registering enterprises in 2002.[107] Tax audits became routine, rather than exceptional. In 2001, the tax administration carried out 440,000 audits on companies and another 311,000 on individuals, bringing in an additional R52 billion in revenue to the consolidated budget, an increase of R4.5 billion from the previous year. Between 2002 and 2005, tax receipts quadrupled from small businesses, taking advantage of a simplified compliance process.[108] Meanwhile, individual taxpayers were finally assigned taxpayer identification numbers (TIN), enabling the state to draw income profiles of households. Between 2000 and 2005, the state's revenue take from personal income taxes quadrupled, from R174 billion to R695 billion.[109]

The government also tried to transform the operational practices of the tax administration in dealings with taxpayers, in order to remake the tax administration into a more professional, rational, and service-oriented state agency. In February 2005, Putin demanded the government impose order on the tax administration, citing numerous complaints about inspectors harassing taxpayers.[110] In response, MinFin pushed through a set of administrative reforms suggested by business groups that more clearly defined the constraints on tax inspectors.[111] In November, the Duma tried unsuccessfully to radicalize the reform by offering amendments, such as criminalizing bureaucratic abuse by tax officials.[112] The fact, however, that this type of reform was announced annually belies the government's commitment to fundamental change. Indeed, the Supreme Arbitrage Court issued no less than three decrees in 2009, admonishing the agency for illegal methods of investigation, violating the taxpayer appeal process, exceeding the statutes of limitation in investigations, and applying "tax blackmail" by blocking financial transactions and license applications to force settlements of disputed claims.[113] As one scholar rightly put it, Russia tax administration reforms were more about "empowering," rather than "rationalizing," the bureaucracy.[114]

By virtually all indicators, Russian state fiscal-administrative capacity at the end of the 2000s was significantly improved from a decade previous. The tax administration more effectively gathered information, monitored transactions, and realized revenue claims. Budgetary revenues flowed into uncharted territories of the state bureaucracy and commercial banks to a much lesser extent. It would be correct to say that the system worked better, but wrong to say that it was fixed. Intrabureaucratic rivalries threatened to unravel the fragile coherence of state finances. Even an empowered Ministry of Finance could not follow capital when it disappeared into the pockets of policemen.

Having been deprived of its historic mission in the battle between socialism and capitalism, the police needed a raison d'être for the transition. By the end of the first decade, the police found a new service mission, dubbed the "economic security of the state." The 1998 fiscal collapse became the event that crystallized the new mission as part of a postcommunist corporate identity.[115] This domestically focused national security concept explicitly linked state strength with economic conditions. State security agents redirected their attention to combating illegal economic activities. The tax police was especially well positioned to play a prominent part. Indeed, the tax police adopted the new security concept as its official agency motto: "On Guard for the Economic Security of the State."

In 2001, a leadership change reinforced this more aggressive pose, when tax police chief Viacheslav Soltanganov was forced into retirement. Soltanganov publicly voiced reservations about coercion: "I have worked in the power structures for three decades, so I speak with authority. Forceful methods are one of the mechanisms that must be utilized by the state, but not the main mechanism.... It is very rare in practice that the tax police pursue punishments, such as incarceration. We are a very humane organization."[116] By contrast, his replacement, Mikhail Fradkov, was a strong advocate of strict application of coercion to encourage tax compliance. The new tax police chief described his task simply: "it is necessary that people are afraid of us."[117] Fradkov proposed legislation that would impose mandatory jail terms and confiscation of property for those found guilty of "large sum" tax crimes. Anything more lenient, he warned, would keep tax evaders in the shadows.[118]

The tax police became more active in the revenue extraction process after the financial collapse. In 1997, the tax police initiated fifty-seven hundred criminal cases; in 1999 (one year after the fiscal collapse), the agency initiated 16,500 criminal cases; and in 2000 the number nearly doubled to thirty-two thousand criminal cases.[119] The target of tax police investigations changed as well; the force was unleashed against the regional and economic elite, who could no longer rely on central patrons for protection. The agency launched investigations into the political machines of the powerful regional governors of Tatarstan and Primorskii Krai, leading to criminal charges and arrests.[120] The tax police next took on the corporate elite, starting criminal tax evasion investigations against the largest companies and richest tycoons. More than three hundred commercial banks were targeted, exposing numerous schemes by which bankers and clients colluded to make "fictitious" tax payments. In Moscow, this campaign led to forty criminal cases, with one alone amounting to R17 million in unpaid taxes.[121] The large state-managed railway and electricity monopolies were investigated as well.[122]

The unleashing of coercion against the economic elite caused a reaction. The business community begged the government for relief from the aggressive tactics of revenue collectors.[123] In 2003, Putin surprised even the tax police director when the fifty-thousand-person force was suddenly stripped of its autonomy. But the hopes of businessmen were soon dashed. The tax police was not dismantled, just reorganized: one-third of the force was subordinated to the economic crimes division of the Interior Ministry, while two-thirds of the force was reassigned to a new narcotics enforcement agency.[124] In 2005, the government said it would meet businessmen halfway by placing some clearly defined limits on the auditing powers of the tax administration, such as imposing time limits on inspections and stopping the practice of repeat inspections.[125] And in 2009 the Duma passed legislation that conditionally decriminalized tax evasion. As long as a delinquent taxpayer agreed to make amends for back taxes and penalties, the matter remained in the jurisdiction of the tax administration, thereby removing the police and the threat of arrest from the investigation. Although these more recent measures promised official restraint in the use of coercion in tax enforcement, state revenue agents still found it difficult to abide by their own rules.

Society Reacts: Cultivating Tax Compliance

How does the state get anyone to willingly give up a portion of their wealth? Not surprisingly, a substantial body of research has been conducted on this question; perhaps surprisingly, there is consensus on the answer.[126] Tax compliance is influenced by a mix of three factors: cost, exchange, contingency. First, the cost of compliance is considered against the risk of evasion. So coercion matters. Even countries that exhibit higher levels of societal consent with state revenue claims are still said to be examples of "quasi-voluntary" compliance, implying that a discreet but credible risk of detection and punishment exists, hence the "quasi."[127] But simple coercion is not sufficient, as research shows diminishing levels of compliance when coercion becomes widespread and heavy-handed.

Second, societal tax compliance is affected by instrumental calculation in the exchange of public goods for private wealth. The belief that you are getting something desirable back for your wealth has a positive effect on societal compliance. Tax contributions should not go to "others"—not to self-servicing bureaucrats, undeserving outsiders, or idling insiders. The belief that taxes are being redistributed to "them" has a negative effect on the compliance of "us." High-compliance communities are associated with economic well-being and social homogeneity.[128] Third, societal compliance is affected by normative consideration, or social contingency. What other people are doing has an effect on what you will do.[129] Who is paying and who is not is a fairness question. The perception that other taxpayers are more or less in compliance has a positive effect on one's compliance, whereas a perception of widespread evasion has a negative effect. The way in which the state treats society also is a contingency factor. Research shows that the behavior of tax collectors influences compliance; a more cooperative and empathetic tone from state agents is associated with higher levels of societal compliance. By assessing these three factors, this section explains why the Polish and Russian states fared differently in cultivating tax compliance in society.

Poland: Cultivating Tax Compliance

STATE COMPLIANCE STRATEGIES

The Polish state needed to gain access to the wealth of petty capitalists and worker households. To do so, both market-liberal and social-democratic governments crafted policies in accord with the factors that promote tax compliance—costs, exchange, and contingency. The Polish state succeeded in encouraging tax compliance, as Polish society accepted its status as taxpayer early in the transition. A public opinion survey in 1993, conducted by the Polish Public Opinion Center (CBOS), showed that two-thirds of respondents believed that it was "natural" to pay taxes.[130] This does not mean that there was no tax evasion in Polish society, because there was; nor does it mean that all taxpayers responded in the same manner to state revenue claims, because they did not. But it does mean that the state's strategies generally had a positive effect on societal compliance.

In calculating the risk/benefit costs of compliance, Polish society recognized rightly that the threat of sanction for underreporting income was low. The tax inspectorate was understaffed and the tax police were unarmed; there was little risk of getting caught. As an example, with almost two million businesses filing tax returns, MinFin reported uncovering only seventy-five hundred cases of fraud in 1994, and a similar number in 1995; that is, less than one-half of 1 percent of all returns.[131] Law enforcement officials confirmed that liberalizing reforms spurred a dramatic increase in tax-related economic crimes, overwhelming tax inspectors and costing the Treasury billions of zloty.[132] Even when criminal arrests were made, court convictions were few. Those found guilty of tax evasion rarely lost their business licenses, and even more rarely went to jail. In 1992 former prime minister Jan Bielecki reported in dismay: "It is true that taxpayers around the world attempt to avoid paying taxes, but in Poland cheating the state has become a dangerously ubiquitous phenomenon," with the threat of punishment so weak that "people often brag about their tax frauds."[133]

Besides coercive risk, the cost of compliance entails economic calculation. The social-democratic government tried to facilitate compliance by gradually easing the burden on taxpayers and simplifying the payment process. Historically, the introduction of personal income taxes has aroused societal resistance in other countries, but not in Poland. In the first year, most wage earners were barely aware that they were part of a new tax regime. The government ordered special wage increases, known as *ubruttowienie*, in both the private and public sectors that corresponded with the new tax burden. The PIT was not resisted by households because it did not have a noticeable effect on their net income. The raise was added to gross salaries and then taxed away.[134] Moreover, wage earners were not forced to sort out the complicated administration of PIT, which was entrusted to their employers. Eventually, as tax awareness grew in society, more than half of wage earners filed individual returns, taking advantage of deductions.

Petty capitalists also were eased into the tax collection system with special treatment. The cost of compliance at first was low. Tax holidays were available for new start-up businesses in the early 1990s; after that, a variety of administrative innovations were tried to keep the costs of compliance reasonable for entrepreneurs. Small businesses were allowed a generous exemption threshold of $50,000 before the VAT went into effect.[135] By mid-decade, however, the threshold was incrementally lowered each year, bringing more entrepreneurs into the VAT system: in 1994: 447,687 taxpayers; in 1995: 632,121 taxpayers; in 1996: 780, 842 taxpayers; in 1997: 900,000+ (est.) taxpayers.[136] In addition, the "revenue lump sum" tax was an administrative device used to capture a share of small-business wealth. It offered entrepreneurs a moderate flat rate and simple self-assessment on gross sales. In its first year, 1994, two-thirds of small businesses opted for this form of income tax. Given the limited monitoring capabilities of the tax administration, this type of "presumptive" tax encouraged small businesses to operate in the legal economy. Tax officials recognized that the "revenue lump sum" would miss a significant amount of entrepreneurial wealth, but it was considered more important to get businesses into the system and paying at least a portion of their tax obligation.

The second factor influencing compliance is the exchange of public goods for private wealth. By dismantling the command economy, it was inevitable that many state-provided goods and services were curtailed. Despite this, the retired, disabled, and unemployed received regular assistance from the state budget to lessen the harsh effects of the new economy.[137] By 1998, the annual cost of pensions and social insurance consumed roughly 15 percent of all budgetary expenses, comparable to the cost of salaries of public sector workers.[138] Poles gradually came to associate the tax burden with social benefits. When the PIT was first proposed, a 1991 CBOS survey found 70 percent of skeptical respondents believing that the tax would only redistribute wealth from households to bureaucrats.[139] But popular perception was modified. When Solidarity oppositionists called for an antigovernment PIT boycott in 1997, more than 70 percent of Poles rejected using taxation as a means of protest.[140] A 1998 CBOS survey asked respondents whether they favored a reduction in the tax burden if it meant reducing the provision of public goods. Although 80 percent of respondents said "yes," they would gladly accept a tax cut rather than pay for the costs of state administration, an overwhelming 90 percent said "no" to tax cuts if it meant a reduction in pensions or health services.[141]

Tax compliance is also influenced by perceptions of fairness: consent is contingent on what others are doing. Perceptions of fairness fluctuated across society, depending on which party controlled state finances. In the early 1990s, public sector employees saw Balcerowicz's market-liberal tax policies as unfair and their compliance declined; in the later 1990s, petty capitalists saw Kolodko's social-democratic tax policies as unfair and their compliance declined. The state was especially successful in cultivating wage-earner compliance with the PIT. Unlike the *popiwek*, which was applied to the public sector but not the private sector, the new PIT was applied evenly. It was difficult to evade because it was collected at the place of employment. It was a progressive tax with three rate brackets, but more than 90 percent of taxpayers fit into the lowest bracket. The new rich, of which there were few, were taxed at a rate more than twice as high.[142] When Balcerowicz proposed a flat-rate PIT in 1998, a CBOS survey found 77 percent of respondents opposed; they said that higher earners should pay higher rates. Only 17 percent of respondents supported the flat-rate tax.[143] Another survey at that time showed 60 percent of respondents believing President Kwasniewski's veto of the flat tax was "just."[144] Another example of Polish society's sensitivity to tax fairness is indicated by the results of a 2002 public opinion poll, which recorded an overwhelming 77 percent of respondents against a government proposal to offer a tax amnesty to those concealing income.[145] When the Constitutional Tribunal struck down the amnesty, it called the proposal "unfair" for giving a "tax bonus to dishonest taxpayers."[146]

Poland's petty capitalists were increasingly critical of the tax regime on all counts—costs, exchange, contingency. As the private sector took on more of the overall tax burden, Polish entrepreneurs complained about the costs of compliance. However, the number of businessmen who identified tax rates as "a problem for doing business" eventually declined in step with the decline in CIT rates: 2002, 82 percent; 2005, 79 percent; 2008, 59 percent.[147] Concerning exchange, businessmen did not view their tax contributions as a fair trade of private wealth for public good, but instead saw their wealth being redistributed to undeserving people and wasteful bureaucrats. Finally, concerning contingency, lax tax enforcement of public sector firms was seen as blatantly unfair, placing a heavier burden on small business.[148] Meanwhile, petty capitalists perceived widespread evasion among their peers in the small-business community. A MinFin survey of three hundred small businessmen found that only 10 percent believed that most entrepreneurs paid taxes honestly. The consensus was that roughly one-third of income was concealed from tax collectors.[149] "Fair tax standards" for the small-business sector was a constant theme of market liberals when they controlled state finances.[150]

Overall, the Polish state employed a nonconfrontational, ever-bending, and gradual approach to cultivating societal tax compliance. In the crucial first years of the new tax regime, the state successfully established precedence for compliance with its new revenue claims. As the economy gradually recovered, state coffers were replenished by wealth from wage-earner households and petty capitalists.

SOCIETAL COMPLIANCE PATTERNS

All tax systems are dynamic, as state and society compete for capital. When the Polish state leaned on its revenue sources, wage earners and petty capitalists found ways to reduce their tax burdens. In the second half of the 1990s, both groups became adept at avoidance. Tax avoidance meant using the letter of the law to violate the spirit of the law.

The cash-poor Polish government used tax policy as an indirect means of providing social assistance to wage-earner households. Because of this, the PIT was revised repeatedly to allow for more deductions. By 1997, close to half of all personal income taxpayers applied for some form of rate reduction, taking advantage of more than one hundred categories of relief. PIT deductions were mostly related to housing, educational, professional, and medical expenses; but at one time or another household tax bills could also be lowered by investing in treasury bills, giving blood, or purchasing theater binoculars (in place of eye glasses). One New Year's Eve, Poland's opticians stayed open extra late to accommodate the long queue of customers, who were either struck by a sudden outbreak of nearsightedness or else had just learned of the tax break for eyeglasses.[151] In 2008, Poles began earning "blood money" when the government created a PIT deduction for donating blood, which could be up to 6 percent of household income.[152] In a twist on the practice of avoiding taxes, some taxpayers intentionally overpaid their taxes when the courts ruled that the tax administration must pay interest on the surplus amount returned at the end of the year—at a rate that turned out to be higher than what savings banks were offering.[153]

The most infamous tax avoidance ploy came from the deduction for charitable donations. The law specified that up to 10 percent of income could be written off, but it was vague about what constituted a charity. In 1996 more than 6.3 million Poles, 27 percent of all PIT tax filers, deducted over 9 billion zloty in personal income by making "charitable" donations to their family and friends.[154] Even though the tax administration threatened to audit familial philanthropists, taxpayers took advantage of the loophole until it was closed by the legislature.[155] Another popular tactic to lower personal income tax payments was simply to declare oneself to be self-employed, and then to be taxed as a small businessman. By 1996, over 1.7 million taxpayers filed as self-employed, but they were not all entrepreneurs; many were just avoiding the higher-rate bracket.[156] With management's cooperation, full-time employees reregistered as self-employed contract workers without really changing jobs.

As a result of the state-labor revenue bargain, the politically protected large state enterprises avoided paying taxes by accumulating tax arrears and then negotiating down their debts. By 1996, roughly twelve thousand firms owed about 1.5 billion zloty in tax arrears to the state budget. The bulk of this overdue bill was held by a couple dozen public sector firms.[157] Beginning in 1994, the Finance Ministry authorized regional tax offices to work out negotiated solutions, which allowed firms to offset tax debts with services or goods rendered to other public institutions, such as schools and hospitals. It also meant writing off a firm's debts. In 1996, almost seventy-five hundred firms reached negotiated settlements with local tax officials, bringing in a meager 10 percent of the total amount that was owed to the state.[158] In 1999, the tax administration canceled 130 million zloty in unpaid corporate income taxes.[159] Tax officials defended the practice of negotiated avoidance by citing political and social concerns. The vice minister for taxes, Waldemar Manugiewicz, stated emphatically that it was impossible to threaten bankruptcy against "strategic enterprises," such as the state-run railway, which routinely topped the list of largest tax debtors.[160]

Although some taxpayers reduced their tax burden partially through legalistic avoidance, others escaped completely through illegal evasion. Poland's main tax evaders were its new entrepreneurs. Small businesses were less likely to get caught and more likely to evade, especially on transaction taxes. MinFin published a breakdown of tax evasion by type of tax for 1995: VAT, excise, and sales taxes, 45 percent; CIT, 31 percent; and PIT, 9 percent.[161] The trend was even stronger seven years later, in 2002: VAT and excise taxes, 67 percent; CIT, 23 percent; and PIT, 7 percent.[162] As the full weight of the tax burden was felt, petty capitalists found a variety of means to conceal income. The most common tactics were keeping bogus books, forging transaction receipts, employing undeclared workers, and moving profits to offshore havens.[163] In 2004, over one billion dollars was invested in Poland from companies registered in Cyprus, where Polish capital could evade Polish taxes.[164]

The estimated size of the "shadow economy" is a common indicator of the level of tax evasion. Using this gauge, the transition economies of Eastern Europe displayed notably higher levels of tax evasion than the more advanced industrial economies of Western Europe. Wide variation, however, is observed among particular cases. In this regard, Poland was in good standing in the East, but not so good in the West. Poland's gray economy is usually calculated within a range from 15 percent to 25 percent of GDP. At the end of the 1990s, estimates were on the lower side of this range, while at the end of the 2000s the estimates were more toward the upper side. Accordingly, Poland placed among the best-performing postcommunist states (just behind the Czech Republic and Slovakia) and the worst-performing EU member states (just ahead of Italy and Greece).[165]

Russia: Cultivating Tax Compliance

STATE COMPLIANCE STRATEGIES

Tax compliance strategy in Russia underwent significant change between the 1990s and 2000s. Under President Yeltsin, the state neglected to develop societal compliance. In contrast to Poland, the Russian state had access to rich revenue-generating commodities for income, so there was little concern about the compliance of households and small businesses. The factors that influence compliance—costs, exchange, contingency—registered negatively. Society responded by shirking its tax obligations and withdrawing from the official economy. By contrast, under President Putin the state made a genuine effort to foster conditions that would encourage tax compliance. The government employed a mixed strategy, where coercive risk was raised and economic cost was lowered, and tax compliance improved.

In the 1990s the costs of compliance ran high for Russian taxpayers, and the risks of evasion were low. The political fragmentation of state finances raised the cost of compliance. Federal, regional, and local administrations competed with one another over the same revenue sources. The tax code included over two hundred taxes, applied at multiple rates, which even the tax administration could not always decipher. So much uncertainty made taxpayers vulnerable—and reluctant to pay. Reporting income often brought increased scrutiny from tax inspectors, who otherwise were in the dark about personal wealth and business transactions. The cost of compliance was especially burdensome for small businesses; even if they wanted to fulfill tax obligations, it meant financial ruin with so many state agents claiming a share.[166]

The risk of punishment, meanwhile, was low. The tax administration readily admitted to having only a distorted and incomplete picture of the income of small businesses and households.[167] The coercive threat posed by the tax police was mostly ineffectual. The procurator's office agreed to pursue less than one quarter of all the criminal cases brought by the tax police.[168] As late as 2001, the tax police saw the successful prosecution of just twenty-seven criminal cases.[169] The state's commitment to coercion was anything but credible: in January 1996, Yeltsin signed a decree allowing firms with tax arrears to postpone payment; in February, Yeltsin signed a decree authorizing the confiscation of property of firms with tax arrears; in March, the government issued a decree authorizing withholding of central subsidies to regions with tax arrears; in May, Yeltsin signed a decree preparing an amnesty for firms with tax arrears.[170] During the 1990s the combination of high cost and low risk reinforced noncompliance.

In the first years of the new tax regime the Russian state neglected offering public goods in exchange for tax payments. The government drastically curtailed its delivery of public services and goods, which had long subsidized households. As revenue dwindled, the wages of public sector employees were delayed or not paid at all. Whereas public spending in Poland increased from 47 to 50 percent of GDP between 1989 and 1995, in Russia public spending for the same period significantly declined from just over 50 percent to 43 percent of GDP.[171] The precipitous decline in public goods adversely affected society's view of taxation. A tax police survey showed that taxpayers both did not trust the state to provide public goods or that fellow taxpayers would pay their taxes.[172] The tax administration's professional journal published the findings of a survey conducted in the Tambov region that showed that almost 60 percent of respondents felt the tax code promoted tax evasion.[173] Notably, there was only a weak association with exchange, as only one-third of respondents believed that paying taxes to the state would provide any benefit to themselves. A series of World Bank surveys found that two-thirds or more of taxpayers routinely said that "it is not clear what collected taxes are spent on."[174]

The early Russian tax regime did not feature contingent consent. There was no sense of fairness in the distribution of the burden. Regional tax revolts of the early 1990s, for example, were prompted by the disparity in tax burdens assigned to Russian oblasts and non-Russian national republics. When the Sverdlovsk region unilaterally upgraded its administrative status from oblast to republic, its governor remarked that "with this decision, we say no to a federation based on unequal subjects."[175] Ordinary taxpayers were regularly reminded of politically favored large taxpayers whose outstanding tax debts were listed in the mass media. The widespread perception among taxpayers was that fellow citizens and large corporations were not paying taxes. Frequent statements to the press by government officials of widespread tax evasion only confirmed this notion. In 1988 the head of the Interior Ministry estimated that as many as sixty million taxpayers (more than 90 percent) were involved in some way in the shadow economy.[176] An official of the beleaguered tax administration lamented: "If we want someday to create a normal government, then we need also to develop a normal sense of citizenship—it's a long process, and it may take another generation before we get to that point."[177]

After the 1998 financial collapse, President Putin revised compliance strategies. The state raised the risk of evasion. This was demonstrated in several high-profile cases against large taxpayers, particularly the 2003 assault on the Yukos oil company. Maybe the state still could not monitor society effectively, but it increased the punitive costs for those without political protection who were caught cheating. Just as notably, the state lowered the cost of compliance by imposing order on competing revenue claimants, simplifying administrative procedures and reducing tax rates. According to IMF research, PIT compliance improved after the flat-tax reform: while estimated compliance rates among lower-level income earners stayed the same, at 74 percent, rates for higher-income earners rose from 52 percent to 68 percent.[178] As a percentage of GDP, PIT increased from 2.5 percent in 1999 to 3.3 percent in 2002.[179] Business taxes were also reduced. The 2002 corporate income tax reform reduced business taxes from 35 percent for industrial and retail firms and 43 percent for financial firms to a flat 24 percent rate. In 2003, a new tax arrangement encouraged small-business activity by establishing a consolidated 15 percent tax rate. Continuing the trend, the Unified Social Tax rate was cut from 36.5 percent to 26 percent in 2005. And, after much interministerial debate, MinFin finally got its way and in March 2007 declared a tax amnesty, which allowed self-employed entrepreneurs and individuals to pay a 13 percent tax to a special account for undeclared income received up to five years before December 2006, without incurring penalties or criminal charges.[180]

The 2000s also saw positive developments in an exchange-based tax compliance strategy. The boom in world energy prices enabled the state to provide more public goods. Public sector employees not only received their wages on time but also received long-overdue raises. The military and the police, in particular, received substantial pay increases.[181] Even during the 2008 financial troubles, Prime Minister Putin increased the wages of federal employees by as much as 30 percent.[182] When local administrations or big businesses failed to pay employees on time, Putin went into good tsar mode by publicly chastising chief executives, after which money for back wages was found.[183] Meanwhile, the government increased its budgetary allotments for social welfare pension funds. When the economy stalled in the late 2000s, the government continued to meet its commitment to raise pensions.[184]

Taking advantage of the state's newfound generosity, government officials tried to cultivate the perception of exchange-based compliance in society. A normative campaign was launched on television, in newspapers, and on billboards that explicitly stressed the connection between paying taxes and having public goods, such as well-funded schools, elderly assistance, and public safety. In addition, the tax administration received an image makeover in an effort to recast the agency as a client-friendly service provider. There was little evidence, however, that society's negative view of state tax collection changed significantly. A 2004 survey found that nearly 80 percent of respondents still believed that "most people evade their taxes," suggesting that taxpayers still remained distrustful that others would pay their share.[185]

SOCIETAL COMPLIANCE PATTERNS

When state met society in Russia's transitional tax regime, society was not anxious to get acquainted. In the transitional tax regime, Russian society responded by dodging the state's new revenue claims. The large extractive and industrial corporations, the state's principal revenue targets, were especially good at concocting elaborate evasion schemes. Small businesses and households also figured out how to avoid the taxman.

The corporate sector reduced its tax burden through barter, special deals, and avoidance schemes. First, in the mid-1990s the overall decline in enterprise profits coincided with the central bank's newfound resolve to maintain a tight monetary policy, resulting in less capital available to the corporate sector.[186] To keep the economy going, interindustrial transactions increasingly took the form of barter. In July 1992 only 10 percent of industrial transactions involved the exchange of goods and services, instead of cash; but in January 1997 barter-type exchanges accounted for 45 percent of industrial transactions.[187] Nonmonetary means of economic exchange inventively appeared that would cover other forms of payment—promissory notes, IOUs, regional script, wage substitutes, and ration coupons.[188]

The use of barter began as a survival strategy for cash-poor enterprises, but the economy's transmogrification into postindustrial feudalism was directly driven by the tax regime.[189] The state's rapacious revenue claims caused many firms to fall behind on taxes, a circumstance compounded by the punitively high penalties that kicked in almost immediately. Once a firm was officially declared to be in arrears, the tax administration had the authority to confiscate the funds in its bank accounts. In reaction, enterprises moved outside the banking sector to carry out transactions, using offshore foreign currency accounts, promissory notes, and barter. In 1994, the government first allowed public firms to satisfy outstanding debts to suppliers by issuing a special treasury coupon, which the supplier could redeem either in a future cash payout or by canceling past due taxes.[190] The offsetting of budgetary expenses and incomes was supposed to make the government's ledgers appear in order, but a troubling precedent was set. Once it was acceptable to satisfy debts through offsets, regional and corporate elites took advantage, using nonmonetary means of payment to fulfill tax obligations to the state center. Tax arrears to the central budget increased accordingly as a percentage of GDP, from 2 percent in 1995, to 4 percent in 1997, to 6 percent in 1998.[191] In 1997 alone, the number of firms classified as "large debtors" grew from eleven hundred at the beginning of the year to over thirty-three hundred at the end.[192]

Second, politically favored corporate and regional elites avoided paying taxes through negotiated deals with state authorities. Sometimes these deals were done formally in negotiation with state actors, but sometimes they were done informally. The capital-rich energy sector was especially active. According to the Finance Ministry, in 1995 special tax exemptions cost the budget roughly $6 billion in lost revenue; in 1996, the cost rose to over $30 billion.[193] By 1998, the amount of revenue lost through tax privileges was close to one-third of the total taxes collected for the consolidated budget, and more than two-thirds of the total taxes collected for the federal budget.[194] Third, large corporations set up sophisticated avoidance systems to hide income. Businesses routinely kept separate books, prepared especially for tax inspectors. Firms were founded, registered, and then became defunct, having carried out no business activity other than to evade taxes. Income was concealed by creating networks of territorially dispersed "shell" companies, which the decentralized tax administration could not keep track of.[195] Also, income moved "offshore" to avoid higher rates. Offshore sometimes meant offshore, to a tax haven such as Cyprus, but offshore also meant downriver, to a tax rate-cutting region such as Kalmykia.

The main beneficiaries of the state-elite revenue bargain turned out to be the most flagrant tax evaders. In 1996, unpaid taxes topped $20 billion, or 5 percent of GDP, with just seventy-three large corporations accounting for over 45 percent of the tax debt to the central state budget.[196] In the regions, in 1996 only six of eighty-nine regions met their designated tax obligations to the central budget, and only thirteen additional regions managed to send in more than 80 percent of their designated tax obligations. More than half of the regions failed to collect 70 percent of their designated tax obligations to the central state budget.[197] By 1998, the donor regions topped the list of regions with the highest tax debt to the federal budget.[198] Nearly one-third of all tax delinquent firms were located on the territories of these ten regions.

Unlike Poland, small businesses and households in Russia were given the opportunity and incentives to opt out of the new tax system. Most new small businesses were not in a position to negotiate special deals, but they still managed to reduce their tax bills through bookkeeping tricks to conceal income. The state's predatory extractive practices chased many small businesses into the shadow economy. Whereas Polish taxpayers preferred to file their own PIT declarations, to take advantage of exemptions, Russian taxpayers preferred to let their employers file on their behalf, to underreport salaries. To hide income from the visible official economy, businesses and households used cash, leaving no record of payments and receipts. The state's estimates of the shadow economy as a percentage of GDP varied depending on who was doing the estimating. The state statistical agency put the number between 20 and 30 percent, the tax administration between 30 and 40 percent, the IMF at 50 percent, and law enforcement agencies between 40 and 60 percent.[199] The shadow economy in Russia was at least two times larger than in Poland, highlighting an essential difference in compliance patterns: Poland displayed widespread avoidance, and Russia displayed widespread evasion.

Transitional Tax Regimes Compared

Transitional tax regimes encompassed both the state's means of extraction and society's compliance patterns. Across the postcommunist states, variation occurred in the particular features of transitional tax regimes, which is revealed in a comparison of Poland and Russia. Poland saw the emergence of a tax regime based on "legalistic consent": the state's means of extraction were effectively constrained and rationalized through legal-institutional mechanisms, while society complied in principle with tax obligations, though it still avoided taxes to the extent it was possible under the law. By contrast, Russia saw the emergence of a tax regime based on "bureaucratic coercion": the state's means of extraction were not effectively constrained with legal-institutional checks, while society responded by opting out of the tax system when possible.

Poland: Legalistic Consent

By the end of the 1990s a tax regime was taking shape in Poland based on "legalistic consent." One observer summed up Polish tax morale this way: "whatever is not prohibited is permitted."[200] Polish citizens accepted their newly assigned status as taxpayers and accepted the state's new revenue claims in principle. Polish society, however, tended to avoid complying in full and instead contrived formal and informal means to reduce its new tax burden in practice.

World Values Surveys (WVS) indicated Poland's gradual movement toward quasi-voluntary compliance.[201] In a comparison of WVSs, the percentage of respondents who said that cheating on taxes was "never justifiable" rose from 49 percent in 1989 to 60 percent in 1999; if one includes the respondents who answered "almost never justifiable," the figure rose from 62 percent to 75 percent. These numbers suggest a growing recognition of civic responsibility regarding tax compliance—in principle. The extent to which Poles practiced the principle is another matter: the 1999 survey also found that more than half of the respondents, 59 percent, believed that "many" of their fellow citizens were cheating on their taxes, while less than 1 percent thought that "almost no one" was cheating. If nothing else, the data imply that an increasing number of Poles accepted the right of the state to claim revenue as well as the right of society to reduce its revenue obligation.

These responses should not suggest that society held a sanguine view of state fiscal policy. Consistently, survey respondents expressed the opinion that taxes were too high and social assistance too low.[202] Table 4.1 provides some perspective on just how strongly Poles felt about cheating on taxes. The survey asked respondents how they rated particular "wrongful" behaviors. Two-thirds of respondents considered cheating on taxes wrongful, which was well below exploiting workers and beating children, but well above cheating on exams and using contraceptives. In terms of civic responsibility, Poles felt strongly that it was wrong to give or accept bribes, an act that gives advantage to those with power and wealth; but they did not feel quite as strongly about underreporting income to the taxman or fare skipping on the tram, behaviors that those with lesser incomes can partake in.

TABLE 4.1   Social opinion of wrongful behaviors in Poland (2005)

TYPE OF BEHAVIOR	ALWAYS WRONG	ALMOST ALWAYS WRONG	TOTAL
Employers exploiting employees	84	12	96
Accepting bribes	81	13	94
Giving bribes	73	18	91
Beating children	67	22	89
Marital infidelity	66	18	84
Homosexuality	56	13	69
Underreporting income on tax forms	**51**	**25**	**76**
Dodging fare on public transport	30	29	59
Divorce	29	25	54
Cheating on exams	20	29	49
Not voting	19	14	33
Premarital sex	15	17	32
Using contraceptives	15	13	28

Source: CBOS, Polish Public Opinion (August 2005), 3.

In social surveys, corruption was increasingly identified as a "big problem," rising from 34 percent of respondents in 1991, to 48 percent in 2000, to 69 percent in 2003.[203] Opportunities for corruption, of course, existed in the new tax regime. Poles distinguished among state officials who were most susceptible. Parliament members rated especially low in the public's esteem. Indeed, political contributions and well-placed bribes were means by which informally connected entrepreneurs dealt with their tax obligations.[204] In one high-profile case in Poznan, local leaders encouraged the business community to help sponsor the underfunded local police. This market-based solution to local law enforcement caused a national scandal and high-office resignations when it was found that some local businessmen provided police with computers, office equipment, prostitutes, and vodka in exchange for protection against tax inspections.[205]

Although the view of Poles toward state officials ran from cynical to hostile, the tax administration was held in higher regard than most state agencies. It was not as if taxpayers had warm feelings toward tax collectors, but they did recognize a higher level of professional competence and personal integrity with the tax administration than they did with most other state actors. A 2004 survey found that half the respondents had had dealings with the tax administration in the past five years, of which more than three-quarters were "satisfied with the results" and "satisfied with how they were spoken to and treated" by tax office personnel.[206] Among businessmen, a 2002 survey found that 70 percent of respondents said the tax administration was a "major constraint" on doing business, but a 2008 follow-up survey found only 26 percent said the same.[207] European Bank for Reconstruction and Development (EBRD) and World Bank surveys of Polish businessmen in the 2000s showed that between one-third to one-half of respondents agreed that state corruption, in general, was "a problem for doing business" (2002: 50 percent; 2005:38 percent); but when it came to the tax administration in particular, respondents were much more positive. Only a few (2002: 5 percent; 2005: 6 percent) said that "bribery is frequent" in dealings with the tax administration, as opposed to other state agencies.[208] Significantly, these numbers are particularly low in comparison with other postcommunist countries, which as a group consistently averaged three times higher than Poland.[209]

The rules of engagement in the transitional tax regime reinforced the Polish state's compliance strategy of legalistic consent. The state bureaucracy was constrained from acting on arbitrary impulse and from using administrative coercion to compel compliance. Polish taxpayers were quick to recognize the formal limits of the means of extraction and to carve out an informal sphere of acceptable behavior. In general, Polish citizens complied with the state's new revenue claims to the minimal extent that they were legally obligated to. Poland experienced what tax regimes in all countries experience—an ongoing attempt by those

TABLE 4.2   Social opinion on tax collectors in Poland

A) FREQUENTLY BRIBED STATE OFFICIALS IN OPINION OF POLISH BUSINESSMEN

STATE AGENCY	2002	2005
Government courts	16	15
Health/safety inspector	13	10
Fire/building inspector	8	7
Tax inspector	**5**	**6**

B) IN YOUR OPINION DOES CORRUPTION OCCUR "VERY OFTEN" AMONG:

PROFESSION	1999	2005
Doctors	43	48
Parliament members	15	42
Police officers	28	35
Judges	17	33
Tax inspectors	**13**	**16**
Bankers	8	13
Teachers	1	6

Sources: (A) EBRD–World Bank, BEEPS, "Poland-at-a-Glance" (2006), 4; (B) Osrodek Badania Opinii Publicznej (OBOP), "Corruption on the Eve of Political Change," no. 062/05 (Warsaw: September 2005), 6.

on whom the burden falls to finesse tax payments and reform tax policy. But it is one thing to whinge and wrangle, and another to reject and resist. For all its shortcomings, Poland's new tax regime exhibited more consent than opposition. The troubles with tax collection were well known yet tolerated by the fiscal agents of the postcommunist state. From the state's perspective, it was more important to legitimize its new revenue claims, and it did so by getting as many taxpayers as possible into the system. They fought outright evasion, but accommodated widespread avoidance. An anonymous tax inspector summed it up well: "Most businesses cheat, but if you take only 20–30 percent from the treasury, then you are still a decent taxpayer and inspectors have no time or energy to bother with you."[210] This remark captures the essence of Poland's tax-compliance strategy of legalistic consent.

Russia: Bureaucratic Coercion

Russia's oft-compromised tax code was once famously likened to a Swiss cheese, because it was so filled with holes. But there was nothing Swiss about the relationship between tax officials and taxpayers.[211] There were few reports of amicable chats with the taxman to straighten things out; instead, relations were acrimonious from the start. The rights of taxpayers were only belatedly acknowledged, and even then inconsistently enforced. Russia's state-society fiscal relations exhibited suspicion and recrimination. As the state increasingly sought to compel compliance through "bureaucratic coercion," mutual hostility between state and society was reinforced.

Table 4.3 shows that social attitudes about tax evasion were not especially strict. Cheating on taxes was not considered nearly as bad as accepting bribes, drunk driving, or littering; still, it was worse than skipping the fare on the tram, and more akin to committing adultery. The cumulative percentage did not rise too much when including respondents who answered that it was "almost never justifiable" to cheat on taxes: 1990, 56 percent; 1995, 51 percent; 1999, 54 percent; 2006, 55 percent.[212]

Among postcommunist states, Russia ranked on the higher side (though by no means the highest) for corruption. The trend over two decades was that an increasing percentage of society viewed the postcommunist state as pervasively corrupt. This opinion became even stronger under Putin than under Yeltsin. It was shown by international organizations and business associations that try to measure corruption, as well as by the Russian government, whose annual anticorruption edicts are as reliable as the December snow.[213] In Russia, unlike Poland, society's cynical views about the government in general spilled over to the tax administration in particular. Table 4.4 presents findings from two World Bank surveys of Russian businessmen regarding taxation and the state. The tax administration ranked as the number-one problem for doing business in 2005, and tax rates ranked number-one in the 2008 survey.[214]

The view of society toward tax authorities was unflattering. The Tambov tax administration conducted a survey of the region's taxpayers in 2001, which asked an unusual zoological question: which member of the dog family most closely resembled the tax inspector. The top responses were sly fox (28%), watch dog (20%), and evil jackal (11%).[215] A widespread assumption was that the tax organs were

TABLE 4.3   Social opinion in Russia on behavior that is "never justifiable"

	1990	1995	1999	2006
Accepting bribes	82.7	79	69.1	72.5
Engaging in homosexuality	82.7	68.9	61.6	59.7
Driving drunk	81.1	NA	74.2	NA
Littering	67.5	NA	74.2	NA
Committing suicide	61.5	63.3	63.2	61.4
Making false benefit claims	59.3	56.2	55	49.8
Skipping fare public transport	49.8	33.2	31.5	35.5
Cheating on taxes	**47.6**	**42.8**	**43.4**	**47.8**
Committing adultery	46.5	NA	47.6	NA

Source: World Values Survey (Russia: 1990, 1995, 1999, 2006)

TABLE 4.4 Survey results on problems with doing business in Russia

	2005	2008
Tax administration	64	54
Tax rates	58	79
Corruption	41	67
Worker skills	39	77
Licenses/permits	38	48
Access to financing	36	61
Courts	34	44
Customs/trade regulations	30	28
Labor regulations	20	27

Sources: EBRD–World Bank, BEEPS, "Russia-at-a-Glance" (Washington, D.C.: World Bank, 2006); EBRD–World Bank, BEEPS, "Russia-at-a-Glance" (January 2010). The 2005 survey included 392 firms (38% trade/33% manufacturing); the 2008 survey included 909 firms (13% trade/78% manufacturing).

involved in corruption, and that tax revenues were diverted into private pockets instead of to public welfare. Thirty percent of businessmen admitted making "informal payments" to government officials to help get something done, of which almost two-thirds (18%) admitted to "giving gifts" specifically to tax inspectors to resolve cases (that figure is nearly four times as high as in Poland).[216]

The rules of engagement in the Russian tax regime were defined more than anything else by the discretionary powers of tax inspectors to apply the law selectively and to mobilize bureaucratic-coercive resources during investigations. The effect on state-business relations was insightfully described by Ella Paneyakh, who conducted more than two hundred in-depth interviews with Russian entrepreneurs.[217] In the course of duty a typical tax inspector has four main concerns: (1) uncover violations to report to the field office; (2) collect overdue taxes and fines; (3) steer clear of well-connected businessmen; and (4) avoid serious complaints from taxpayers. The typical entrepreneur, meanwhile, has three main concerns when the taxman calls: (1) do not give cause to inspectors to initiate a comprehensive audit; (2) do not deviate from informal norms concerning violations that the inspector expects to find; and (3) do not deviate from informal norms concerning payment of overdue taxes and fines. The following excerpt from one entrepreneur illustrates a "good" relationship:

> Everybody knows that nobody pays all taxes. I come to my inspector and she says explicitly to me: "Look, I know I am accepting a piece of bullshit from you. I know you fake cashier's receipts, don't you?" I say. "I do." Of course, but I do it reasonably. Because in the previous year, I tricked it so blatantly that they said to me, "Oh dear, let's be reasonable and show some more." I said, "How much?" They said, "Let it be at least 18,000 rubles ($600) more." I have friendly relations with my tax

inspector. When I come to her, she says to me, "Would you please make some mistakes. I am required to impose some additional taxes on you, if I am checking you." So, when I am filing my tax declarations, I write down some mistakes.

This interview anecdote is consistent with a survey of three hundred small businessmen, who were asked how they deal with unfair treatment by tax inspectors: two-thirds answered that they "try to reach a compromise with inspectors."[218] In the rules of engagement, both parties seek to avoid costly and time-consuming investigations. If it was a profitable quarter, then the entrepreneur comes out ahead; if not, then it will take some convincing.

The state's view of society was no more gracious. Tax officials bemoaned society's low-tax culture and pervasive tax evasion. They most often spoke of tax collection in zero-sum terms between state and society. One tax policeman likened the state-taxpayer relationship to a "cat and mouse game."[219] In interviews with the tax police in 1998, a particular view of state and society was clearly and consistently expressed, in which the state was depicted as a civilizing source of social order without which economic life must inevitably be chaotic and violent.[220] The state can only play its anointed role, however, if people pay taxes. Yet people will pay taxes only if a credible threat of punishment exists. As one tax police major put it: "We're the Russian Untouchables, you know, Eliot Ness. Without us, nobody would pay their taxes."[221]

Consistent with this view, in 1998 the tax administration launched a high-profile mass media campaign to make society fully aware of the state's resolve to collect taxes.[222] The series of television spots that aired during income tax season nicely captured the gist of the bureaucratic-coercive compliance strategy. The campaign featured a retelling of the medieval tale of Princess Olga, whose response to defiant tax-scoffing villagers was to burn their homes to the ground; a circus clown, who laughingly tore up his income tax form, went to jail, and made the other clowns cry; and, a burly businessman, whose tax evasion-induced anxiety left him unable to focus attention on the half-naked woman in his bed. The message to taxpayers was clear: if you evade taxes, the state will have you incarcerated, ostracized, dispossessed, and emasculated.

To its advantage, the Polish state did not experience a fragmentation of bureaucratic-administrative resources. Because it needed to extract small amounts of revenue from a large number of sources, the means of extraction were not organized for "taking" wealth; instead, the state had to cultivate tax compliance by "trading" for wealth. Poland's "legalistic consent" tax regime represented a minimalist form of quasi-voluntary compliance. "Legalistic consent" set Poland apart from other postcommunist states in two crucial aspects: first, it enjoyed a higher degree of noncoerced compliance with new revenue claims; and second, it provided a foundation for the strengthening of state fiscal capacity. By contrast, in Russia the means of extraction were designed to accommodate political interests first, and economic interests second. Russian governments made little effort to cultivate tax compliance. The reaction of society was to ignore, avoid, and evade their revenue obligations. And the state's inclination to extract revenue by "taking" was revived. In Russia, capital was not protected from coercion; society's wealth was vulnerable to state predation. The "bureaucratic-coercive" tax regime failed to expand the revenue base or to sustain state fiscal capacity.

BUILDING FISCAL CAPACITY IN POSTCOMMUNIST STATES

In early modern Europe the attractiveness of "the state" as an alternative model of organizing political power was based largely on its impressive capacity to mobilize capital. The chief advantage of state-building monarchs over feudal princes and holy emperors was the ability to raise revenue, which could be used to bolster war-making and territorial administration.[1] The success of this model eventually led to its institutionalization across the continent. The basic components of state finance have not since changed much: income, credit, and currency. At the foundation of state fiscal capacity is income. The modern state prototype, the Italian city-states, prospered until their main source of wealth, profits from eastern Mediterranean trade routes, were closed off by the Ottomans.[2] The first great modern state, Imperial Spain, became a transoceanic superpower from the plunder of the New World's precious metal. Still, it took several centuries before the design of the modern "fiscal-military" state was introduced in the Dutch Republic and then perfected in George Downing's England in the late seventeenth century.[3] Access to reliable and sufficient sources of income was needed to stay on top. Steady income ensured the value of the currency and assured access to credit. But, if income declined and debts went unpaid, then states faced fiscal crisis. The options were few: renegotiate debts, renege on debts, or repay debts with devalued currency.

This chapter compares the process of building fiscal capacity in postcommunist Poland and Russia. It uses two test cases provided by international finance to gauge fiscal capacity. First, in 1998 Eastern Europe was struck by a worldwide financial run on emerging market economies, which began in East Asia the previous year. Although the worst was feared for all transition economies, the effects turned out to be uneven. Poland's transition economy not only avoided financial collapse but recorded modest growth. By contrast, the Russian state succumbed to fiscal collapse when hit by the international financial crisis. The second test, in 2008, came from the opposite direction, when the bubble burst on a series of speculative Wall Street investment ventures. Once more a wave of international financial crisis reached Eastern Europe, undermining the value of assets and causing a shortage of capital. In this case, however, Polish and Russian responses were not fundamentally different. The fiscal capacity of the Polish state again proved resilient. The Russian economy was badly shaken by the crisis, but state fiscal capacity was strong enough to withstand financial collapse.

Crawling from the Wreckage: Fiscal Trends, 1990–1998

Postcommunist states began the transition amid fiscal crisis. The command economy's failure to regenerate growth, and, hence, to provide income, was compounded by unpaid debts and devalued notes. The first postcommunist governments struggled to restore stability to state finances by rescheduling outstanding debts, stabilizing currency values, and securing reliable sources of income. A defining feature of all postcommunist states is that they rested on a narrow revenue base; thus, expanding the revenue base was a critical challenge of the early transition. If they were successful, borrowing would be less burdensome and inflation less worrisome: state fiscal capacity would be strengthened. If they were unsuccessful, states would remain vulnerable to fiscal crisis. It was a challenge that Poland overcame, and that Russia did not.

Poland: Expanding the Revenue Base

At the outset of the transition, Poland's domestic economy did not contain prosperous and easily exploitable income sources. The natural resource base lacked coveted commodities, and the manufacturing sector lagged behind global standards. Its former communist trade partners were no longer compelled to take Polish goods. Beyond the bloc, there was not great profits to be had from coal, canned hams, and outdated industrial stock. What the new Polish state had in plenty was outstanding debt and devalued currency. But with the successful expansion of the revenue base, fiscal capacity was strengthened: by decade's end, Poland was creditworthy and zloty-stable.

The Polish state at first teetered at the edge of a fiscal abyss. Finance Minister Leszek Balcerowicz inherited a desperate situation. Emergency fiscal measures were enacted. First, an austerity program targeted social payments and industrial subsidies. Whereas enterprise subsidies accounted for one-third of state budgetary expenditures in 1988, in 1990 the figure was reduced by almost a half to 16.9 percent, and in 1991 reduced further to 9.4 percent.[4] Second, the procapitalist government secured relief from Western creditors for its $30 billion foreign debt, which was in default. It was both a goodwill gesture and good business, as the Polish market opened to Western investors. Finally, the currency was devalued. The worth of a Polish zloty was established by making it convertible to the U.S. dollar; the zloty's value quickly fell, from fourteen hundred zloty to one dollar in September 1989 to ninety-five hundred zloty to one dollar in January 1990.[5] It was a good start, but the government still needed to find new sources of income.

The Balcerowicz team designed a tax system intended to facilitate both the growth of capitalism and the demise of socialism. By 1992, 3.5 million new jobs were created in the private sector, yet more than twelve million workers still remained in the state sector. The communist state was long accustomed to extracting revenue straight from its industrial sector; the postcommunist state recklessly sundered this relationship. The share of central state tax revenue as a percentage of GDP dropped from 28 percent in 1990 to 23 percent in 1991, causing the budget deficit to spike to 6 percent of GDP in 1992.[6] The steep revenue drop forced the government back to the familiar state sector. Unlike the emerging private sector, state enterprises were well known to the tax administration, which squeezed more revenue from the public sector. In 1991, the public sector contributed 72 percent to the private sector's 28 percent of the state's corporate revenue take.[7]

With state enterprise profits in decline, the government instead targeted the wages of state enterprise employees. The excess wage tax, the *popiwek*, was supposed to serve as a check on inflation, but it became a vital revenue source. In 1990, the *popiwek* and the dividend taxes together made up 11 percent of the state's total revenue take; in 1991, the figure reached 17 percent.[8] Government budget planners originally estimated that the state would collect three trillion zloty from the *popiwek* in 1991, but in November the figure was revised upward to twenty-three trillion zloty.[9] The percentage of the *popiwek* on the total tax burden of state industry increased accordingly: 1989, 4 percent, 1990, 12.5 percent; 1991, 25.5 percent.[10] Even liberal economists criticized the government's onerous taxes on state enterprises. Citing "excessive tax fiscalism" as a principal cause of industrial recession, an editorial in *Zycie Gospodarcze*, an influential promarket newspaper, complained that "Polish firms in the so-called socialized sector pay the highest taxes in the world."[11]

The political reaction to shock therapy led to the departure of the free-market government and the return of the political Left. But Balcerowicz had already made an invaluable contribution to the postcommunist state through policies that encouraged private enterprise. When Balcerowicz left office in 1992, the private sector was still a fuzzy gosling, but the fisc would soon have a golden goose. The social-democratic government displayed a softer touch toward the state sector. Instead of punitive wage taxes, they gently introduced the personal income tax, easing the burden at first. They also extended the state's revenue claims to the new private sector in incremental fashion, trying not to elicit too loud a hiss. By establishing revenue claims on worker households and petty capitalists, the Polish state expanded its revenue base.

Fiscal fortunes follow economic trends: if there is more wealth, there is more to tax. Poland's transition economy was the first in the postcommunist realm to start to grow again. Polish productivity increased every year between 1992 and 1998, marking seven consecutive years of growth for the first time since the 1970s.[12] By 1995, Poland's GDP had returned to the pretransition level; and by 1998 its GDP was roughly 20 percent higher than the pretransition level.[13] By expanding the revenue base, the state shored up the foundation of fiscal capacity—income. Total revenue receipts (including social security) as a percentage of GDP barely declined at all during the transition decade. Poland's ability to maintain steady income levels was a notable accomplishment among early postcommunist states.

The main taxation trends of the 1990s were from corporations to households, from the public to the private sector, from large to small firms, and from

TABLE 5.1 Poland—Macroeconomic and fiscal trends, 1991–1997

A) ECONOMIC GROWTH, 1991–1997 (% CHANGE OVER PRECEDING YEAR)

	1991	1992	1993	1994	1995	1996	1997
Real GDP	−7.0	2.6	3.8	5.2	7.0	6.1	6.9
Capital investment	−4.5	2.8	2.9	9.2	18.5	21.6	21.9
Industrial output	−11.9	2.8	6.4	12.1	9.7	8.5	10.8
Consumption	−7.5	3.5	4.6	3.9	4.1	7.2	6.2

B) STATE BUDGET, 1991–1997 (% OF GDP)

	1991	1992	1993	1994	1995	1996	1997
Revenue	26.1	27.2	29.5	30	29.3	27.5	27
Expenditures	29.9	33.2	32.3	32.7	31.9	30	28.3
Budget deficit	−3.8	−6	−2.8	−2.7	−2.6	−2.5	−1.3

Sources: World Economy Research Institute, *Polish International Economic Report, 1997/98* (Warsaw: Warsaw School of Economics, 1998), 42; *OECD Economic Surveys: Poland*, 1997 (Paris, OECD: 1997), 38, 40. Budget figures do not include social security funds.

direct to indirect taxation. In 1990 the corporate income tax alone accounted for 43 percent of taxes collected for the state budget, but by 1994 that figure was reduced to little more than 10 percent.[14] Meanwhile, household wealth was tapped to fill the void. The personal income tax accounted for 1 percent of taxes collected for the state budget in 1990, but they shot up to more than 25 percent by the mid-1990s, and remained stable for the rest of the decade.[15] Following a general transition pattern, economic activity increasingly shifted away from the public sector during the 1990s. Poland was a particular case in that economic growth was not led by privatized state enterprises, but by a rash of new start-up small businesses, where more than 60 percent of the workforce was found.[16] Whereas in 1990 taxes on households and transactions accounted for less than half of the total tax take, by mid-decade they made up two-thirds of all tax receipts.[17]

The expanded revenue base provided income from two main sources: small businesses and wage-earner households. First, the Polish economy experienced a surge in petty capitalist activity. The new entrepreneurial private sector became the driving force in the recovery of the Polish economy. The private incentive policies of Finance Minister Balcerowicz encouraged hundreds of thousands of Poles to organize as small-business entrepreneurs. Most notably, by 1995 new start-ups accounted for 50 percent of GDP, the highest rate in Eastern Europe.[18] Many of the new entrepreneurs benefited from an initial phase (usually three years) of income and transaction tax breaks to help them get going; by mid-decade, however, the small-business sector began to contribute an increasingly larger share to the state's total tax take. Between 1993 and 1994, tax income generated by small businesses increased in real value by nearly 30 percent.[19] At the start of the Polish transition, roughly seventy-five hundred state enterprises provided over 80 percent of total revenues.[20] By the mid-1990s more than 1.8 million small and medium businesses were registered with the tax authorities and making some form of payment to the state budget.

TABLE 5.2 Poland—Breakdown of tax revenue (as % of total state revenue)

	1990	1991	1992	1993	1994	1995	1996	1997
VAT/excise taxes	21	29	32	39	41	42	47	46
Corporate income tax	43	24	21	17	15	13	11	11
Personal income tax	1	2	21	23	25	25	24	25
Excess wage tax	20	22	8	2	1	—	—	—
Other	14	23	20	19	17	20	18	18

Sources: *OECD Economic Survey: Poland, 1994* (Paris, OECD: 1994), 37; *OECD Economic Survey: Poland, 1997* (Paris, OECD: 1997), 40; *OECD Economic Surveys: Poland, 1998* (Paris, OECD: 1998), 39. The "other" category includes privatization revenues.

Second, the personal income of wage earners became a new revenue source for the state. Labor could not move its assets the way entrepreneurs could. The understaffed tax administration may have had trouble keeping pace with the book-keeping tricks of petty capitalists, but it had a much easier time catching up to the pay envelopes of industrial workers and salaried employees, especially those in the less opaque public sector.[21] This was openly admitted by the government's vice minister for taxes, Witold Modzelewski, who expressed concern that an over-reliance on households would undermine the civic morale needed to pay taxes.[22] Employers were compelled to deduct the state's revenue claim from employee paychecks, making it difficult for workers to escape the notice of tax officials, at least without management's cooperation. The implementation of the PIT in 1992 had an immediate effect on the revenue base.

It was paramount to find new sources of income because the state-labor revenue bargain put pressure on state finances. The social-democratic government reaffirmed state commitments to the unemployed, retired, and disabled. In 1990, the state subsidized seven million pensioners (retired and disabled), but by 1998 the number had risen to 9.5 million. Moreover, the value of pensions increased from 53 percent of the average public wage in 1989 to 67 percent in 1998.[23] Nearly 15 percent of Poland's GDP was invested in pensions—twice as much as the OECD average. Budgetary expenditures in 1997 amounted to 45 percent of Poland's GDP, comparable to its prosperous neighbor Germany and more than 5 percent higher than the OECD average; Poland's total revenue take, however, was only 40 percent.[24] Meanwhile, the state-labor revenue bargain used tax exemptions to subsidize wage-earner households. The loss of PIT income because of exemptions was significant: a whopping 24 percent in 1996, 15 percent in 1997, and 14 percent in 1998. The PIT rate brackets ranged from an upper 40 percent to a lower 19 percent, but with all the exemptions the real PIT tax rate for the whole economy in 1998 was 12.5 percent.[25]

The cost of social subsidies overextended the budget. To cover the difference, the government turned to the credit market for relief. Poland began the transition in debt and in default, but quickly took action. President Walesa's first visit abroad as head of state was to the United States to appeal for a reduction in Poland's debt obligations. In 1990, the Paris Club agreed to reschedule Poland's debt obligations and, eventually, forgave nearly half of Poland's outstanding debt.[26] In 1994, Poland reached agreement with the London Club, which forgave nearly half of Poland's $14 billion in debt to Western commercial banks.[27] The rescheduling of Polish debt to the West removed a huge fiscal constraint. By mid-decade the heavy burden on state finances was significantly eased as a result of Poland's successful petitions for foreign debt relief. Whereas debt service represented 78.5 percent of GDP in 1990, it was halved to 39 percent in 1993, and to only

6.5 percent by 1997.[28] The income generated by the new tax system allowed for regular payments for rescheduled debts. As a result, Poland's credit rating was raised, and new lines of credit were made available to cover budget deficits. With steady income and credit restored, the Polish state did not need to devalue its currency. The government pursued a policy of gradual disinflation. Annual inflation rates declined from 47 percent in 1991 to 15 percent in 1997. Moderate increases in the money supply were consistent with economic growth trends.[29] By mid-decade, the zloty was stable.

In charting a path from the fiscal wreck of the old regime, the Polish state stood out among its postcommunist peers for successfully expanding its revenue base. The dispersion of economic activity from large industrial conglomerates of thousands of workers to small retail trade and service businesses of ten or fewer employees dramatically restructured the revenue base. The amounts of revenue available from any small entrepreneur or individual wage earner were miniscule, but when amassed these two groups offered significant income sources. By the late 1990s, Poland's transitional tax regime was in place. It was flawed, it was contested—and it was bringing in enough revenue to keep the postcommunist state operating with manageable deficits. As a result, state fiscal capacity was strengthened.

Russia: The Incredible Shrinking Revenue Base

Like Poland, Russia entered the transition in fiscal crisis, desperately needing capital. And, like Poland, Russia inherited a narrow revenue base from the old regime. But the similarities ended there. Unlike Poland, the Russian revenue base contained lucrative and accessible income sources—minerals, metals, oil and gas—that had already been developed in the Soviet period. The Russian state remained more dependent on commodity exports, and more vulnerable to external conditions. Russia's transitional tax regime did not promote an expansion of the revenue base, but a contraction. State fiscal practices contributed to the demonetarization of the transition economy. Instead of money-based market capitalism, Russia lurched toward barter-driven postindustrial feudalism.

The Gaidar government focused its collection efforts on a select set of big revenue targets, particularly in the energy export sector.[30] The tax reforms introduced at the outset of the transition placed the heaviest burden on these corporations. As an indication of this continuity, in 1989 the turnover tax and the profits tax accounted for 64 percent of total revenue; in 1993, after the first year of radical reform, the VAT and the profits tax accounted for 60 percent of total revenue.[31] By the mid-1990s, Russia's twenty most profitable corporations accounted for more than two-thirds of central state income.[32] A handful of firms in the energy sector provided one-quarter of the tax revenues collected at all levels of government.[33] This arrangement was intended to facilitate the state's efforts to locate and collect revenues given its limited administrative capabilities, but it also made the state revenue-dependent on a few large corporations.

Economic trends in the transition decade were decidedly negative. The Russian economy contracted by roughly 40 percent between 1991 and 1997.[34] The transition economy languished in depression. In mid-decade the corporate sector suffered further from external economic conditions, sending profits downward and making revenue even scarcer. Official figures indicated that corporate profits in 1996 fell to almost half of what they had been in 1995.[35] The steep decline in corporate profits tore a gaping hole in the budget. According to the government's 1996 designated income targets, the central state underfulfilled its budgetary tax collection goal by nearly 20 percent, but the profits tax was underfulfilled by more than 33 percent. Whereas the profits tax accounted for almost 30 percent of total tax income to the central state in 1995, it plummeted to just 18 percent in 1996.[36] The central state budget, meanwhile, suffered a steeper drop in its revenue take as a percentage of GDP, from 16.6 percent in 1992 to 10.7 percent in 1998.[37] And with a constant barrage of demands from capital-starved industries, poor regions, and fiscal populists, the Chernomyrdin government could not maintain tight spending limits. Unmanageable budget deficits were a chronic feature of the transition decade.

Even more alarming, the revenue fount of petro-capital was reduced to a trickle. While the old industrial sector declined, the energy sector increased as a

TABLE 5.3   Russia—Macroeconomic and fiscal trends, 1991–1997

A) ECONOMIC GROWTH, 1991–1997 (% CHANGE OVER PRECEDING YEAR)

	1991	1992	1993	1994	1995	1996	1997
Real GDP	−5.5	−19.4	−8.7	−12.6	−4.1	−3.3	+0.9
Capital investment	−3.1	−39.5	−28.1	−29.6	−10.4	−20.6	−3.6
Industrial output	−8.0	−18.5	−13.3	−20.9	−3.3	−4.0	+1.9
Total consumption	−4.9	−5.5	−1.0	−2.5	−3.1	−3.1	+3.0

B) CONSOLIDATED STATE BUDGET, 1992–1998 (% OF GDP)

	1992	1993	1994	1995	1996	1997	1998
Revenue	28.0	29.0	28.2	28.4	26.0	28.2	24.5
Expenditures	31.4	33.6	37.7	31.6	30.4	33.3	28.1
Budget deficit	−3.4	−4.6	−10.7	−3.2	−4.4	−5.1	−3.6

Sources: *Finansy v Rossii: Statisticheskii sbornik, 2000* (Moscow: Goskomstat, 2000), 15; IMF, *IMF Staff Country Report* no. 99/100, "Russian Federation: Recent Economic Developments" (Washington, D.C., September 1999), 6, 37, 38; *Rossiya v tsifrakh: Ofitsial' noe izdanie* (Moscow: Goskomstat, 1999), 28. Revenue and expenditure figures include federal, regional, and local budgets; they do not include social security funds.

percentage of economic activity. Energy products rose from roughly 40 percent of all exports in 1992 to 50 percent in 1997. The flow of Russian oil and natural gas into world commodity markets rose by more than 50 percent in this period as well.[38] By mid-decade the postcommunist state was dependent on energy exports for more than one quarter of its budgetary income. The fiscal danger of a narrow revenue base became clearly apparent when energy income sources plummeted. World energy prices dropped to twenty-year lows: the price for a barrel of Urals crude was $18 in 1997 and just $11 in 1998.[39]

Meanwhile, the state's new revenue claims on small and medium enterprise (SME) business transactions and personal income (PIT) remained underdeveloped and often beyond the reach of tax collectors. First, the SME sector experienced stunted growth. The number of SMEs initially jumped from 560,000 (with seven million employees) in 1992 to 860,000 (with 8.6 million employees) in 1993, but there were only 840,000 (with 6.3 million employees) in 1996.[40] Small business was the most dynamic sector in Poland, accounting for more than 50 percent of GDP; but in Russia small businesses contributed only 12 percent of GDP by 1997 and less than 8 percent of total taxes collected.[41] When the central state enacted a simplified, single-rate-tax scheme to promote SME compliance in 1995, regional officials delayed and obstructed its implementation.[42] Likewise, the state had great difficulty collecting PIT from households. In 1994, in a labor force of seventy million, less than three million individuals filed income tax statements. By 1996, only 16 percent of taxpayers paid on time and in full, and another 34 percent did not pay at all.[43]

By the mid-1990s, the transition economy was short of cash. Barter increasingly replaced money as a means of exchange in Russian industry, topping more than 50 percent of the transactions in the ferrous metals, petrochemicals, and machine-building sectors.[44] Accordingly, the Chernomyrdin government authorized tax payments in goods and services. In effect, state-elite revenue bargaining was driving the demonetarization of the revenue base. Large corporations had

TABLE 5.4   Russia—Breakdown of tax revenue to consolidated budget

	1992	1993	1994	1995	1996	1997
VAT/excise taxes	40	28	28	28	35	34
Profits tax	28	36	31	27	17	15
Personal income tax	0.75	1	2	8	10	10
Energy excise tax*	—	—	—	7.5	16.5	12.5

Sources: *Finansy v Rossii: Statisticheskii sbornik, 2000* (Moscow: Goskomstat, 2000), 22–24; IMF, "Russian Federation: Recent Economic Developments," *IMF Staff Report*, no. 99/100 (Washington, D.C.: International Monetary Fund, 1999), 68.

* As percentage of total revenues to federal budget.

an incentive to accumulate tax arrears, penalties and all, instead of paying on time and in cash, knowing that the Chernomyrdin government would authorize debt swaps and barter schemes that would clear their tax debts without touching their cash assets.[45] Meanwhile, regional leaders used similar schemes to finance the local public sector. Regional leaders shared the same incentives as local enterprises to hang on to their cash assets, keeping them in the region instead of sending them to Moscow. The percentage of nonmonetary means in the total tax receipts to the central state rose from 10 percent in 1995 to 42 percent in 1997.[46]

Since income was not going to cover expenses, the government looked to currency and credit to help finance the state. By the mid-1990s, Yeltsin's only economic boast was that the government had managed to control inflation. This was no small accomplishment after the hyperinflation of the early 1990s and the "Black Tuesday" twenty-seven percent devaluation of the ruble in 1994.[47] The Russian ruble was overvalued, but the government feared the return of inflation that would accompany currency reform. As a result, the artificially strong ruble unintentionally made domestic producers less competitive in consumer markets and effectively stalled the pace of economic recovery. Political constraints put the kibosh on currency reform, leaving credit as the only available option.

Like Poland, Russia inherited an onerous foreign debt burden from the old regime; unlike Poland, Russia received little debt forgiveness, and instead added more to the total. It was bad enough that Russia assumed the Soviet debt, but Prime Minister Chernomyrdin during a 1996 visit to Paris even agreed to repay about $400 million of tsarist-era debt to French creditors.[48] The government finally reached agreement on a manageable long-term repayment schedule with the Paris Club in 1996 and the London Club in 1997.[49] By this time the new Russian state had borrowed twenty-four billion dollars in addition to the one hundred billion in Soviet debt that it was responsible for.[50] While Poland's foreign debt burden by 1997 was about 20 percent lighter than when the old regime fell, Russia's foreign debt burden by 1997 was about 25 percent heavier. The Russian state looked to the domestic market for new sources of credit. By the mid-1990s, Russia's new financiers were an integral part of state fiscal policy. The financiers, however, did not constitute a new source of tax revenue. Rather they became the main suppliers of credit, as the principal purchasers of short-term debt issues.[51] Indeed, the rules of the debt auctions, at least at first, were written so that Russia's commercial banks would not have to compete against wealthier international financiers.[52]

Russia's transitional tax regime was fundamentally flawed. Unlike Poland, the postcommunist Russian state did not expand its revenue base in the 1990s. In legislation, tax policy reformers may have cast a wide revenue net over society; but in practice tax collectors still patrolled the same narrow revenue ground.

Throughout the decade, the Russian state remained dependent on a concentrated and lucrative revenue base—the energy export sector, large manufacturing and processing, and the rich donor regions. It was lucrative, but not reliable.

Threat from the East: The 1998 Financial Crisis of Emerging Markets

Beginning in the summer of 1997, the dynamic economies of East Asia saw their financial systems fall like dominoes. East Asian bankers and governments were left holding billions of dollars in bad debt as a consequence of a sudden run on global capital. The collapse of East Asian financial and currency markets signaled that the investment boom was over for high-growth, high-risk emerging market economies, which were left vulnerable as panicky investors took flight.[53] In 1998, the contagion effects spread to Eastern Europe, whose transition economies were jolted by the sudden drop in foreign capital and credit. This international financial crisis tested the fiscal capacity of the postcommunist states, and not all of them passed. When the crisis reached Poland in 1998, the state remained solvent. Its resilience to capital crisis was not because of good fortune, but because of good policy enacted by postcommunist elites, who in the late 1990s came to a consensus on prudent management of state finances. By contrast, Russia was more vulnerable to capital crisis, a situation compounded by the unwillingness of postcommunist elites to make individual compromises for the general good of state finances.

Poland: Elite Consensus and Surviving Financial Crisis

In 1997, Poland benefited from yet another elite consensus, with the promulgation of a postcommunist constitution. In January, a draft constitution outlining a mixed political system, which tipped the power balance in favor of parliament, was introduced for public debate. The draft was delivered by a special parliamentary commission, which had worked on the document for nearly three years. The commission comprised the four major political blocs in the 1993 Sejm: social democrats (SDL, or Party of the Democratic Left), free-market liberals (UD, Democratic Union), the peasant party (PSL, or Polish People's Party), and the trade union bloc (UL, Union of Labor).

To become the law of the land, the draft had to be debated, amended, and accepted by both houses of parliament, and then approved in a nationwide referendum. But Solidarity and the Catholic Church raised objections: the former, still obsessed with punishing former communists and collaborators, wanted explicit rejection of the old regime; and, the latter, still concerned with preventing a secular state, wanted explicit recognition of a higher power. They threatened to obstruct the process unless their demands were met. Negotiations were convened, as political leaders urged compromise. Sejm Speaker Josef Zych made a nationally televised plea to rally popular support for the draft constitution.[54] Prime Minister Wlodimierz Cimoszewicz stressed that the draft reflected the willingness of partisan political actors to find common agreement even when divided by particular interests and he urged that others should do the same.[55] And President Kwasniewski went further, saying that "the draft does not correspond 100 percent to a single author, because this work rests on many ideas and on compromise, which is the great virtue of the constitution."[56] Consensus prevailed; the challengers were appeased with modest concessions. In July, Poland at last had a postcommunist constitution after its approval by the parliament and by a referendum of the people.

The constitution not only delineated a division of power in the postcommunist state, it also provided a legal framework for the management of state finances. Party leaders agreed on the need to establish a set of formal institutional constraints on fiscal policy, which became law in the constitution and in several follow-up financial reform acts. The adoption of fiscal institutional reform formalized the basically sound fiscal practices of the social-democratic government. And when the social democrats strayed too far from fiscal discipline, market liberals in parliamentary opposition were quick to act as a political check on borrowing and spending. Although the constitutional codification of fiscal prudence reflected the concerns of influential domestic political actors, it also was an assuring gesture to European Union technocrats, skeptical about Poland's commitment to fiscal responsibility. The new measures were intended to depoliticize the fiscal policy process as well as to limit the ability of state financial policymakers to opt for populist fiscal measures.

First, fiscal institutional reform restricted the influence of political actors and enhanced the role of policy experts in the fiscal policy process. The constitution curtailed the powers of the president, taking away the presidential veto over the state budget. The parliament, meanwhile, was no longer allowed to amend monetary policy. The powers of the National Bank were scaled back as well, as the constitution forbade it from lending capital to finance budget deficits. Real responsibility for the national currency was entrusted to a new Monetary Policy Council (MPC), which oversaw the implementation of monetary policy. The MPC was chaired by the head of the National Bank, and composed of nine financial experts, three each nominated by the president, the Sejm, and the

Senate. To further insulate fiscal policy from politics, MPC members served fixed six-year terms, subject to recall only under extraordinary circumstances.[57]

Second, new restrictions were placed on budgetary policy. The range of options for financing the state budget were explicitly defined and limited: the government must rely on income, not currency or credit. It was not a strict "pay-as-you-go" policy, but it encouraged a more cautious approach toward the expenditure side of the state ledger. The new constitution erected a debt ceiling for state finances at 60 percent of GDP. In May 1998, more elaborate rules were announced by which a series of corrective measures and spending freezes would go into effect if the debt exceeded 50 percent of tax income. The government was no longer permitted to include one-off items, such as privatization sales, as budgetary revenue, since these were not regular income sources. Meanwhile, further down the administrative chain, tighter controls were placed on the spending and borrowing practices of local governments.[58]

The big test for Polish state finances came in the 1998 capital crisis of emerging market economies. The first smallish tremors were felt in January: Korean investors pulled out of a multimillion-dollar joint venture deal, and the Warsaw Stock Exchange dropped 5 percent in value.[59] The MPC was forced to make a minor devaluation of the zloty; the currency correction calmed foreign investors, who returned in February. In May, an EBRD official praised Poland as the only emerging market economy in Eastern Europe unscathed by the Asian crisis; in June, Merrill Lynch touted Polish short-term treasury bills as an attractive and safe foreign investment opportunity.[60] But in August, the resounding fiscal crash of postcommunist neighbor Russia sent shockwaves through Poland's transition economy.

Political leaders from across party lines (the social-democratic president, Solidarity bloc prime minister, and free-market finance minister) quickly found common purpose in preventing a panic. On television, in the press, before business audiences, to whomever would listen, they talked up the economy's underlying strengths and played down investors' rising fears.[61] They consulted on strategy with international financial organizations in the West, and coordinated tactics with fellow postcommunist governments in the East. They renegotiated the 1999 state budget, cutting back previously planned spending increases and lowering revenue projections. Even if basic macroindicators were sound, political actors on all sides recognized that the mind-set of investors could rattle the foundations of state finance and threaten fiscal crisis.

Despite the assurances, the initial response of foreign capital was to flee. On the day after the Russian crash, the Finance Ministry held an auction for foreign buyers of short-term treasury bills. Nobody showed up.[62] In the fortnight that followed, foreign investors cashed out over one billion dollars from the financial system. The accumulated value of traded shares on the Warsaw Stock Exchange tumbled to a 30 percent loss. Under pressure to adjust the exchange rate again, the MPC authorized another small devaluation of the zloty. The currency devaluation was meant to help those Polish producers, especially in agriculture, that were still dependent on former Soviet markets. The foreign trade deficit leapt from $250 million in August to $1.5 billion in September.[63]

But the political campaign to convince foreign capital to stay put was not a baseless appeal. By 1998, Polish state finances really were in good shape. First, Polish state coffers were regularly replenished from the new sources of income. While income as a percentage of GDP declined one point (from 42 to 41 percent) from the previous year, GDP was growing, so the state's total revenue take in 1998 actually increased by 14 percent from the previous year (from 197 billion zloty to 225 billion zloty).[64] The 1998 budget deficit remained a manageable 2.5 percent (although the next year it climbed back over 3 percent). Polish businesses remained profitable; Polish trade relations were reoriented to the West.[65] Second, Poland was not overextended with credit. The once crippling costs of foreign debt service fell from nearly 70 percent as a percentage of GDP in 1991 to less than 7 percent in 1997.[66] Even if foreign creditors were now to leave en masse, the state was not reliant on their capital. By 1998, Polish households, enticed by personal income tax deductions, were the main purchasers of government bonds.[67] Foreign investors owned only 8 percent of short-term Treasury bills and 21 percent of long-term bonds.[68] Foreign investors did not rush to buy MinFin's latest T-bill offerings, but they did not cash out the bonds they were already holding. As an indication of the state's manageable credit situation, interest rates on short-term debt remained moderate and stable throughout the summer and fall of 1998, suggesting relatively low risk.[69] Third, since the state was not overextended on credit, it was not forced to undercut the zloty. In August, the MPC approved a small devaluation to help Polish exporters. By mid-September, the head of the National Bank, Hanna Gronkiewicz-Waltz, reported that the financial system was still in good shape and that the zloty had withstood the crisis, retained its value, and was stable.[70] Indeed, by the year's end, the value of the zloty had appreciated.

The fiscal capacity of the postcommunist Polish state in the 1990s was strong enough to withstand the capital crisis of emerging market economies. Poland did not experience any massive flight of foreign investment.[71] State fiscal managers neither defaulted on debt obligations nor undertook drastic devaluations of currency. Even though business activity slowed in 1998, the economy still registered nearly 5 percent growth for the year. People paid taxes; maybe not all that they owed, but enough to keep the state solvent. And, perhaps most notable, underlying Poland's strengthened fiscal capacity was an elite consensus on responsible management of state finances.

Russia: Elite Conflict and Succumbing to Financial Crisis

At the same time that Poland's elites were coming to agreement on state finances, Russia's elites were moving further apart. The show of common cause in Yeltsin's reelection in 1996 was not sustained in policy matters thereafter. Russian elites were divided among themselves, competing to win special fiscal favors from the central state. Following the presidential election, however, new personnel were put in charge of state finances who were determined to combat tax-delinquent corporate and regional elites. In his second term, Yeltsin assembled an "anti-crisis" government to straighten out state finances. The government's chief patron of elite bargaining, Viktor Chernomyrdin, was eventually forced out of power. The "anti-crisis" government included Anatoly Chubais, as finance minister and deputy prime minister; Boris Nemtsov, as deputy prime minister; Boris Fedorov, as head of the tax administration; and Sergei Kiriyenko, as Chernomyrdin's successor as prime minister. Upon his appointment, Chubais described their main task: "Our bankers think that they are the bosses. Even after the election, they will keep trying to take advantage of us. We need to sock them in the teeth for once in our lives. We won't achieve anything unless we do this."[72]

In contrast to Poland, Russia's "anti-crisis" government opted for unilateral solutions and confrontation, rather than multilateral negotiations and consensus, to strengthen state fiscal capacity. In October 1996, President Yeltsin decreed the formation of a special commission, the Temporary Extraordinary Commission for Strengthening Tax Collection, "to bring to account the heads of the subjects of the federation, and heads of state enterprises and joint stock companies for violations of tax legislation." The commission was referred to by its acronym, VChK, or the Tax Cheka, an appropriation of the name of the original Bolshevik secret police force, a symbolic touch emphasizing that this time the president really meant it.[73] With its special powers to initiate bankruptcy proceedings, the Tax Cheka tried to intimidate large corporate taxpayers into settling their outstanding debts to the state budget. But the Tax Cheka turned out to be more bark than bite. By the end of 1997, it managed to have one middle-level revenue official sacked from the customs agency and initiated bankruptcy proceedings against one firm.[74] In the summer of 1998, it gave four major industrial producers a one-month ultimatum to pay their tax arrears or be forced into bankruptcy, but then never acted on the threat.[75] In 1998, another government commission found that of the more than fourteen hundred tax-delinquent firms under investigation since the first half of the year, bankruptcy proceedings were initiated against less than 5 percent.[76]

Meanwhile, the central state's extractive efforts were energized by the arrival of the pugnacious economist Boris Fedorov. He purged the tax administration of senior cadres, whom he claimed were either incompetent or corrupt. He tried to recentralize state finances, pushing a consolidation of the state's three main revenue organs—tax administration, tax police, and customs committee—into an overarching Ministry of Incomes.[77] The police, however, had no interest in working for civilians and nixed this initiative. Fedorov launched a multimedia campaign to impress the public that the state was serious about collecting taxes. He publicized a "blacklist" to shame the worst tax delinquents, who, he vowed, would either pay up or end up in jail. He promised tax audits for Russia's thousand richest citizens, who, if found guilty of evasion, would face a public show trial. "I simply think it is time to start monitoring the tax history of prominent people, who must set the example of a taxpaying culture for the rest of the citizens," Federov explained.[78]

The "anti-crisis" government tried to expand its revenue reach to new sources of income and to hike the rates on existing taxes in an effort to scrape up more rubles. After failure in the legislature, the president and government began simply to issue special decrees. The land tax was doubled, import duties on foreign goods from outside the Commonwealth of Independent States (the consortium of most of the FSU) were doubled, pension fund contributions were tripled, a regional sales tax was imposed, and VAT taxes now went into effect when goods were delivered instead of when payments were received. Foreign employees living in Russia were targeted, as the government made claim to an estimated $5 billion worth of untaxed personal income in the ex-pat community. A new state-managed alcohol company, Rosspiritprom, was formed to reclaim the state's former monopoly on vodka sales and add a few more drops of income to the budget. Even the state's list of three thousand untouchable "strategic" enterprises was revised, making three-quarters of these firms available for privatization sales. These unilateral revenue measures were resisted by the legislature, the business elite, and regional leaders. Konstantin Titov, Samara governor and head of the Federation Council's budget committee, requested that the Constitutional Court determine their legality. And the communist-controlled Duma added it to the long list of the reasons why Yeltsin should be impeached.

The fate of the "anti-crisis" government was ultimately decided in a showdown with Russia's richest and most powerful corporation, Gazprom. The energy giant accounted for roughly 15–20 percent of total tax income to the federal budget. Earlier, Prime Minister Chernomyrdin allowed Gazprom head Rem

Vyakhirev the right to represent the state's 35 percent ownership stake in the firm. With Chernomyrdin's consent, the tax administration negotiated a special deal with Gazprom: the firm would continue to supply public institutions that could not pay their energy bill, and in exchange Gazprom would not pay more than R2.4 billion per month in cash in taxes. The new "anti-crisis" government refused to recognize this elite bargain.

In June 1998, Fedorov delivered to Gazprom a monthly tax bill for R4.2 billion, due in cash. Gazprom responded by paying only R800 million. Fedorov vowed to freeze the company's bank accounts and seize its assets, reclaim state control over its 35 percent ownership share, and suggested breaking up the supersized energy conglomerate. Vyakhirev opposed the "forcible extraction of debts" and complained that reckless taxation was going "to bury the gas industry."[79] He pointedly reminded the government of the thousands of public organizations and enterprises that could not pay their fuels bills and whose operations were dependent on Gazprom's generosity. In late June, Fedorov ordered tax officials in Orenburg and the Urals to seize the assets of Gazprom subsidiaries.[80] Gazprom responded by cutting the gas supply to St. Petersburg's main power plant by 40 percent and curtailing gas supplies to 170 public institutions in the Urals.[81]

President Yeltsin intervened, making a televised national appeal: "all companies, small and large, must pay their full share of taxes."[82] The president urged Gazprom to cooperate with the tax administration, saying "we must break the cycle of non-payment."[83] But the stalemate continued. Ever hostile to Yeltsin, the Duma denounced the government and voted 370–0 against the sanctions against Gazprom. Kiriyenko postponed further action. In late July, the government and Gazprom finally met in closed session and produced a one-sided compromise. Instead of the R4.2 billion that the tax administration insisted on, the firm paid only R3.1 billion, of which R600 million would come from the Finance Ministry to cover the public sector's unpaid gas bills. Thus, Gazprom was to pay R2.5 billion in cash to the state budget, and Fedorov was told to leave the company alone. The "anti-crisis" government failed to break the constraints of elite revenue bargaining.

The fiscal vulnerability of the Russian state was exposed in the 1998 international financial crisis. In July, the state statistical agency reported that virtually every economic indicator had turned negative: GDP registered its largest monthly decline since 1996; real income was 9 percent lower than it had been the previous year; industrial output, oil production, exports were down; wage arrears, unemployment, inflation were up. Public sector workers protested unpaid wages by taking to the streets, or the tracks—coal miner demonstrations in West Siberia effectively shut down the Trans-Siberian Railway. Meanwhile, the "anti-crisis" government's campaign to increase revenue succeeded in reversing the decline, but only slightly. The Finance Ministry reported that budgetary income exceeded expenses (by 0.4 percent) for the first time in more than a year.[84] But that figure did not take into account debt repayment. There simply was not enough capital to pay debts and wages. Thus, the final act of the "anti-crisis" government was an attempt to renegotiate the debt.

For almost two years, the Russian government survived on capital obtained through short-term, high-interest credit. The Chernomyrdin government used three-month debt issues to cover chronic budget deficits. This credit scheme offered a quick fix for revenue shortfalls, but it started a vicious cycle in which the costs of paying off the interest consumed ever larger amounts of income. The government responded by issuing more debt at more attractive rates. By the spring of 1998, Russian state finances were sustained by a short-term-debt pyramid scheme.[85] The central bank jacked interest rates higher and higher to tempt investors to stay in for another round: 30 percent on May 1, 50 percent on May 18, and 150 percent on May 28. But these rate hikes prompted panic instead of pounds. The international financial community lowered Russia's credit rating. The cost to service the short-term-debt issues that were due in August was over R35 billion, while the budget took in less than R25 billion for the month.[86]

The Kiriyenko government now focused its efforts on debt restructuring. The recently disgraced Chubais was returned to favor and dispatched to Washington to secure a $100 billion pledge from the IMF. The money was supposed to bail out the Russian government by converting its debilitating short-term, high-interest debts into more manageable long-term, low-interest Eurobonds. Meanwhile, by midsummer the Russian government owed $400 billion in internal debt. Kiriyenko met with a group of Russian financiers who held the largest shares of domestic short-term debt to persuade them to accept the debt swap or face devaluation. Unlike elites in Poland, those in Russia were not inclined to compromise personal interest for the public good. They refused the government's proposal.

In late August, Kiriyenko announced that the government was initiating currency devaluation and unilateral debt restructuring. In response, Russia's biggest bankers triggered a run on their own banks. The country's financial system crashed. The ruble was in free fall. Cash disappeared from the economy. The "anti-crisis" government was in fiscal crisis, which quickly turned into a political crisis. Yeltsin dismissed Kiriyenko as prime minister and reappointed Chernomyrdin, whose instincts were to curtail elite confrontation and restore elite bargaining. The "young reformers" were forced out of state finances, again. But the image of old apparatchiks back in charge did not calm things. The communist-led Duma immediately launched a power grab against the executive branch and demanded the president's resignation. Military and police units around Moscow were mobilized in case of "mass disturbances."[87] Only the appointment of compromise candidate Evgeny Primakov as prime minister restored a semblance of order. In trying to sort out state finances, the new Primakov government renegotiated outstanding tax debts with the largest corporate tax delinquents and worked out acceptable nonmonetary means of payment such as the delivery of gas and other fuels.[88] That is, the system of state-elite revenue bargaining was again dictating fiscal policy. The recently sacked deputy prime minister, Boris Nemtsov, told a reporter that he needed a vacation, but he also warned that unless Russia's big business tycoons started paying their taxes, they would soon come to regret their fate.[89] It was a prophetic remark.

Threat from the West: 2008 Global Financial Meltdown

A decade after the crisis of emerging markets came another international financial menace, originating in the advanced capitalist West. In a contemporary revival of extraordinary popular delusions and the madness of crowds, Wall Street was transformed from a community of savvy investors into wild-eyed speculators, chasing paper profits in tidied-up bundles of bad debt. When the bubble burst, trading houses caught holding the worthless assets collapsed. In a scenario already familiar to postcommunist Russia, American financier-oligarchs underwent a shakeout and reconsolidation. Venerable Wall Street investment firms were declared bankrupt, and then were gobbled up by financially more-solvent and politically better-connected firms. Meanwhile, billions of dollars of paper wealth became simply paper, and the once deep pool of international investment capital dried up. Because the cross-national networks along which capital flows had become so extensive, a global financial meltdown followed.

The Organisation for Economic Co-operation and Development (OECD) recorded the largest collective drop in GDP since 1960, when the statistics were first kept.[90] In Eastern Europe, the 2008 financial crisis hit harder than the 1998 crisis. The contraction of capital caused a contraction of production: In 2009, GDP in Hungary, Bulgaria, Romania, and Moldova declined by nearly 10 percent, in Estonia and Ukraine by nearly 15 percent, and in Latvia and Lithuania by nearly 20 percent. Postcommunist states once again were threatened by fiscal crisis, as income declined, credit departed, currency inflated, and deficits increased. Like 1998, Polish state finances managed to defy the trends and remain solvent; unlike 1998, Russian state finances did as well.

Poland: Surviving Fiscal Crisis, Again

In 1998, Poland had good fiscal fortune because it had good fiscal policy. But the transition economy did not go unscathed. For the next year or so, there was less investment capital, higher borrowing costs, and lower output levels. When economic growth slowed, state budget deficits ballooned past 5 percent annually in the early 2000s. At that time, the inherent tensions between political and fiscal interests, contained in the state-labor revenue bargain, could no longer be suppressed. The costs of maintaining the revenue bargain, particularly the use of tax exemptions as social subsidies, cut into budgetary income. But the economic slowdown proved short-lived, and by mid-decade Poland boasted one of Europe's strongest growth rates, which the state successfully claimed a share of. Postcommunist Poland benefitted from both dynamic economic growth and capable fiscal management. In 2008, when another international financial crisis struck, state fiscal capacity once again managed to absorb the blow.

In 2008, Poland's government was in the hands of liberal democrats. Prime Minister Donald Tusk entrusted state finances to Jacek Rostowski, who continued the postcommunist trend of capable, strong-willed finance ministers. His first official act was to have the portraits of communist-era finance ministers removed from the ministry and consigned to a museum.[91] Rostowski's background impressed: the British-born and Western-trained economics professor founded the influential Polish think-tank CASE, worked with Balcerowicz at the Finance Ministry and National Bank, and even advised the Russian government on fiscal reforms. His appointment, however, was controversial. Still smarting from

TABLE 5.5 Poland—Macroeconomic and fiscal trends, 2001–2009

A) ECONOMIC GROWTH, 2001–2009 (% CHANGE OVER PRECEDING YEAR)

	2000	2001	2002	2003	2004	2005	2006	2007	2008	2009
Real GDP	4.3	1.2	1.4	3.9	5.3	3.6	6.2	6.8	5.1	1.7
Investment	3.9	−13.4	−7.2	3.3	14.7	1.4	16.1	24.3	4.0	−13.4
Industrial output	6.3	−0.8	−0.5	7.8	10.5	3.5	10.0	10.1	6.8	−0.3
Consumption	2.9	2.3	3.0	2.7	4.3	2.7	5.2	4.6	6.1	2.0

B) CONSOLIDATED STATE BUDGET, 2001–2009 (% OF GDP)

	2001	2002	2003	2004	2005	2006	2007	2008	2009
Revenue	36.5	37.1	36.7	38.6	38.6	39.1	39.6	41.3	40.3	40.2
Expenses	39.3	42.0	42.5	43.8	43.2	41.7	41.7	41.2	41.9	44.0
Deficit	−2.8	−4.9	−5.7	−5.2	−4.5	−2.6	−2.1	+0.1	−1.6	−3.8

Source: Rocznik statystyczny Rzeczypospolitej Polskiej, 2009 (Warsaw: Glowny urzand statystyczny (GUS), 2010), 642, 696.

See website: http://www.stat.gov.pl/gus/5207_ENG_HTML.htm.

electoral defeat, the conservative populists questioned Rostowski's patriotic credentials: How can a foreigner who does not pay taxes in Poland possibly manage MinFin? Among market liberals, Rostowski was assailed by disgruntled rivals for not being a real party member or authentic neoliberal.[92] And, former finance minister Zila Gilowska ridiculed Rostowski for not holding a doctorate degree.[93] Unlike previous finance ministers, Rostowski appeared to lack political clout, since he was not named deputy prime minister. What he did have, however, was the full confidence of his friend, the prime minister.

Rostowski came into office with a mostly liberal policy agenda: controlling social spending, trimming tax rates, deregulating the business sector, and joining the Eurozone. He was a genuine fiscal conservative, not a knee-jerk free marketeer. Although Rostowski pushed for personal and corporate income tax cuts, he was careful not to disrupt revenue flow to the state budget.[94] First, he removed the flat-tax reform from the policy agenda, citing a need be both fiscally and socially responsible. Second, he opposed the elimination of the capital gains tax, arguing that it was the most effective means to assure that Poland's very rich pay taxes. Third, he supported the "50+" initiative, which promised incrementally higher pension rates for each year that a worker stays on past retirement. This policy was intended to sustain the PIT as a revenue source by encouraging people to work longer. Fourth, he seized income-generating ventures that existed discreetly within state officialdom. In particular, he targeted for privatization a chain of hotels run by the Military Property Agency. When the Defense Ministry protested, he caustically countered that liberating the military from the tourist trade would not undermine national security. Finally, he refused to lower sales taxes to encourage consumption because of the need to maintain budgetary income. This last issue almost forced his resignation.

Poland's conservative populists did not care much for the finance minister, and the feeling was mutual.[95] Rostowski was openly derisive of the Kaczynskis' chauvinistic rhetoric, saying that it harmed Poland's standing in Europe.[96] The international financial crisis provided the opportunity for Rostowski's critics to act. In June 2008, Jaroslaw Kaczynski, leader of the Law and Justice Party in the Sejm, insisted that the government cut the petrol tax (which his government had previously raised); Rostowski refused even to consider the proposal, saying the measure would only benefit the fuel industry.[97] Kaczynski threatened that if the tax was not cut, he would initiate a no-confidence vote.[98] Neither side budged. The populists went ahead with the no-confidence vote in the Sejm, which Rostowski survived by a vote of 235 to 150.[99] A year later, the Kaczynskis tried again. Rostowski's 2009 budget was based on an overly optimistic growth assessment and had to be readjusted several times. This led to charges of amateurism and mismanagement. The Law and Justice deputy head of the Sejm public finance committee asserted that Rostowski's budget read more like "science fiction" than state finance.[100] The conservative populists instigated another no-confidence vote, this time with support from the social democrats. Rostowski survived yet again, though by a narrower margin, 223 to 193.[101]

At the start of 2009, Rostowski was pilloried by parliament; by the end of 2009, he was hailed as Europe's "Finance Minister of the Year."[102] Unlike the rest of Europe, Rostowski refused to shed market liberalism for crisis Keynesianism. To begin, he insisted that the real economy was strong, and would withstand the worst effects of the financial crisis. Next, when the economy began to slow, he resisted using state funds to stimulate activity, citing the detrimental long-term effect of large budget deficits. Finally, he shot down all parliamentary proposals for populist tax breaks. These policies incurred rancor and ridicule, but eventually were vindicated. In 2009, Poland was the only country in Europe to escape recession, scoring nearly 2 percent positive growth. Economic activity slowed, but did not stop; credit became tighter, but banks did not fail.

Though unwilling to make dramatic public gestures to cue private actors, Rostowski was keenly aware of the effect that state fiscal capacity had on the economy as a whole. When the stability and credibility of state finances were threatened, he did not hesitate to intervene.[103] To compensate for income lost from slower growth rates, Rostowski moved to privatize more state-operated entities, including power companies and the Warsaw Stock Exchange. When a run on the currency began, he used the government's special savings to buy up zloty. The daring move succeeded in restoring confidence in the currency, saving it from freefall. The value of the zloty fluctuated before settling down at a modestly lower value, which benefitted domestic producers. Rostowski made further fiscal adjustments, such as linking VAT rate hikes to cover borrowing above the constitutionally set debt ceiling.[104] Unlike its neighbors, Poland's economy experienced neither a sharp rise in inflation nor a major drop in household consumption. The budget deficit increased, surpassing the EU-mandated 3 percent ceiling. The government made up the difference by issuing long-term, low-interest bonds and securing a generous credit line from the EU.[105]

The Polish economy was not overly dependent on foreign capital and trade, and thus it was less vulnerable to external shock. Poland's institutions of state finance, the National Bank, the Monetary Policy Committee, and the Finance Ministry, provided a coordinated and flexible response that insulated the domestic economy from the international financial crisis. Underlying state fiscal capacity was the steady flow of income. Because of this, even when budget deficits rose, the state was able to gain access to credit at manageable interest rates and did not have to resort to currency devaluation. In 2010, the World Economic Forum promoted Poland to thirty-ninth place on its annual Global Competitiveness Index, stating, "This significant improvement for a second year in a row reflects the country's relatively stronger resistance to the economic crisis as a result of more prudent economic policies and its growing domestic market size."[106]

Russia: Surviving Fiscal Crisis, at Last

It is hard to imagine a policy area in which the Yeltsin presidency failed more miserably than state finance. Instead of enforcing revenue claims, economic resources were traded for political support to the detriment of fiscal capacity; while budget shortcomings were covered with reckless short-term borrowing. One of the more impressive policy accomplishments of Putin's presidency was the reform of state finances, conducted by his stalwart finance minister, Aleksei Kudrin. Between 2000 and 2008, the Russian state treasury measured eight straight years of budget surpluses. That was quite a reversal of fiscal fortune.

The foundation of the state's strengthened fiscal capacity was income. In the 2000s, the state collected significantly more revenue than in the 1990s.[107] There are several reasons for this. First, state finances in the new millennium profited from changing economic conditions in general and the price of a barrel of oil in particular. For a state that was income-dependent on energy exports, the quadrupling of world prices was the main cause of replenished coffers. Second, policy mattered too. The "Russian Tax Revolution" strengthened extractive capacity by streamlining the tax code, and making it easier and less costly for taxpayers to comply. For Kudrin, however, tax cutting did not come at the expense of balancing budgets, paying down debts, and building reserve funds. He especially favored raising additional revenue by taxing the "superprofits" of the energy sector. Finally, previous governments failed when they challenged Russia's corporate elite to pay their taxes, but Putin's tax collectors fared better. The state radically altered the terms of revenue bargaining with its business elite, and, in so doing, was able to capture a larger share of corporate profits.

As it turned out, the 1998 financial collapse was not all bad for Russia. In particular, the ruble's 75 percent drop in value helped make Russian goods significantly cheaper and more attractive to Russian consumers, giving Russian producers a boost. Meanwhile, in the global marketplace Russian export commodities were about to take off. The economy registered 5 percent positive growth in 1999, followed by 9 percent in 2000. These were the highest growth rates in Russia in more than thirty years, and they continued for ten years more, until 2009.[108] Table 5 provides a glimpse of the robust upward trend in macroeco-

TABLE 5.6   Russia—Macroeconomic and fiscal trends, 2001–2009

A) ECONOMIC GROWTH, 2001–2009 (% CHANGE OVER PRECEDING YEAR)

	2001	2002	2003	2004	2005	2006	2007	2008	2009
Real GDP	5.0	4.7	7.3	7.2	6.4	7.4	8.1	5.2	−7.9
Investment	–	2.8	12.5	13.7	10.9	16.7	22.1	9.9	−16.2
Industrial output	2.9	3.1	8.9	8.0	5.1	6.3	6.8	0.6	−9.3
Consumption	–	–	–	9.2	8.8	9.0	11.1	8.6	−5.1

B) CONSOLIDATED STATE BUDGET, 2001–2009 (% OF GDP)

	2001	2002	2003	2004	2005	2006	2007	2008	2009
Revenue*	29.7	32.5	31.2	32.0	39.7	39.5	40.5	38.6	34.8
Expenses	26.8	31.6	29.9	27.4	31.6	31.1	34.5	33.8	41.1
Surplus/deficit	2.9	0.9	1.3	4.5	8.1	8.4	6.0	4.9	−6.3

Source: *Finansy v Rossii: Statisticheskii sbornik* (Moscow: Goskomstat), 2002 (table 1.1); 2006 (table 2.2); 2008 (table 1.1). Goskomstat of Russian Federation website: http://www.gks.ru/free_doc/new_site/finans/fin29g.htm.

*Before 2005, social security is not included; after 2005, social security is included.

nomic and fiscal indicators. In the 2000s the Russian economy was transformed from roadkill to Siberian Tiger.

The driving force of economic growth was, of course, the producers and exporters of Russia's energy and mineral wealth. Opposite of Poland, where wealth was dispersed, in Russia wealth remained concentrated throughout the 2000s. Twenty financial-industrial groups controlled 40 percent of Russian industry.[109] But in the 2000s wealth spilled over the commanding heights. The government finally achieved success promoting small-business development and coaxing private entrepreneurs to enter the official economy. The long-stymied small-business sector began to grow again. In 2003, the state registered roughly eight hundred thousand small-medium businesses; in 2005, the number of SMEs finally exceeded one million.[110] More important, the state managed to gain access to this new revenue source.

The Russian state still remained reliant on long-familiar revenue sources. Tax reform measures in Putin's second term expanded revenue claims on the energy sector. Tax rates were steadily increased as world prices remained high. In the spring of 2003 the government unilaterally imposed increased fees on the export of metals and oil.[111] During the 2000s profit taxes, export taxes, and natural resource user fees rose steadily as a percentage of the total tax take, combining for about 25 percent of the tax take in 2002 and rising to nearly 45 percent in 2006; the percentage of VAT and PIT revenues, meanwhile, declined.[112] In October 2006, Shatalov announced in a speech to the Union of Industrialists and Entrepreneurs that tax reform was near an end and that tax stability had finally been achieved in the economy.[113] The remarks of Russia's most prominent tax reformer did not go over well with Russia's most powerful business lobby. From the government's perspective, the major tax reforms necessary to strengthen state fiscal capacity were in place. Kudrin's team resolutely redefined the state-elite revenue bargain against the interests of the corporate elite, and successfully transformed the transitional tax regime.

Kudrin also made it a priority to repay outstanding debts and restore Russia's creditworthy status. The London Club agreed to convert $20 billion of Russian debt into $30 billion in long-term, low-interest Eurobonds.[114] Then, in 2000, the Paris Club agreed to forgive some of Russia's debt in exchange for a long-term payback schedule, with interest guaranteed. At the time, it seemed like a good deal, but shortly afterward the suddenly cash-rich Russian government was in position to settle up entirely.[115] In 2006, Russia finally put to rest Soviet-era debts.[116] By paying fourteen years ahead of schedule, Russia paid a $1 billion penalty, but avoided $12 billion in interest costs. In the 2000s, the state's outstanding debt as a percentage of GDP fell precipitously: 1999: 57 percent; 2002: 39 percent; 2004: 24 percent; 2006: 10 percent; 2008: 5 percent.[117] When the 2008 financial meltdown caused a financial collapse in Iceland, Russia assumed a reverse role as rich savior, discussing a $4 billion bailout. Fiscal reality, however, soon caught up to Russian officials, who in the end offered a more modest $300 million loan.

Finally, Kudrin used the windfall profits from energy production to create capital savings funds. Russia stockpiled foreign currency reserves worth hundreds of billions of dollars. By 2008, Russia had the world's third largest cache of foreign currency reserves, after China and Japan.[118] In 2004, MinFin created a new Stabilization Fund with oil revenues, to provide a financial cushion against future fluctuations in world commodity markets. MinFin built up the fund quickly by generously helping itself to 90 percent of the revenue generated above $20 per barrel. In just three years, its value climbed past $100 billion, more than 10 percent of GDP.[119] All that wealth locked up in the state treasure-house was coveted by regional and economic elites. Moscow mayor Yury Luzhkov was a relentless critic of Kudrin's policy of "accumulation for its own sake," and the head of the country's largest industrial lobby, Arkady Volsky, referred to Kudrin's fiscal conservatism as "blockheadedness."[120] In 2008, when the fund passed $150 billion, it was reorganized into two separate funds: about 80 percent of the capital would be put into a Reserve Fund, which was put into conservative long-term investment, and the remaining 20 percent was put into a National Welfare Fund, which was used to promote Russian industry and bolster social programs.[121]

In 2000, President Putin declared a goal of doubling Russian GDP by 2010. The 2008 international financial crisis ended any hope of reaching that mark.

By midsummer, foreign and domestic investment in the Russian economy dropped sharply. In September, the Russian stock exchange shed more than 50 percent of its corporate worth, and several times suspended trading.[122] Russia's stockpile of foreign currency reserves shrank by two-thirds from peak value. In the second half of 2008 foreign currency reserves fell from $386 billion to $170 billion. And, the ruble lost 35 percent of its value relative to the dollar. Because the economy was still dominated by energy exports, a recession-induced drop in world oil prices had devastating effects. In July 2008, Urals crude sold for nearly $150 a barrel, but by the end of the year it was selling for less than $50 a barrel. Economic decline continued through the next year, as GDP contracted by almost 8 percent. Positive growth only resumed in the third quarter of 2009.

But the 2008 financial crisis was not a replay of the 1998 crisis. It was not the state, but the private economy, in collapse, and this time the state was prepared to act. Unlike Poland's cautious monetarist approach, the Russian government intervened with an aggressive fiscal approach. To stimulate economic activity, the government invested capital totaling nearly 2.5 percent of GDP.[123] The Central Bank acted to defend the currency, whose value was fixed in relation to a dollar-euro basket. The bank spent 25 percent of its foreign exchange reserves to buy rubles. Between September 2008 and January 2009 the Central Bank made twenty-one small adjustments in the exchange rate, gradually loosening the exchange rate from thirty rubles to forty rubles to the basket.[124] These economic developments adversely affected state finances. The government's defiant fiscal policy strained state coffers. With its main sources of income curtailed, the government deficit rose to 8 percent of GDP in 2009. To encourage economic activity, Kudrin finally gave in to pressure and lowered the VAT tax rate. In a search for nontax sources of income, the government proposed to sell off state assets, reversing a five-year trend toward greater state ownership. Politics eventually caught up with Kudrin in 2011, when he was forced to resign by President Dmitry Medvedev after publicly criticizing the president's plan to triple investment in the military.

Unlike 1998, the Russian state's strengthened fiscal capacity withstood the 2008 financial crisis. The state did not go deeply into debt to finance the deficit. The Finance Ministry's fat reserve funds covered most of the costs. The remaining deficit was managed through credit. The government did not plead for help from international lenders; instead, it raised capital from domestic markets. In 2009 the government borrowed roughly 1 percent of GDP, a modest amount compared to what other European states borrowed to finance their stimulus investments.[125] In April 2010, Russia returned in grand fashion to international capital markets. The government put up $5.5 billion in bonds for sale, the second largest debt offering on record for an emerging market economy.

Taking advantage of the low rates in world bond markets, Russia offered five-year bonds for 3.7 percent interest, and ten-year bonds for 5.1 percent interest. With a Standard and Poor's medium-risk credit rating of BBB, Russia's bond sale was notable for the relatively low interest rate, indicating the guarded confidence of international capital markets in Russian finances.[126] With confidence returning, in June 2010 the Russian Central Bank commemorated its 150th anniversary by issuing a limited-edition fifty-thousand-ruble gold coin, weighing five kilograms and bearing the likeness of the bank's founder, Alexander II, the reformer tsar.

The means by which the modern state pays for its warfare and welfare have not changed fundamentally in more than two hundred years—claiming income, obtaining credit, and manipulating currency. Postcommunist states faced the challenge of finding the right mix of income, credit, and currency to overcome fiscal crisis in the early transition. Indicators of state fiscal capacity include items such as revenue takes, budget deficits, credit ratings, and exchange rates. But the real test of fiscal capacity for the postcommunist states came when financial crises beyond their borders caused a run on foreign capital and credit in their domestic economies. This chapter compared state fiscal capacity in Poland and Russia, as revealed by their responses to the 1998 and 2008 international financial crises.

The 1998 financial crisis of emerging market economies exposed disparities in fiscal capacity between Poland and Russia. By creating new sources of income, the Polish state strengthened fiscal capacity during the transition decade, mainly by expanding its revenue base and depoliticizing state finances. In contrast, the new Russian state exploited a narrow revenue base, which was lucrative but less reliable. In the late 1990s, the risks of this approach became clear when the state experienced a severe revenue decline. The financial crisis of emerging markets hit hard: the Russian state declared bankruptcy, reneged on its debts, and devalued its currency. Ten years later, the 2008 global financial meltdown seeped across Eastern Europe. As in 1998, Poland proved resilient; unlike 1998, Russia did as well. In the 2000s, Poland's transitional tax regime continued to provide a firm foundation for state fiscal capacity. The Polish state generated most of its revenue from domestic consumption, which was sustained through the crisis. State finances underwent a decline in tax income and an increase in the budget deficit, but it was manageable. In 2009, European economies were stagnant or contracting, all except Poland. In Russia, the 2008 capital crisis heavily stressed state finances, and once again exposed the state's fiscal vulnerability to energy exports. Unlike 1998, however, Russian state finances survived. After nearly a decade of windfall energy profits and conservative fiscal management, state fiscal capacity was sufficiently strengthened to withstand the worst effects. The state responded to the financial emergency with an infusion of capital into the banking sector and big industry. It was enough to keep the economy going until late 2009, when the price of oil began to rise again and the economy showed signs of renewed growth. Underlying fiscal capacity was each state's transitional tax regime: Poland's "legalistic consent" cultivated conditions leading to an expansion of the revenue base and, hence, a wider spread of wealth; Russia's "bureaucratic coercion" promoted conditions ultimately leading to the state's deeper penetration of the wealth generated by a narrow revenue base.

TAXATION AND THE RECONFIGURATION OF STATE AND SOCIETY

If coercion is at the foundation of state power, then capital is at the foundation of civil society. What makes postcommunist state building such a unique historical experience is that the flow of power resources runs from state to society, instead of the other way round. Ultimately, this process *might* lead to the consolidation of civil society, the social realm of private interaction and organization formally protected from state penetration and interference. A recurring theme in postcommunist studies, however, is the woeful weakness of civil society.[1] This is hardly surprising given the extensive monopolization of power resources long enjoyed by the communist state. But at least some postcommunist countries have made considerable progress toward building the foundations of civil society. In these cases, power resources were reorganized into new institutional forms, autonomous and insulated from direct state intervention. Toward this end, battles over taxation played a major role in determining whether nascent civil society could stand up to the postcommunist state.

This chapter examines the tangible effect that the fisc had on postcommunist state-society relations in the contrasting cases of Poland and Russia. It first compares taxation and power, more specifically, state coercive power. In Poland, efforts to mobilize coercive threat and bureaucratic clout to curtail tax avoidance came to naught; instead, state coercion was subsumed into a system of legal-administrative checks that promoted the rule of law, the institutional embodiment of "legalistic consent." In Russia, by comparison, police and bureaucrats were not routinely restrained in tax collection; the legal system was not a reliable check on state coercive power, but rather abetted the rule by law, the institutional embodiment of "bureaucratic coercion." Second, taxation and wealth, or capital, is examined. Poland and Russia took divergent paths to very different types of postcommunist capitalism. In Poland, the tax system contributed directly to the consolidation of "social-market capitalism," an economy that embraces both the free market and social protection. In Russia, the tax system led directly to the consolidation of "concessions capitalism," a two-tiered economy in which, on one level, the state continues to own the most lucrative economic assets, and, on the other level, the state espouses private property and entrepreneurship. Finally, the influence of taxation on the realignment of power resources between state and society is considered. In Poland, taxation helped to reinforce society's claims on economic, organizational, and ideological power resources, which cumulatively led to the emergence of a "civil society," legally protected and institutionally autonomous from the postcommunist state. In Russia, taxation enabled the state to undermine societal claims on economic, organizational, and ideological resources, which led to a "dependent society," exposed and vulnerable to intervention and predation by the postcommunist state.

Taxation and Coercion

"We can observe then, that in cities where there is most police and the greatest number of regulations concerning it," Adam Smith once noted, "there is not always the greatest security."[2] Smith's observation of police and security was made about eighteenth-century Paris and London, but it just as well could be said about contemporary Russia and Poland. Postcommunist Russia was overloaded with law enforcement, but often looked lawless; while Poland had the rule of law, without a lot of law enforcers. In Russia, state coercion, embodied by police and bureaucrats, acted all too frequently outside the constraints of the legal system, while in Poland state coercion was effectively tamed by the legal system. The state-society competition for capital that occurred in the tax regime was a critical determinant of these contrasting coercion outcomes. Most everyone by now has heard of Mikhail Khodorkovsky, Putin's pet prisoner whose incarceration inspired international indignation, but only a few people outside Poland know who Roman Kluska is. They both were successful businessmen; they epitomized postcommunism's nouveau riche; they were antagonistic toward political authority; and they orchestrated elaborate tax-avoidance schemes. The similarities ended, however, when each became the target of tax collectors. The opposing manner in which their cases were resolved reveals the fundamental differences in the role of state coercion in postcommunist Poland and Russia.

The Rule of Law in Poland

TAMING COERCION IN THE TAX REGIME

Among postcommunist states, Poland was one of the most successful in subordinating coercive resources to civilian political control.[3] During Poland's negotiated regime transition, Solidarity carefully avoided antagonistic confrontation with communism's coercive agents. In the early transition, elite consensus assured that there would be no retribution dramas; instead, the old regime's security forces were gently vetted and reorganized. The taming of state coercion was achieved by offering incentives to security personnel and erecting legal-institutional checks.

In April 1990 the Polish Police Act began the reform process, which included depoliticizing state coercive agencies; making coercive agencies accountable to civilian authority; separating the security forces from the regular police; transforming regular police from a military-style militia to a civilian-style police force; and appointing civilian leadership at the Ministry of Interior.[4] The size of the elite security forces (that is, the secret police) was cut by three-fourths, from twenty-four thousand to six thousand. The revamped security agency was subordinated to the Interior Ministry and made answerable to the prime minister; its activities were monitored by a half dozen political, legal, and administrative institutions. The new government wanted old regime soldiers to fade away, and used enticing retirement packages to make it happen. The special social insurance fund for "uniformed" state employees (police and military) was one of the most generous social benefit programs in the state budget, and it allowed policemen to retire after only fifteen years of service.[5]

To make sure that the state's revenue agents did not overstep their authority in dealings with taxpayers, several checking mechanisms existed. First, the Supreme Administrative Court (*Naczelny Sad Administracyjny*, or NSA) was an office of appeal within the state bureaucracy.[6] It heard complaints from those who felt they had been wronged by a state agency and was empowered to overturn administrative acts. The NSA was a popular option for aggrieved taxpayers, who prevailed in roughly one-third of the cases brought before it.[7] Next, the Ombudsman was an independent office, elected by the Sejm and approved by the Senate for a five-year term; those selected to serve were recognized experts in constitutional law.[8] The Ombudsman's office monitored the separation of powers within the state and guarded against transgressions by state agents on the civil rights of Polish citizens. Finally, the Constitutional Tribunal acted as an interpreter of the constitution and arbiter in constitutional disputes.[9] It is an independent body of fifteen judges, chosen by the Sejm for nine-year terms.[10] All three bodies contributed to the taming of coercion within a framework of rules, rather than leaving coercion to the discretion of state officials. In the 1990s, as the relationship between coercion and capital was still taking shape, these institutional checks managed to stand up to political challenges.[11] Even when decisions went against the government, they were most often respected by state officials.

In the formative years of the Polish transition, state-society conflicts over taxation were resolved by "third branch" arbitrators. Most notably, the Ombudsman (*Rzecznik*) and Constitutional Tribunal acted to limit the reach of the postcommunist state. These two bodies promoted strict adherence to the rule of law in battles over capital. In so doing, they effectively decriminalized tax avoidance, and reinforced the emergence of a Polish tax regime based on "legalistic consent." They did so by curbing fiscal-administrative fiat and promoting norms of fairness and civility in state-society fiscal relations. Early in the transition, several seemingly small tax disputes proved to be big tests for the Ombudsman and the Constitutional Tribunal. These disputes did not involve dramatic displays of coercion, but mundane instances of bureaucratic overreach. Nonetheless, what was at stake was significant—could the state get away with it?

The role of the Ombudsman as a trusted guardian of civil rights was shaped by Tadeusz Zielinski, who was the first to hold the post in the postcommunist regime. In 1993, Zielinski argued three cases before the Constitutional Tribunal in which he charged the state with exceeding its legal mandate to increase the amount of revenue collected from society. First was the attempt by the Sejm to tax housing loans, which enterprises were giving to employees as a way to dodge wage taxes. The Constitutional Tribunal did not disagree with the state's assessment that these loans were really intended to supplement income, but it rejected the tax administration's attempt to make retroactive revenue claims on the income.[12] Next was a similar case in which the Sejm tried to restrict the personal income tax exemption on capital gains. The Constitutional Tribunal again forbade state tax officials from making retroactive claims after the tax code was revised.

Finally, MinFin was obligated to index wage ceilings annually in accordance with the three rate brackets for personal income tax. As it was, 91 percent of taxpayers already were in the lowest rate bracket. But in 1993 MinFin instead tried to freeze wage tax ceilings, which would have had the fiscal effect of increasing the number of taxpayers in the middle and upper rate brackets.[13] The Ombudsman appealed this act to the Constitutional Tribunal. MinFin and Sejm representatives declared that their actions were dictated by dire budget needs, and maintained that it was impossible to retract the taxes because more than seven trillion zloty already had been collected from more than seventeen million taxpayers.

The Tribunal was unmoved, and ruled the action unconstitutional, saying that "the government has the right to raise taxes, but it must be done by proper procedures, and the taxpayer must be given time to adjust to changing regulations."[14]

The behavior of state officials in these particular cases was a counterreaction to recover lost income with retroactive revenue claims or readjusted tax rates. Even when it was obvious that an unintended ambiguity in the law created a hole in the collection net, state officials were made to abide by the political-legal process for making revenue claims. They were required to revise legislation, rather than simply issue administrative edicts. The actions of the Ombudsman and the Constitutional Tribunal legitimated tax avoidance in these cases, rather than condone bureaucratic overreach, and, as a result, reinforced the rule of law.

This approach was captured nicely in several later Tribunal rulings. In 2002, the Tribunal shot down legislation that placed a 2 percent tax on any funds transferred out of Poland. The Tribunal stated: "the regulations are imprecise and ambiguous. One has no idea who or how this tax will be paid because it is not specified." In 2004, the Tribunal restricted the power of the Finance Ministry and tax administration to make broad interpretations of tax law and act on them simply because of the presumption of taxpayer guilt. The ruling argued that the constitutional obligation to pay taxes does not constitute an obligation to pay the maximum amount, nor a prohibition to take advantage of lawful methods of tax optimization."[15] These rulings illustrated a defining feature of the Polish tax regime: the burden is not on society to comply with the intentions of state officials, but on state officials to get the rules right.

The Ombudsman and the Constitutional Tribunal also promoted norms of fairness in state-society fiscal relations. The Ombudsman was consistently rated by the public as one of the most trusted institutions in Poland, while the Constitutional Tribunal was recognized as a legitimate arbiter of revenue disputes, making decisions on the merits of each case.[16] The actors who staffed these institutions were consciously engaged in cultivating norms of fairness and mutual respect. As an example, in January 1995 the social-democratic government bypassed the Sejm and announced a revised PIT rate schedule. But President Lech Walesa objected, arguing that the government's actions were unconstitutional and asking the Constitutional Tribunal to intervene. The Tribunal concurred and revoked the new tax rates, saying that only the legislature had the power to effect such a change. Walesa's legislative success was not a political success, however. The official guardians of the constitution were clearly irked by the president's attempt to politicize their work. Ombudsman Zielinski issued a sharp public rebuke to the president for trying to intimidate the Tribunal and for "abusing the law." Zielinski went on to say that "everybody, especially government officials, must respect the rulings of courts and tribunals."[17] Just before his term was over,

Zielinski in an official statement addressed the issue again: "It is the undeniable right and duty of the tax office to exercise control over the honesty of tax declaration and to start penal proceedings against dishonest taxpayers. But tax officials must be guided by the principle that the state has confidence in its citizens, and fiscal officers have no right to presume a priori the dishonesty of every taxpayer's declaration."[18] For a tax regime to develop norms of consent, there must be at least a minimum level of mutual understanding between tax collector and taxpayer.

The Supreme Administrative Court (NSA), meanwhile, was the state's internal checking mechanism, which heard citizen complaints against the tax administration. The NSA decided against the tax administration in several controversial cases. In 2005, for example, the NSA determined that if the tax administration had overcharged a citizen, then the citizen was entitled to not only the return of the overcharged amount but to interest on that amount as well.[19] Ten years earlier, in 1995, the NSA was involved in a politically charged tax fraud case brought by the Gdansk tax office against Lech Walesa, who was accused of concealing one million dollars of personal income. The money in question was given to Walesa by Hollywood's Warner Brothers film studio for the exclusive rights to his life story.[20] Walesa appealed to the NSA, which dismissed the charge, stating that the legal-administrative process had been violated since the five-year statute of limitations had already run out. "There is justice," crowed Walesa, "there are autonomous courts."[21] Indeed, there were.

THE LIMITS OF COERCION: THE OPTIMUS AFFAIR

The legal constraints on the use of state coercion in revenue extraction were tested in 2002 when the state prosecutor charged Poland's richest businessman, Roman Kluska, with tax fraud. The Polish tycoon's dramatic confrontation with state tax collectors helped to fortify the line between public prerogative and private property in postcommunist Poland.

Kluska began the transition as a thirty-three-year-old unemployed factory manager, building computers in his attic. Taking advantage of the communist regime's economic liberalization, in 1988 he created a private company, Optimus, for the manufacture and sale of personal computers. Under Kluska's direction, the business rapidly became one of the most innovative and profitable information technology companies in East Central Europe. In 1994, Optimus was the first private start-up to be listed on the Warsaw Stock Exchange. In 1996, it was the first Polish firm to spin off a successful corporate subsidiary, Grupa Onet.pl, which began as an Internet service provider but blossomed into a multimedia entertainment and information services giant.[22] By 1998, Optimus controlled one-third of the market for personal computers in Poland. Kluska became a millionaire, and then a billionaire, among the wealthiest men in Eastern Europe. Since 1989, the *Warsaw Voice*, the popular English-language Polish newspaper, annually selects a "Chair of the Year," an award that goes to the person that has "had most influence directing the events of the previous twelve months in Poland." In 1997, the paper named Kluska as "Chair of the *Decade*."

Kluska epitomized postcommunism's nouveau riche, whose fortunes were made from the rubble of the command economy and the opportunity presented by the transition economy. His commercial accomplishments were especially noteworthy since Optimus was a private firm built from scratch, not a privatized ex-nomenklatura business. Kluska was neither beholden to political patrons nor a broker in party politics. He was a generous patron of civil society, a fervent proponent of private enterprise, and a loud critic of official corruption. As a magnanimous benefactor of the Catholic Church, Kluska aligned himself with the most determined political antagonist of the ruling social democrats. He donated sixteen million zloty to the building of the modernly majestic Church of Divine Mercy in Krakow on the occasion of Pope John Paul's canonization of Poland's Catholic heroine Sister Faustina.[23] Political independence and personal devoutness, Kluska claimed, were the motives that led to his arrest in 2002. The prosecutor said it was tax evasion.

By this time, Kluska had sold his controlling shares in Optimus to pursue new business ventures, though it was his past dealings that interested tax authorities. At issue was a multimillion dollar contract Optimus won to provide personal computers to the Ministry of Education. Instead of a direct sale, the computers were first exported to Slovakia and then imported back to Poland, thereby taking advantage of a high-tech tax loophole that enabled the company to receive a VAT exemption. In July 2002, the tax administration finished presenting its evidence to the court, which agreed with its assessment that Kluska had willfully conducted the circuitous sale for no other reason than to shortchange the treasury of more than sixteen million zloty. Police arrested Kluska, who spent the next forty-eight hours in jail.[24] He was released only after posting an exorbitant eight million zloty bail bond. Police also snared four business associates for tax fraud, and seized Optimus funds and property.[25] They demanded nine million more zloty from the company to cover lost VAT dues, along with financial penalties for the illegal export-import scheme. In February, the Novy Sacz tax office issued new accusations, which brought the amount of taxes and fines owed to twenty-seven million zloty (almost seven million dollars).[26]

The Optimus case attracted great attention. Polish businessmen anxiously viewed the affair as an attempt by state agents to bring down one of its leaders and, in so doing, establish a precedent that could be applied to any one of them next. State officials recognized that their new get-tough approach to tax evasion was on trial as well. Optimus filed an appeal to the Supreme Administrative Court. Kluska insisted that his actions were perfectly legal, according to both tax experts and local revenue agents, who originally ruled favorably on the transaction.[27] In a side story to the main case, Kluska claimed that prior to his arrest an anonymous individual offered to intervene on his behalf with tax officials to settle the dispute—for a hefty fee; while Kluska's defenders wanted to believe it, the insinuation of bribery was never substantiated. The frustrated prosecutor, meanwhile, threatened the uncooperative Optimus legal team with five years in jail for obstructing justice, because they refused to testify against their client.[28]

After nearly a year of delays and deliberations, the NSA issued a verdict: Roman Kluska was cleared of tax evasion charges.[29] It also ordered the state to release all monies seized, plus pay interest. The defeated prosecution team talked of appealing the verdict or of bringing new charges against Kluska, but dropped the case instead. Vindicated and emboldened, Kluska brought his own charges against the tax administration, demanding 1.5 million zloty as recompense for his illegal incarceration and interest on his bail bond. Now the court sided with the prosecutor and dismissed most of the charges, except for awarding Kluska a token five thousand zloty for unlawful detention.[30]

The repercussions of the Optimus Affair spread beyond the court ruling. The NSA's verdict was a stinging rebuke to the state's efforts to enhance the use of coercion in the fight against tax evasion. A high-ranking social democrat who had enthusiastically endorsed the public display of coercion against Kluska, the deputy finance minister and head of Tax Control, Wieslaw Ciesielski, was forced to resign as the government's case came undone.[31] If the state meant to send a signal to businessmen, it was not the one intended. The number of court cases challenging the tax administration rose sharply in the year following the Optimus case.[32] The use of coercion against Optimus did not have the effect of weakening the private sector in relation to the state, just the opposite: civil society was strengthened by the showdown. The Polish Confederation of Private Employers was inspired by the Kluska case to create its own "civic ombudsman for private business," to expose cases of state administration misconduct, to draft proposals for legal changes, and to support private firms in tax disputes in court.[33] Kluska, meanwhile, attained a status of free market martyr. In 2007, in alliance with the social-conservative Kaczynski government, he assisted in the preparation of a set of administrative reforms, known as the "Kluska Package," which promised to help private entrepreneurs by easing regulatory rules, simplifying registration requirements, and limiting on-site inspections, particularly by the tax administration. It was necessary, Kluska said, because "the bureaucratic monster is determined to return to power."[34]

The resolution of the Optimus case was consistent with Poland's "legalistic consent" tax regime. Clearly, Kluska was violating the spirit of the law, while following the letter of the law. He was avoiding taxes, but in Poland tax avoidance was legal. The state-society contest over the legal limits of coercion was an ongoing issue in Polish politics. But, in the end, the Polish state never made coercion a credible feature of tax collection. The use of state coercion against society was regulated by explicit rules of engagement, which were closely monitored and faithfully enforced by politically independent legal-administrative organs. The Optimus case is illustrative of how state-society revenue battles reinforced the establishment of the rule of law in postcommunist Poland.

Rule by Law in Russia

UNLEASHING COERCION IN THE TAX REGIME

The Soviet state was dedicated to the cultivation of coercive resources, including over one million uniformed political and civilian police. The communist regime was considered to have been generally effective at keeping this extensive coercive apparatus under civilian political control. But political constraints on coercive forces began to fray in the late Soviet period, and they were nearly severed after the old regime's collapse. Russia's transition was marked by impromptu privatization and decentralization of the coercive resources of the communist state into the hands of "violent entrepreneurs."[35] The several hundred thousand agents remaining in state employ, meanwhile, faced an uncertain future. Yeltsin broke up the KGB into a half dozen agencies with limited mandates. Without a cold war to wage or a proletarian democracy to defend, demoralized police lost their sacred service mission. With the state continuously strapped for revenue, security operations were curtailed and personal livelihoods were crimped. And the possibility that there could be a settling of past accounts, as happened to some other communist bloc security forces, left Russia's police vulnerable to retribution.

In the transition, the police were released from Communist Party oversight, but they were not effectively checked by new civilian political-legal institutions. Early initiatives to subordinate the state's security forces to parliamentary oversight were ultimately quashed.[36] The 1993 Constitution ended the uncertainty over the institutional fit of coercive agents. In the restructured political order, the security apparatus was placed under the person of the president, beyond parliament or cabinet oversight. This arrangement was consistent with past patterns of power in Russia in which the police were placed under the personal discretion of the central executive, insulated from politically independent and legally based institutional control. Yeltsin and the police shared a mutual interest in keeping the security forces shielded on the executive side. Still, Yeltsin's authority over the state's coercive agents was tenuous, and he was careful not to antagonize them.

After Russia's 1998 fiscal collapse, revenue extraction more consistently reflected the state's preference for bureaucratic coercion. The trend was driven by presidential succession. In contrast to his predecessor, Vladimir Putin was both less constrained politically and less inhibited personally in using the coercive resources attached to the office. The central state's fiscal imperative was reinvigorated. As a result, the fine line of legal technicality that separates evasion from avoidance was smudged over by police and prosecutors, who determined that any violation of tax law, whether of the letter or of the spirit, was punishable.

In the 1990s, law enforcers repeatedly ranted that the fight against tax evasion was being undermined by legislative imprecision. Tax legislation was rewritten and tax avoidance schemes were declared illegal. In the mid-1990s only two articles of the criminal code dealt with tax evasion, but by 2002 the number had increased to fifty-three articles.[37] As a warning to the corporate elite, especially in the energy sector, the expanded mandate of tax enforcers was broadcast loudly from executive quarters as the following examples show. Ministry of Economic Development (December 2003): "Besides the fact that the oil companies acquired huge properties in just a few years, they still use tax optimization schemes worth billions of dollars annually. Our patience has run out." Ministry of Finance (January 2004): "We will continue to pursue oil groups for unpaid taxes. The use of measures with retroactive force cannot be ruled out." Presidential administration (October 2004): "Everyone who uses tax optimization schemes illegally must be called to account for their actions."[38]

One by one, favorite avoidance schemes were outlawed. In 2001, internal tax havens and special tax-exempt cities, which had been created by the Yeltsin administration to garner political support and help out economically distressed regions, were abolished. By registering in a tax haven, oil companies had reduced their profit tax rate from 35 percent to 11 percent. MinFin estimated that closing down tax havens increased income to the 2001 state budget by 1.6 percent of GDP.[39] In 2002, the transfer pricing scheme, in which oil companies paid fewer taxes by selling at reduced prices to their own subsidiaries, was eliminated, when the state replaced the sales tax with a fixed-rate tax on production.[40] Also in 2002, the movie tax exemption, another oil company favorite, was canceled. Here corporate profits were invested in "Russian" films (that is, films about Russia, made in Russia, directed by Russians, and sanctioned by the Russian Ministry of Culture). In the role of Max Bialystock, the Slavneft oil company submitted multimillion-dollar exemption claims for dozens of "Russian" films that were either made for significantly less or not made at all. During the two-year life of this exemption, the Ministry of Culture issued seven hundred national seals of approval, but only 180 "Russian" epics were shot.[41]

As in Poland, legal-institutional checks existed to arbitrate state-society tax battles. The 1993 Constitution created a Constitutional Court, a system of arbitrage courts, and an Audit Chamber. Indeed, in the 1990s the Constitutional Court and the arbitrage courts earned reputations for protecting taxpayers from tax collectors who had exceeded their mandate.[42] The Constitutional Court, for example, put the kibosh on attempts by revenue agents to apply tax laws retroactively, to seize property without court approval, to assess disproportionately large fines, and to make managers personally liable for corporate disputes. The Arbitrage Court, meanwhile, was concerned with commercial activities, including state-business relations.[43] In the 1990s, the Arbitrage Court was a safe haven for taxpayers. As tax collectors became more aggressive in enforcing revenue claims in the late nineties, taxpayers became more adept at using the Arbitrage Court. By the tax administration's accounting, in 2000 the arbitrage courts favored taxpayers in more than two-thirds of the cases decided.[44]

Tax enforcers at first had a hard time learning to work the new legal system. As of 2000, the tax police could persuade the prosecutor's office to pursue less than one quarter of the criminal cases it had sent.[45] In the summer of 2000, the tax police finally took on corporate titans Lukoil and Avtovaz, filing criminal charges for tax evasion and demanding back payments and fines in the hundreds of millions of dollars. But they did not get far: the prosecutor general ordered the case against Avtovaz closed for insufficient evidence, and the Moscow Arbitrage Court threw out almost every charge against Lukoil, reducing to a pittance the amount of back taxes owed.[46] According to Director Mikhail Fradkov, the tax police in 2001 successfully prosecuted only twenty-seven criminal cases.[47] He attributed the poor showing to both the ambiguity of the law and the ingenuity of evaders. "Several times we did not gather enough evidence and the court refused our case," Fradkov acknowledged. "In the past, we simply hammered out a number of cases. Now each case is thoroughly reviewed by a legal expert to determine if it will hold up in court."[48]

In the 2000s, the state's ostensibly independent legal system was co-opted into reinforcing the practice of bureaucratic coercion. The Constitutional Court readily constructed a legal foundation for bureaucratic coercion. In 2000, taxpayer challenges to the expanding mandate of the tax police led the Constitutional Court to reaffirm the agency's power to put firms in double jeopardy by launching investigations independent of the tax administration, to gain access to a wide array of personal financial information, and to conduct surprise searches, surreptitious surveillance, and secret audits of taxpayers.[49] In 2004, the Constitutional Court upheld the power of tax authorities to apply Article 169 of the Civil

Code to tax evasion. This article stated that any economic transaction deemed "anti-social" or "immoral" could be declared criminal and the assets received thereof confiscated.[50] In 2005, the Constitutional Court ruled that the three-year statute of limitations on tax evasion crimes, explicitly stated in the tax code, did not apply in cases of "deliberate" tax evasion. One district judge summed up the new approach when his verdict openly acknowledged that the actions of a company director on trial for tax evasion "fell within the boundaries of the law" and then handed him an eight-year jail term anyway.[51] A similar reverse trend was seen in the findings of the Arbitrage Court. Whereas taxpayers won 64 percent of the court cases in 2000, the tax authorities won 83 percent of the cases in 2006.[52]

Instead of politically independent judges, Russia's police-packed government showed a preference for centralized bureaucratic checking mechanisms. In state finances, the most effective instrument of bureaucratic control was the Audit Chamber. Under the capable leadership of Sergei Stepashin, whose résumé included stints as police chief and prime minister, the Audit Chamber vigorously investigated the misuse of state funds and nonpayment of taxes by regional and economic elites.[53] The Audit Chamber was not endowed with law enforcement powers, but it was charged with the investigation of wrongdoing and with alerting the police and the public of its findings. Because Stepashin was an authoritative figure, both for his professional experience and his personal integrity, the Audit Chamber was not easily intimidated when investigating elite actors.[54] The Audit Chamber was originally subordinate to the Duma. President Putin, however, concluded that the Audit Chamber should be relocated to the executive side under presidential supervision. Although Stepashin and the legislature at first resisted, in 2004 the Audit Chamber was made subordinate to central executive control.

In the 2000s, state-society revenue battles in Russia reflected an increasing tendency toward rule by law, rather than the rule of law. This was most evident in the criminalization of tax avoidance. In the tradition of Soviet criminal justice, and in sharp contrast to Poland, the accused was presumed guilty until proven innocent. The Constitution's legal-administrative checks on state coercion worked some of the time; the problem was that they did not work all of the time. The institutions intended to protect societal capital from state coercion were vulnerable to political pressure, as revealed in the Yukos Affair.

THE LIMITS OF COERCION: THE YUKOS AFFAIR

This brings us to the case involving Mikhail Khodorkovsky. The former communist youth leader enjoyed a phenomenal rise to riches during the Yeltsin years by adeptly manipulating insider access to political patronage and economic assets.

Through the Menatep Bank, Khodorkovsky gained access to Communist Party bank accounts, and then through the "loans-for-shares" scheme he acquired the Yukos Oil Company. By 2003, he was the wealthiest man in Russia. When President Putin tried more vigorously to assert the fiscal interests of the central state, the confident Khodorkovsky acted to protect his prospering business fiefdom. In this effort, he was the most visibly ambitious tycoon seeking to impose limits on the central state's ability to intervene in and make claims on the wealth of the postcommunist economic elite.[55]

First, when the government tried to raise the excise tax rates on oil exports in the 2002 Duma, Khodorkovsky orchestrated an alliance of communist and liberal deputies to reject the proposal. It was a rare legislative defeat for Putin's government that year. Second, Khodorkovsky led a private initiative to expand the overwhelmed and outdated pipeline infrastructure. But this venture threatened to undermine the existing state monopoly over oil transport, which provided the government with information about transactions and revenue from user fees. Third, Khodorkovsky sought to check the powers of the central state through financial support to opposition parties and nongovernmental organizations, thereby helping to build societal-based organizational capacity. In the 2003 Duma campaign, he publicly endorsed the pro-business platform of the Union of Right Forces, which advocated lower taxes, private property rights, and a reduced state presence in the economy.[56] He founded his own nongovernmental organization (NGO), Open Russia, with the explicit goal of promoting civil society in Russia. Finally, Khodorkovsky endeared his company to foreign capitalists by promising to adopt international financial standards of corporate governance and by wooing new investment partners. The more a Russian firm becomes embedded in a network of foreign capital, the less easily it can be manipulated by the state. In sum, Khodorkovsky's actions represented an attempt to draw a clear line between the public realm and the private realm, defining bounded limits on state prerogative.

In February 2003, Putin gathered the corporate elite in Catherine's Hall in the Kremlin, where he spoke about efforts to improve the performance of the state administration. At the meeting, Khodorkovsky was outspoken in his criticisms of official corruption. Putin replied that Khodorkovsky had his own problems with paying taxes, and then explicitly linked the government's poor governance with business's tax evasion.[57] Five months later, a close business associate of Khodorkovsky was arrested for improprieties related to the privatization of a fertilizer firm in the early nineties. The Yukos Affair had begun. In October, masked commandos seized Khodorkovsky from his private plane at a Siberian airport. The case against Yukos involved several core allegations: defrauding the state of privatization revenues, setting up an illegal offshore company to hide oil profits, evading corporate and personal income taxes, and stiffing the pension fund. The company was hit with bills for unpaid taxes and fines, covering the years 2000–2003, for more than $15 billion; Khodorkovsky's personal debt to the state was nearly $2 billion.[58]

The Yukos Affair was a showcase of unchecked bureaucratic coercion. The formidable forces of the secret police, the justice ministry, the audit chamber, the tax police, and the tax administration were collectively mobilized to compile a succession of criminal cases against the company and its top directors. The legal system provided no protection against this assault. The courts followed the prosecutor's recommendations in close step. Due process was ignored. The accused were not permitted adequate time to review the charges in order to prepare a defense. On the rare occasion when an arbitrage judge decided in favor of the defendant on a procedural matter, she was quickly removed from the case, and fired from her post shortly thereafter.[59] Yukos bank accounts were frozen and its assets seized; the firm's business operations were paralyzed. Even the media was an instrument of the state offensive, airing a documentary that tied Khodorkovsky to Chechen terrorists and murdered journalists. Abuses of the legal system were so frequent and blatant that the Yukos Affair inspired a new popular term, "Basmanny justice," named for the district court in which the case was tried. Attempts by Yukos to reach a settlement and a repayment schedule were rejected by the tax authorities. Instead, Khodorkovsky and his principal partner, Platon Lebedev, were found guilty of tax evasion in May 2005 and given a nine-year jail sentence. Two years later, the state played double jeopardy, filing more charges of tax evasion and embezzlement against the pair. The second trial, which ended in 2010, increased the original sentence to twelve years. Meanwhile, Yukos was dismantled and its multibillion-dollar assets were redistributed to state-owned Rosneft and a few other more compliant members of the corporate elite.[60] Unlike the Optimus Affair in Poland, which reinforced the rule of law, the Yukos Affair served to consolidate rule by law in the postcommunist Russian state.

Taxation and Capital

"If finances have created and formed the modern state," Joseph Schumpeter observed, "so now the modern state forms them—deep into the flesh of the private economy."[61] Fiscal sociology assumes that the particular way in which a state extracts revenue influences the organization of economic activity more generally. How power interacts with wealth is revealed through the tax system. Neoliberal-inspired reform was supposed to create some version of the market economies found in the West; instead, it produced a variety of transition capitalisms in the

East, ranging from Friedmanism to Caponeism. Here again Poland and Russia provide a study in contrasts, where different systems of revenue extraction influenced different types of transition economy. In Poland, "legalistic consent" facilitated the emergence of "social-market capitalism," while in Russia, "bureaucratic coercion" gave shape to "concessions capitalism."

Social-Market Capitalism in Poland

Elite consensus was displayed in the Polish transition with the adoption of the 1997 constitution. The new constitution was an outstanding landmark on the path to democratic consolidation. Poland's new basic law not only codified the organization of political power, civil rights, and bureaucratic-coercive agencies, it also defined the social character of the distribution of economic resources. This consensus formed around the notion of "social-market capitalism," through which Poland's political elite expressed a commitment to both free enterprise *and* social justice. The constitution proclaimed that Poland should be "a social market economy based on the freedom of economic activity, private ownership, and solidarity, dialogue and cooperation of social partners."[62]

Social-market capitalism was a Polish version of welfare capitalism.[63] It was inspired by Poland's neighbors, the prosperous welfare states of northern Europe; by Poland's past, the institutional inheritance of community-based social-economic organization; and by Poland's present, the structural constraints of the transition economy. What was particular about the Polish welfare state was the firm commitment to social benefits despite the scarcity of wealth in the transition economy, which led to the tax system serving as a means of subsidizing living standards. Its elaboration was associated with social-democratic political actors, such as Finance Minister Grzegorz Kolodko and Labor Minister Jerzy Hausner, and like-minded left-wing economists.[64] Meeting in June 2008, in Gdansk, the city of Solidarity, the Standing Conference on the Social Economy of Poland issued a manifesto that defined social-market capitalism as "a set of institutions that have in common the fact that they try to reach certain social objectives using market economy tools."[65]

As an economic concept, social-market capitalism was a kind of "third way" economy, incorporating elements of capitalism and socialism, while avoiding the extremes of the free market and the command economy. In principle, the model combined economic liberalism with social protection. It assumed that economic growth is positively correlated with social cohesion; contrarily, weak social cohesion is a drag on economic growth. The strength or weakness of social cohesion was directly influenced by levels of wealth disparity, unemployment, poverty, health care, and education.[66] As a political concept, social-market capitalism was an affirmation of the solidarity of the Polish nation, as expressed through an explicit commitment to maintain a level of social dignity and self-worth among all members of the community. According to one version, "social economy has no political affiliation, it is a place where different ideologies can peacefully meet, and does not require a choice between freedom and solidarity."[67] It was notable that before the concept was enshrined in the Constitution, it was first invoked at the 1989 Round Table negotiations, in the "Position Statement on Social and Economic Policy and Systems Reform," one of three major documents produced in the historic agreement.[68]

Social-market capitalism was rooted in Polish historical precedence, dating back before communism to the Second Republic of the interwar period.[69] Under the influence of Marshal Jozef Pilsudski, Poland moved toward a dirigiste state-society model. To shore up the image of the newly independent nation, Pilsudski's government sought to acquire the modern status symbols of early twentieth-century European states, including an unsparing social welfare system. By the 1930s, the Polish state featured a centralized social insurance bureaucracy that oversaw welfare and pension programs covering over two million citizens. This administrative apparatus was co-opted by the communist regime, and operated with only minor modifications right up until the transition. The long-term institutional effects were apparent in the views of Polish society about the postcommunist transition. Like the interwar experience, postcommunist Poland was committed to a relatively generous welfare policy, despite being one of the poorer countries in Europe.

Of course, it was good politics too. Some version of social-market capitalism was endorsed by almost every major political party, including conservative Catholics, Solidarity trade unionists, smallholding farmers, and ex-communist social democrats; only the free market liberals rejected what they understood as an inherently contradictory notion of a "socially just free market." Polish society overwhelmingly supported social-market capitalism. Throughout the postcommunist transition, public opinion surveys repeatedly showed dissatisfaction with the performance of market capitalism and a strong preference for the state to play an economic role. Survey findings showed an early optimism about free market capitalism, which steadily eroded over the course of the transition. Instead, Poles increasingly favored some form of state protection from the free market, as indicated in 1997 by the nearly two-thirds of survey respondents who answered that the main goal of privatizations should not be economic efficiency, but that "no one should get hurt."[70] Moreover, Poles generally favored more state spending on public assistance, especially for those most vulnerable to the free market: the poor, elderly, and disabled.[71]

Poles were fairly consistent in their opinions of how the state should intervene in the economy: wealth redistribution, social protection, and market preparation. In terms of wealth redistribution, a majority of Poles consistently believed that the people with high incomes were not paying enough taxes. Roughly three-quarters of Poles responded affirmatively to the statement that "it should be the government's responsibility to reduce the differences between those who earn a lot and those who earn a little" (by 71 percent in 1994, 76 percent in 1998, and 80 percent in 2000.).[72] In terms of social protection, "profamily" tax relief remained one of the most popular features of the Polish welfare state. Finally, in terms of market preparation, survey respondents did not support taxation in exchange for unconditional welfare benefits, but rather taxation as a means of enabling people to take advantage of the new market economy. Public surveys showed that two-thirds of respondents routinely supported tax relief for businesses that created jobs.[73]

Tax policy reinforced Poland's social-market capitalism. On the market side, a series of incentives were transmitted to economic actors via the tax system. Tax policy was used to promote private initiative, especially for new small businesses. The checks on the tax administration, meanwhile, attempted to provide a professional and predictable revenue extraction process. The legal guardians of the new order, the Ombudsman and the Constitutional Tribunal, resolved tax disputes so as to protect societal wealth from state predation. The results of the numerous small-scale state-society conflicts over economic resources that took place in the tax regime had the large-scale cumulative effect of consolidating the institutions that support a market economy—state coercion constrained by the rule of law and societal capital organized as private property. Upon this institutional basis, postcommunist Poland developed a dynamic domestic consumer market economy, which generated new wealth and proved to be self-sustaining.

On the social side, Polish political elites were committed to maintaining a generous welfare state, but they did not have the resources to do so. Instead of direct economic payouts, tax deductions and exemptions were systematically enacted as an alternative form of social subsidy to households. In effect, tax breaks made up for low wages and high prices. In addition, the seemingly lax attitude that certain governments took toward collecting tax arrears from large public firms was another means of social subsidy, without having to shell out investment capital. Even after Poland joined the EU, which forbade such practices, successive governments continued to use the tax system as a surrogate means of providing social welfare. Thus, through taxation the postcommunist state assumed a paternalistic role as mediator between market and society in the consolidation of Poland's social-market capitalist economy.

Concessions Capitalism in Russia

Russia's economic transition did not lead to *market* capitalism, but to *concessions* capitalism.[74] The concept of concessions capitalism puts emphasis on what distinguishes it from command socialism and market capitalism. The most valued economic resources of the communist state were not fully redistributed to society in the form of private property; these assets were made into state concessions.[75] Postcommunist Russia's concessions capitalism is a kind of "upstairs-downstairs" economy, in which upstairs are strategic industries in the form of large corporations that remain directly or indirectly subordinated to the state sector, while downstairs are mass consumption retail and trade in the form of small and medium enterprises that are organized into a regulated private sector. Russia's concessions capitalism was a direct outcome of the state's revenue-extraction practices.

This organizational scheme first appeared under Yeltsin, but it was institutionally consolidated under Putin. When the postcommunist business elite pushed to convert its acquisitions into private property, they were rudely disabused of this aspiration by Putin. The economic resources found upstairs belonged to the state. State concessions come mainly in three forms: lucrative natural resources, large manufacturing firms, and public monopolies. Most state concessions are not managed directly by state ministries and agencies, as was the case in the command economy. They are not regulated by enforceable contracts, but by the personal discretion of high-level state actors. Concessions are farmed out to politically favored corporate executives, who are charged with generating profits while navigating the pitfalls of global capitalism and fulfilling the obligations of the central state. The underlying political logic of the concessions economy comes into clearer focus when examining the main developments in state–big business relations under Putin.

First, in the redistribution of the communist state's economic resources, the line between public and private property was not distinctly delineated. Under Yeltsin, the state was generous in granting economic concessions, but it was vague about formalizing the proprietary claims of private actors and thereby creating a recognized protective boundary. With Putin, the line between private and public not only remained blurred but also shifted to the advantage of the state. Second, the economic elite in Russia is not autonomous, but a state creation. Power and wealth relations may have been a bit fuzzy under Yeltsin, whose impulsive leadership style and frequent absences allowed favored tycoons to gain influence in state policymaking; but the relationship between power and wealth was made crystal clear under the more resolute and steady Putin. Russia's postcommunist economic elite do not own their wealth, they are concessionaires. They lack the power resources to assert autonomy; they are too weak either to capture the state or to bargain with it as equals. Third, economic concessions come with obligations of state service, which mainly means revenue. Here, leadership style matters. The politically embattled Yeltsin was lax in forcing the business elite to fulfill its social obligations, but the politically secure Putin coerced the business elite to pay taxes to the state and to bestow gifts on the nation, in the form of recovering lost art treasures, funding health clinics, and outfitting sports teams. Not to comply meant to risk losing it all.

Although concessions capitalism is distinct from market capitalism and command socialism, it is not an unprecedented form of economic organization in Russian history, where those who controlled coercive resources have also long controlled economic resources. Instead of a division of coercive and economic resources between state and society, as occurred in some early modern European states, there was a concentration of these power resources within the Russian realm. The state claimed ownership over the most valuable assets in the economy and, as a result, determined the criteria for conferring elite status in society. The relationship between ruling tsars and elite aristocrats reflected this system of wealth and power in medieval and imperial Russia.[76] Those aristocrats who played the game well prospered, but any leadership change meant that the rules of the game could change as well, and fortunes and honors were revoked for those concessionaires who resisted. This system of power and wealth operated right up to the final years of the old regime. The concessions strategy was employed to facilitate industrialization in the late imperial period, for example in Russian railway construction and the economic development of the Far East.[77]

In postcommunist Russia, the state's reimposition of a concessions-based economy was announced with a barrage of official bombast at the time of the Yukos Affair. Boris Gryzlov, the former Ministry of the Interior militia head turned parliament speaker, stated that "the country's natural resources do not belong to any corporation or particular person, but to all the people of Russia."[78] Evgenii Primakov, former prime minister turned corporate lobbyist, said that Russia's energy resources "were given by God to all the people." And if there was still a question as to how "all the people" would exercise ownership, it was soon made clear. Sergei Ivanov, KGB cop turned defense minister, asserted that Russia's natural wealth "belongs to the state, they are not private property."[79] It was not a coincidence that the state campaign to reclaim economic assets from the business elite coincided with an election campaign for parliament. Survey findings showed consistent social support for two particular features of the concessions economy. First, the economy's rich natural resources and large Soviet-era manufacturing complexes should belong to the nation, that is, the state. Second, state power should predominate over the big business elite.[80]

The fiscal needs of the state were at the core of the concessions economy. Historically, Russian rulers have long relied on economic commodities that could be directly taxed—forests, land, minerals. They have not been terribly troubled, past or present, to pursue moveable assets through indirect taxation of transactions, preferring instead to concentrate on fixed assets in a way that would yield readily extractable rents. The introduction of a transition economy diverted economic resources away from the public to the private realm. But the postcommunist state failed miserably in its initial attempt to collect tax revenue from private actors. The concessions economy, thus, emerged as an "upstairs/downstairs" compromise. The Russian state remained fiscally dependent on the wealth generated by the "upstairs" economy.

The bureaucratic-coercive tax regime was the means by which the state consolidated its claim on the economic wealth contained in the "upstairs" economy. State investigators leveled tax evasion charges against scores of big businesses, along with confiscatory claims of back taxes and penalties. The outstanding tax debts were settled only when a state-run enterprise finally acquired a sizable, often controlling, stake in the ownership of the targeted firm. After a decade of decline, the state sector began to grow again, as indicated by the increase of state-owned shares (from 20% in 2003 to 35% in 2007) on the Russian stock market.[81] In 2005 alone, Gazprom grabbed up 75 percent of oil giant Sibneft; Rosneft captured 99 percent of Yuganskneftegaz, a lucrative subsidiary of Yukos; and Rosoboroneksport, the state arms manufacturer, found itself with 60 percent of Avtovaz, the country's largest car manufacturer.[82]

With state control now more firmly established, the Finance Ministry was able to dictate fiscal policy to big business, when the political will existed. A commission headed by Finance Minister Kudrin concluded that Russia's major exporters, especially in the energy sector, would have to give more of their income to the state.[83] With the help of the Audit Chamber, the Finance Ministry gained direct access to the exports of Alrosa, which monopolized the diamond industry.[84] MinFin decided whether and how much Russia's concession companies could borrow investment capital from abroad.[85]

The concessions economy not only serves the fiscal interests of the state but the personal interests of particular state actors. In the 2000s, the state security forces unleashed against the tax-avoiding economic elite became directly involved with managing the richest corporations. The police did not uproot the system of informal takings of economic resources; they supplanted those who created it. The expanded operational mandate that went with the new "economic security" service mission of the police provided an opportunity for coercion to gain direct access to capital through a new form of state predation. In this postcommunist protection racket, the security forces profited from the creation of a quasi-formal collections agency, staffed by former policemen and authorized to confiscate property from firms that are either in financial difficulty or in trouble with the law. The process was cryptically referred to as "velvet reprivatization," but it was in effect a state-sanctioned extortion racket.[86]

Bureaucratic coercion served the state's short-term revenue needs, but at the cost of long-term economic development, especially in the "downstairs" economy. As the Putin administration was expanding state intervention in the "upstairs" economy, it tried to restrict state predation on the "downstairs" economy. Putin ordered the government to make a genuine effort to limit coercion and use other means to induce small businesses to come out of the shadow. The government lowered the cost of tax compliance, reduced tax rates, and eased the regulatory burden. The government also tried to restrain the powers of tax inspectors, tax policemen, and regional authorities. But it is not so easy to maintain differing policies simultaneously upstairs and downstairs. The restraint that the center urged on local agents often went unheeded, especially when shown the example of unchecked coercion by the state center.

The concessions economy is a recurring structural pattern in Russia. It is not the result of some invisible cultural force, but of the organization of power resources, namely the concentration of coercion and capital. Russia's contemporary concessions economy is sustained by the same three sources as was its imperial predecessor: fiscal needs, in that the state is served by the existence of readily extractable rents from fixed assets; political needs, in that one of the main threats to the continued dominance of Russia's semiauthoritarian regime of former cops is the emergence of autonomous centers of wealth in society; and economic needs, in that big business elites who wish to maintain wealth and status are reluctant to challenge the state.

Taxation and Society

The fall of communism was characterized by a redistribution of power resources from state to society. Most significant in this process was the fate of coercion and capital. But these are not the only power resources that either state or society can possess. Beyond coercion and capital, the communist state also controlled the sources of status, means of organization, and standards of morality. These additional power resources also were redistributed in Eastern Europe's postcommunist transitions. In some cases, the state relinquished sufficient power resources for society to consolidate its own private realm; in other cases, the state held on to power resources in an attempt to continue making society subordinate. Poland and Russia, here again, represent contrasting types. The Polish state facilitated the development of a legal-institutional framework to uphold a "civil society." The Russian state systematically undermined the legal-institutional bases of societal autonomy, thereby reinforcing a "dependent society." The tax regime supported or undermined the development of civil society in three areas of societal autonomy: (1) economic resources and elite status; (2) organizational resources and civic association; and (3) ideological resources and moral authority.

Civil Society in Poland

ECONOMIC RESOURCES AND ELITE STATUS

Poland is among the few postcommunist cases that successfully reestablished civil society. This notable transition outcome was made possible by the autonomy of Polish economic elites. Poland was no different from other postcommunist countries in that the dismantling of the social-leveling command economy created the conditions for a nouveau riche social stratum to emerge. Poland was different, however, regarding the new economic elite's sources of wealth, organizational capacity, and relationship to the state.

Poland's new rich made their fortunes from new business ventures, in retail, media, electronics, telecommunications, and finance. They got their start in the late communist period, when restrictions on private activity were eased. They may have had political allies, but not political patrons. They were not strategically placed heirs of existing sources of wealth. They were entrepreneurs who started small and scored big, taking advantage of society's pent-up consumer needs. Given these constraints, Poland's elite were not among postcommunism's superrich. In 2002, Poland's one hundred richest people were worth an estimated 53.5 billion zloty, which was one-third more than Russia's richest individual.[87] A 2007 list of Eastern Europe's one hundred richest people included twelve Poles, but not one of them was in the top fifty.[88] Finally, wealth was not regionally concentrated. Of course, there were richer and poorer regions, but the new rich were located across the country. Although Warsaw was wealthier than the rest of Poland, economic capital was not concentrated in the political capital to nearly the same extent as in Russia, because Polish economic elites were not dependent on the state.

The annual lists of Poland's richest people are consistent with this profile. In 2009, for example, not one individual in the top ten was beholden to the state for wealth; instead, all of them found fortune in the private sector.[89] The richest entrepreneur, Zygmunt Solorz-Zak, made his fortune in broadcasting, using satellite technology to create Polsat, the country's first commercial television station. After years of prudish programming, he brought Baywatch to the Baltic. The second richest, Leszek Czarnecki, was fresh out of engineering school in 1986 when he formed his first business. In 1991, he founded European Leasing Fund, renting cars, computers, and industrial equipment. By decade's end, he sold Poland's largest leasing firm to French banking giant Credit Agricole, and moved into real estate. The third richest, Michal Solowow, invested his life savings of $10,000 in a construction company in the early 1990s, which he sold for $44 million in 2002. He then founded the Echo investment firm, which buys and restructures struggling private companies.[90]

Poland's new entrepreneurial class was divided over the organization of state-business relations. Devoted capitalists advocated a strict division of labor between the market and the state. They viewed state-business relations in antagonistic terms, and expressed a preference for a competitive "survival of the fittest" business community and a minimalist hands-off state. Alternatively, other business-men wanted an interactive relationship with the state, preferring some version of continental-style corporatism. This model assumed that state and business were institutionally independent of one another, but had mutual interests in mechanisms of cooperation for coordinating economic goals, channeling policy input, and administering tax collection. The conflict over competing models was waged through the successive attempts of social-democratic governments to pass a proposed Business Association Bill, which would formalize a corporatist structure in state-business relations.

The main proponent of this legislation was the National Chamber of Commerce (KIG), which served as an umbrella organization for 150 different business organizations and maintained ties with the social democrats. The KIG helped draft the legislation, which would have compelled hundreds of individual business associations to become members of one giant organization. According to KIG head Andrej Andarski, the legislation was "vital for civil society," in that the business community, once united, would gain direct access to the policy process and would bolster self-governance by assuming responsibility for taxation, registration, and licensing.[91] In opposition to these proposals, the vice president of the Adam Smith Centre, Andrej Sadowski, stressed that Polish entrepreneurs did not need a closer relationship to the state, but rather to get away from the state's "socialistic inclination" to overregulate, overtax, and redistribute.[92] Much of the business community agreed with Sadowski's counterargument that business self-governance would be best served by less state involvement, not more. They successfully fought the effort to create a state-sanctioned business association with compulsory membership. There was no elite consensus for corporatist-style state-business relations.

Poland's entrepreneurs organized into competing business associations, which engaged the state on taxation: proposing legislative reform to political elites, providing advice to individual businesses, and monitoring the actions of the tax administration.[93] The Polish Business Roundtable represented the upper stratum of economic elites; its exclusive invitation-only membership included Poland's largest private businesses and richest businessmen. They did not have trouble gaining access to high government officials; in 2008, for example, they hosted the vice prime minister and finance minister on separate occasions for stately dinners and informal chats about tax policy.[94] By contrast, any new start-up could join the Business Centre Club (BCC). The BCC acted as a watchdog in state-business interactions and provided legal counsel to businesses disputing the tax administration. The Lodz-based BCC lobbied for tax administration reform, calling for shorter time limits on investigations, which eventually passed.[95]

Finally, private wealth in Poland was defended by a robust professional community of tax policy advocates and tax law specialists, dedicated to protecting private wealth from state power. The Polish Association of Taxpayers (PAT), for example, was a prominent tax advocacy group. Headquartered in Krakow, PAT consulted the Finance Ministry on tax legislation, held workshops to teach businesses how to lower tax costs and react to tax audits, and disseminated opinions to the general public. PAT published a semiregular magazine, which kept tax experts up to date on tax administration practices, and handed out an annual "Golden Zloty" award to an organization or publication that helped raise tax awareness.[96] Poland also hosted a large community of tax lawyers and consultants. Attempts by the state to organize this community into a state-sanctioned body failed; instead, they formed an autonomous professional organization, the Polish Association of Legal Counselors (PALC). When the state prosecutor threatened to imprison reticent company lawyers in the Optima case, PALC defended the right of the defendant's lawyers to remain silent, arguing that attorney-client confidentiality was the "foundation of the profession and of the rule of law."[97] In 2008, a grassroots movement supporting a "Polish Taxpayers Charter" was organized to promote further checks on the tax administration.[98]

ORGANIZATIONAL RESOURCES AND CIVIC ASSOCIATION

A necessary condition of civil society is the capacity for self-organization by private actors. In the Polish transition, the competition for capital in the tax regime strengthened organizational capacity in society. The postcommunist state did not resist this development; it helped to promote it, using tax policy to do so.[99]

In Poland, the nongovernmental sector of clubs, charities, and professional associations is referred to as the "third sector," apart from state and market. In the early 1990s, Polish society was poor in both economic and organizational resources. The government offered modest tax exemptions to encourage donors, international and domestic, to invest in the third sector. By the early 2000s, more than thirty thousand nongovernmental organizations were registered. The number was much larger if religious and professional groups were included: eighteen thousand trade unions, fifteen thousand Church organs, five thousand professional associations, and fifteen thousand volunteer fire brigades. Still, the third sector lacked financial resources and organizational strength. At this point, the state began to more actively support civil society development.

Tax policy was mobilized in the service of civil society through the Public Benefit Law. This legislation created a "percentage" system, by which taxpayers were allowed to allocate 1 percent of their total personal income tax to a societal organization, instead of to the state. Poland was not the first East Central European state to adopt this policy, whose origins go back to the nineteenth century as a solution to the conundrum of separating church and state in predominantly Catholic countries.[100] In Poland, the impetus to enact a fiscal percentage system came from below, from the nascent NGO sector. The Association for the Forum of Non-Governmental Initiatives (FIP), an umbrella group of large and small NGOs, was the driving force. With support from over 250 NGOs, FIP presented a draft proposal to the government in September 2001, and then followed up with an intensive lobbying effort of the political parties and an extensive advocacy campaign across the country.[101] Poland's version of a "percentage" system included a much longer list of eligible NGOs than other Eastern European countries, including not only charity and educational organizations but also cultural, environmental, and rural organizations.[102] Social-democratic President Kwasniewski and Finance Minister Belka declared their support for the civil-society-promoting fiscal reform. It took more than a year to filter through the Sejm, until spring 2003, when it became law.

The Public Benefit Law allocated a state subsidy raised from the 1 percent tax as well as expanded the number of tax exemptions available to qualifying NGOs.[103] To qualify, an NGO had to demonstrate that it provided critical social services benefiting either society in general or a hardship group in particular. The Ministry of Labor and Social Policy was responsible for overseeing the NGO sector and giving official accreditation to "public beneficial organizations" (PBO). Those receiving the coveted PBO status included not only cultural and charitable organizations but also explicitly political organizations that supported human rights, free speech, and political watchdog groups. Since the law went into effect, the number of registered NGOs increased from roughly 36,500 in 2002 to 55,000 in 2006; also, the number of foundations increased from five thousand in 2002 to eight thousand in 2006.[104] The number of taxpayers who participated in the program increased in the first three years: from 80,000 in 2004, to 680,000 in 2005, to 1,256,000 in 2006. The amount of income available to qualifying NGOs increased from ten million zloty in 2004, to 42 million zloty in 2005, to 62 million zloty in 2006.[105] In 2007, the liberal-democratic government of Donald Tusk simplified the administration of the "percentage" system to encourage more taxpayers to participate. Instead of sending the amount directly to the NGO and then waiting months to be reimbursed by the government, taxpayers now could specify the contribution on their tax declarations and entrust the tax administration to pass along the funds. Tusk promoted the reform by publicizing his personal NGO contribution to the Hospice of Saint Faustina in Sopot.

A by-product of the Public Benefit Law was the issuance of a set of "Rules for Social Dialogue," a goodwill gesture on behalf of the government that obliged state administrators to consult with NGOs in matters that concerned their areas of operation. Bureaucratic intransigence was a common complaint from organized society.[106] The enhanced capacity for NGO self-organization was put to the test almost immediately, in 2004, when the government proposed eliminating personal income tax exemptions for charitable donations. Roughly ten million Poles make charitable donations each year, the main source of NGO income. Having just gained a new source of income, Polish NGOs did not want to give up an older and more reliable one. The FIP waged a vigorous lobbying campaign against the proposal. In the end, a compromise was reached, in which the deduction for charitable donation was retained, but the amount of the exemption was slightly reduced. By such means, the self-organizing capacity of Polish civil society was reinforced by taxation.

IDEOLOGICAL RESOURCES AND MORAL AUTHORITY

Civil society is further bolstered by institutionalized sources of moral authority, independent of the state. In modern times, the Catholic Church played such a role in Europe in general, and in Poland in particular. Even when the Church's influence on society had long waned elsewhere, it remained strong in Poland. Close to 90 percent of Poles today identify as Catholic, while close to 60 percent identify as actively so. This makes Poland atypical among postcommunist countries. Even under the communist regime, the Polish Church maintained relative autonomy from the state. In postcommunist Poland, battles over church-state relations are less about establishing institutional independence for the Church, and more about defining limits on the political role of the Church. At stake was the very character of the postcommunist state, as strictly secular or particularly religious.

The Church was never a subordinate instrument of the state. Because the Church possessed the ideological power resource of moral authority, Polish rulers regularly sought its legitimating blessings; in exchange, it received special privileges, including exemptions from tax obligations on property and wealth. Whereas such an arrangement was long commonplace in the Catholic countries of Western Europe, it was unique in Communist Europe. The Polish Church retained relative autonomy under communism, especially after the 1956 reforms, although it was not free of state revenue claims. It was only during the desperate last years of the old regime that the Church was released from political constraints and revenue obligations through the Statute on Freedom of Conscience and Creed. The statute accorded the Church a special legal-fiscal status, exempting it from income, property, and communal taxes as well as customs duties.[107] This tax deal was contested in the postcommunist transition.

The principal combatants in the battle over the secular/religious disposition of the postcommunist state were the ex-communist social democrats and the emboldened Catholic Church. Lingering acrimony from the communist period infused the conflict. In autumn 1993, the social democrats became the dominant bloc in the Sejm, and quickly targeted the fiscal privileges of the Church. In December, the Sejm's Budget and Finance Committee, led by social democrat Maciej Manicki, proposed that the Church be stripped of its special fiscal status, be required to register all income with the state, and be forced to give up its tax-exempt commercial operations, including tobacco and alcohol sales.[108] Manicki insisted that the Church was no different than other social organization, such as a trade union or a political party, and thus undeserving of a special status. The Church hierarchy answered with sanctimonious hyperbole: the primate of Poland, Jozef Cardinal Glemp, rued "a return to communist times," while the secretary of the episcopate, Bishop Tadeusz Pieronek, pilloried the proposal as "Stalinist."[109] The Sejm passed a mild version of the proposal, in which the Church was obligated to register and pay corporate income tax on its commercial operations, but it retained special exemptions on income for routine expenses and charity work.

The church-state power struggle continued throughout the 1990s. When the social-democratic Sejm liberalized abortion restrictions, the Church called for a nationwide tax boycott, which went unheeded.[110] In 1996, the Church was caught in a tax evasion scandal when the Central Statistical Office reported that the Church had requested over four thousand exemptions on imported cars in 1995, totaling more than 8.5 million zloty in lost customs duties. As it turned out, the cars were actually for "gift-giving" parishioners seeking to avoid the import duty. Customs officials knew of the scam, but were reluctant to challenge the Church.[111] In reaction, social-democratic backbenchers called for the abolition of the Church's special fiscal status, but the more pragmatic social-democratic leadership came up with a compromise.

They proposed a "Church Tax" that would allow taxpayers to specify on tax returns that a small percentage of their payment should be allocated to the Church. The benefits to the state were threefold: the elimination of easily abused tax privileges, the penetration of Church finances, and, most important, an alignment of Church-state fiscal interests. The benefits for the Church were the retention of a special fiscal status and a steady source of income. The model for the Church Tax was borrowed from Germany and Hungary, where taxpayers were permitted to designate 1 or 2 percent of their state revenue obligations to the Church instead. Cardinal Glemp and the Polish Catholic hierarchy endorsed the compromise.[112] Polish society, however, showed that a majority (59 percent) was pro-choice on charitable donations.[113] So, in the end, the Church Tax was subsumed into the NGO tax legislation, enabling taxpayers to support either secular or religious nonstate charitable organizations in society.

The Church remained an independent moral authority to a large number of Polish citizens. Even consensus-minded social-democratic leaders came to recognize that it was better to try to co-opt the Church than to antagonize it. Indeed, the social democrats asked for the Church's blessing to confer legitimacy on the postcommunist order. Most notably, in 1997 the Church was persuaded, after much wooing, to give its support to the new Constitution. The Church's support, however, demanded the substitution of the draft document's clear language on separation of church and state in favor of a vague-sounding passage assuring "mutual impartiality" between church and state. In 1998, the Polish Sejm finally ratified a concordat with the Vatican concerning the conduct of church-state relations. As part of that agreement, decisions relating to church-state fiscal affairs were to be resolved through a special joint commission.

Historically, Poland's Catholic Church was and has been the institutional embodiment of civil society. Attempts by secular-minded political actors to use fiscal policy to enforce a strict separation of church and state and to make the Church equal among rather than above societal actors have been ineffective. Instead, the Church managed to retain some special tax exemptions, to receive state subsidies for its educational and social services, and to make good on most all of its property restitution claims. In this way state fiscal policy effectively reinforced the institutional autonomy of Polish society's most influential source of moral authority.

Dependent Society in Russia

ECONOMIC RESOURCES AND ELITE STATUS

The organization of Russia's concessions economy directly shaped the relationship between the postcommunist state and economic elites. Earlier in the transition, economic elites tried to consolidate their newly acquired wealth in the form of private property that was recognized by the state and protected from state predation, but this attempt failed. The postcommunist state was covetous of its economic resources and vigilant not to allow them to move beyond its control. Russia's new economic elite was created by and dependent on the state; they had little choice but to go along. They were not capitalist barons, but state concessionaires, and the epitome of dependent society.

The concessions economy was reinforced by the material and status interests of the economic elite. To play the game well meant to be attuned to the cues of central state leaders, who might change the rules at any time. Part of the game is that state concessions come with obligations of state service. In the 1990s, Yeltsin's service demands on the new economic elite were minimal: support his political ambitions, which the elite usually did, and pay taxes to the state, which the elite sometimes did not. In the 2000s, under President Putin, the rules changed. His administration made clear its intentions to forcibly reclaim and redistribute economic resources unless elites provided various forms of fiscal service to the state: paying more taxes to the treasury; making philanthropic donations to social and cultural institutions; and sharing their profits with central state insiders. A concessionaire must adjust to changes when they occur, else fortune and freedom may be lost. An elite actor who tries to restrain the state runs the risk of falling from favor and getting cut out of the spoils; this tangible threat keeps economic elites divided against one another in dealings with the state.

In sharp contrast to Poland, a look at Russia's richest businessmen and sources of wealth shows their dependence on the state. They did not build new private businesses, but rather gained controlling interest in Soviet-built industrial enterprises, mainly in energy, metals, and manufacturing. In the 2000s, the state reasserted its interest, either formally by reclaiming ownership shares or informally by intimidating corporate directors. The top ten richest Russians in 2010 all had derived their wealth from privatized industrial holdings in energy or metallurgy, businesses that were penetrated by the state.[114]

State-business relations in postcommunist Russia reflect the particularities of power and wealth in a concessions economy. In the 1990s, under President Yeltsin, state-business fiscal relations were idiosyncratic and ad hoc; revenue claims were negotiated on an individual basis. Private economic actors organized professional business associations. The new small-businesses sector displayed self-organization in the creation of several professional associations to pursue their interests.[115] The old state sector organized into a large, influential group, the Russian Union of Industrialists and Entrepreneurs (RUIE). The new tycoons, meanwhile, did not bother organizing, because they had personal ties to policymakers. In the 2000s, under President Putin, state-business relations were reorganized. Russia's many business associations were consolidated and centralized. In corporatist fashion, the state preferred to deal with a few large actors, particularly on tax issues. RUIE was the preferred organ for business association. In 2001, the big tycoons were forced to join.[116] By the mid-2000s, RUIE included over one hundred major professional business organizations that represented all major economic sectors. Its members accounted for two-thirds of Russian GDP.

Russia's most powerful business association, RUIE, has known only two lead-ers, Arkady Volsky and Alexander Shokhin, both of whom were state insiders. In the old regime, Volsky was a party boss in the auto industry. He came to promi-nence in the late communist period as an economic adviser to the political lead-ership.[117] Volsky thrived in Yeltsin's elite-bargaining style, but clashed with Putin's state-corporatist style. He was replaced as head of RUIE by Alexander Shokhin, who, like Volsky, was short on business experience and long on political connec-tions. Shokhin's résumé revealed the consummate insider: vice prime minister, economics minister, labor minister, Duma deputy, party boss. The deputy leader of RUIE, meanwhile, was Igor Yurgens, the head of the country's largest trade union. It was noteworthy that business and labor interests were consolidated into one organization. It was an indication not only of the weakness of organized labor but of Putin's penchant for using state-controlled institutions to organize society.

Unlike Poland, Russian business associations were connected to and subor-dinated to the state. Moreover, by keeping economic wealth organized as state concessions instead of private property, the postcommunist state deprived eco-nomic elites of the opportunity to accumulate capital as a potentially autono-mous power resource.

ORGANIZATIONAL RESOURCES AND CIVIC ASSOCIATION

Like the state, civil society rests upon infrastructural capacity. For society to re-main autonomous from the state, it needs an independent organizational base. The Russian state under President Putin used the bureaucratic-coercive tax re-gime to weaken the infrastructural capacity of newly established nongovernmen-tal organizations. Because of postcommunist society's limited resources, most prominent NGOs were started with internationally provided organizational and financial means. The international ties of the NGO sector, however, aroused the suspicions of veteran security agents who under Putin occupied high-level central state posts. In June 2001, Putin told a gathering of NGOs that their "dependence on foreign funds does not do us any good."[118] In particular, NGOs concerned with such issues as democracy, press freedom, and the environment were apt to clash with those on the state side of the divide. The state's hostility toward the NGO sector intensified following the episodes of internationally assisted protest politics that caused regime changes in neighboring Georgia and Ukraine.

The first effort to use fiscal policy to constrain NGOs came in 2002, when the new tax code changed the fiscal status of NGOs, eliminating their special exemp-tions and making them liable to pay corporate income tax, even if they were not engaged in commercial activity.[119] A number of NGOs, however, negotiated an extension of their exempt status from the government at this time. The second effort, coming after the "color" revolutions, was more determined. In 2006, the independence of the NGO sector was reined in further with a new regulatory regime that saddled them with an onerous financial-reporting burden. To comply with the new regulations, for example, the Carnegie Foundation was forced to produce a copy of the 1919 death certificate of founder Andrew Carnegie. Tax inspectors were empowered to penalize any NGOs that made even the smallest errors on their income/expense statements. In a third effort, in 2008, a government decree revised the state-approved list of NGOs that still maintained a tax-exempt status; the list was reduced from more than one hundred organizations to just twelve. Those NGOs losing protected status were forced to pay a 24 percent corporate income tax on all grant monies allocated for projects inside Russia.

Bureaucratic coercion was used to inhibit the development of an independent NGO societal sector. As early as 1998, the St. Petersburg tax police were unleashed on the Bellona Foundation, an Oslo-based environmental NGO, whose lawyers had acted in a well-publicized trial involving the FSB (Federal Security Service) and environmental activist Aleksandr Nikitin. After the 2006 reform, charges of improper financial reporting were brought against a number of NGOs, including human rights organizations (Memorial Society), environmental groups (Bellona, Dront), and press freedom monitors (Educated Media Foundation). And, not surprisingly, Khodorkovsky's civil society-promoting, George Soros-influenced NGO, Open Russia, was raided by tax authorities four times in the year and a half following the oil tycoon's arrest, while tax investigations were launched on Open Russia's twenty-three partner organizations.[120]

The number of NGOs in the 1990s numbered close to a half million, but in the 2000s the number of officially registered NGOs fell to less than half that number.[121] The decline in NGOs was not just the result of the state's hostile intent but also society's benign consent. A 2005 survey conducted by the Donors Forum on NGO activities provided insight into public perceptions on the state-society relationship. Two-thirds of respondents said providing social assistance to the needy was the main role of NGOs, while less than half said promoting democracy; meanwhile, 55 percent believed that NGOs were involved in money laundering. When asked who should first undertake charity work, nearly 60 percent said the state, while only 25 percent said private persons, and less than 10 percent said foreign charity organizations. Most notably, nearly three-quarters of the respondents agreed that the activities of NGOs should be coordinated by the state.[122]

Instead of an autonomous civil society, Putin expressed a preference for a "well-ordered civil society."[123] In 2000, an effort by the state was made to organize Russia's newly independent social actors in the Civic Forum, a loosely coordinated body of over five thousand NGOs, which proved too unwieldy for the central state. In 2004, a new initiative was put forth at the president's urging.

The resulting Public Chamber was composed of 126 individual representatives from a short list of government-approved nonstate organizations; one-third of the members were chosen directly by presidential decree. It brought together a select group of societal elites, drawn from business associations, professional organizations and trade unions, academic institutions, culture and the arts, into a single institutional framework, in which the state established the parameters and goals of social group activity. There were seventeen businessmen elected to the Chamber, the largest professional bloc. The Chamber was organized into seventeen functionally distinct commissions. The first head of the body, nuclear scientist Yevgeny Velikhov, said that "the motto of the chamber's work should not be confrontation but cooperation with authorities."[124]

The Public Chamber did not turn out to be quite as compliant as expected. It used its status to provide a voice of discontent, especially concerning legislative and administrative assaults on civil society. The Public Chamber's first act, in November 2005, was to protest the Duma's efforts to further restrict the activities of NGOs. At least some members of the Public Chamber recognized how tax policy undermined the autonomy of civil society. Chess master Anatoly Karpov protested the elimination of tax exemptions for NGOs doing charity work, arguing that tax benefits enabled private organizations to perform good deeds that the state was not always capable of.[125] The deputy secretary of the Public Chamber and head of the Union of Industrialists and Entrepreneurs, Aleksandr Shokhin, appealed to the president to soften regulations intended to give the tax administration greater powers of investigation against businesses. Shokhin instead proposed a "fair practice" policy, by which tax inspectors would be held accountable for wrongful accusations of tax fraud.[126] The Public Chamber also consistently called for amendment of the criminal code for tax evasion, which enabled the police to imprison tax delinquents even if they had paid their tax debts.[127] But the Public Chamber was not an instrument of independent civil society; it was a state-sanctioned voice in the policy process, and its opinion, when inconvenient, was simply ignored.

Like Russia's economic elites, NGOs did not have deep roots in society, which made it easier for the state to seize potential power resources from them. Under President Putin, the state actively sought to undermine an independent civil society and to keep society-based actors constrained within a state-based institutional framework. As part of this effort, the state used its bureaucratic-coercive tax regime to prevent the consolidation of organizational resources in autonomous society-based civic associations.

IDEOLOGICAL RESOURCES AND MORAL AUTHORITY

Finally, civil society can be sustained from independent institutional sources of moral authority, particularly the Church. But church-state relations in Russia displayed a different pattern than in Poland. The Russian Orthodox Church was closely tied to political power and, from the time of Peter the Great, in service to the state. After the communist regime collapsed, indications were that the Church might begin to act more independently of political power. Although less than one-fifth of Russians were active church members, more than two-thirds identified themselves as Orthodox Christians. In terms of moral authority, the Church consistently ranked among the most trusted institutions in postcommunist public opinion polls. In this regard, the Orthodox Church appeared to be a potential ideological power resource in postcommunist Russia. But as events played out, the Church did not emerge as an independent societal actor; instead, it achieved limited institutional autonomy and remained closely attuned to state interests. Toward this outcome, taxation was used to reinforce this interdependent state-church relationship.

At the highest levels especially, church and state found mutual accommodation. For state leaders, the Church conferred its moral authority on the new power arrangements. Yeltsin cultivated a public relationship with the Church's spiritual head, Patriarch Aleksei II, who was on hand to consecrate his presidential inauguration. Putin immediately included in his first inauguration a visit to the Kremlin's Annunciation Cathedral, where Aleksei presented him with a holy icon of medieval hero-prince Alexander Nevsky.[128] When Putin declared that he would hang around as prime minister after his presidential term ran out, Aleksei went on nationwide television to say "it was a great blessing for Russia." For the Church, postcommunist state leaders showed public respect toward the institution, following decades of official disdain. Unlike the communist period, the Orthodox Church received a special tax status from the postcommunist state. Its charity-based tax exemption enabled the Church to develop profitable side businesses, such as importing duty-free cigarettes as a form of "humanitarian assistance." In addition, bureaucratic coercion was used against recently arrived proselytizing spiritual rivals. Scientologists, Pentecostals, and Jehovah's Witnesses were set upon by the tax police.

The state sought to harness the moral authority of the Orthodox Church in service to revenue extraction. After the 1998 fiscal collapse, the state used the Church to promote a normative appeal for tax compliance. To legitimate state revenue claims, for example, tax collectors received blessings from the Orthodox Church. In November 1999, a memorial to tax policemen slain in the line of duty was unveiled at a solemn ceremony presided over by the head of the church. Patriarch Aleksei II used the event to present the Icon of Kazan, which had been kept in a monastery beyond the Volga for more than a century, to the leadership of the tax police to protect them from harm while serving the Motherland. The Orthodox Church again bestowed its blessings when it named the apostle Matthew, a Roman tax collector before turning Christian disciple, as patron saint of the tax police. A tax police source noted that these special benedictions were received in exchange for the agency's consent to finance the renovation of a Moscow cathedral.[129]

These politically orchestrated displays of state-church cooperativeness were performed by the hierarchy. In local parishes and monasteries, however, Orthodox priests were not always so deferential to the interests of the postcommunist state. In the early 2000s the Church was involved in a peculiar tax resistance movement. The dispute was not over rubles, but souls. When the tax administration first tried to introduce a taxpayer identification number (TIN) in 1999, it met an unlikely opponent in Orthodox fundamentalists, who stirred up popular protest against the measure. These priests urged the faithful to refuse the state's attempt to assign citizens a personal fiscal identity, arguing that it would supplant their given Christian identity (most Russian first names are also saint names); to do otherwise was a sacrilege, with eternal implications. The Orthodox protest claimed that the state's attempt to assign TINs was really part of a coordinated effort of American imperialism, the international Masonic conspiracy, and servants of the Antichrist to fool good Christians into rejecting their faith before the Last Judgment. Protest demonstrations were organized across Russia, and church and political officials were deluged with petitions. By the end of 2001, a tax ministry spokesman estimated that the protest had involved nearly a million people. Tax officials threatened to withhold state-provided services to churches, such as heat and hot water, but many believers still resisted the TIN. Instead, a well-publicized meeting between government and church leaders was organized, after which the patriarch assured the faithful that accepting the TIN would not mean the loss of afterlife salvation, just here-and-now income.[130]

Postcommunist state building was unique in that the process entailed redistributing, rather than accumulating, power resources. Indeed, the experience might better be called society building, instead of state building. This chapter compared how the battles between state and society over tax revenue contributed to the macroinstitutional reconfiguration of state and society in Poland and Russia, focusing on coercion, capital, and society.

In Poland, the rules governing the use of coercion were routinely enforced. The counterelites who came to power in Poland after the fall of communism were united on the fundamental issues of the transition, including protecting society from the coercive powers of the state. This was most evident in the area of revenue extraction. Tax avoidance was not criminalized, but protected by a set of legal-administrative organs. Through taxation, state coercion was restrained and channeled into the "rule of law." Further, the Polish tax system contributed directly to the consolidation of "social-market capitalism," an economy that embraces both free markets and social protections. Finally, the Polish case was noteworthy for the reestablishment of "civil society." Taxation helped enable Polish elites to maintain sources of wealth and status independent from the state, to bolster the capacity for self-organization of civic associations, and to reinforce the autonomy of the Church.

In Russia, the rules regarding coercion were enforced only sometimes, and certainly not if political authority intervened. Russia's postcommunist elites were divided among themselves, and could never come to agreement on the reconfiguration of power and wealth between state and society. State actors were covetous of the old regime's inheritance of power resources, and resisted their redistribution to society. This was clearly shown in the new tax regime, where tax avoidance was criminalized as state prerogative prevailed over the legal protection of the private realm. As such, taxation in Russia contributed to "rule by law." Regarding capital, the tax system led directly to consolidation of "concessions capitalism," a two-tiered economy in which, on one level, the state continues to own the most lucrative economic assets and, on the other level, the state espouses private property and entrepreneurship. The Russian tax regime undermined institutions that might protect private wealth, and kept postcommunist elites dependent on the state. Civil society requires an independent basis of elite status, civic association, and moral authority. But none of these developed in Russia, where instead the state used taxation to consolidate a "dependent society."

CONCLUSIONS

The postcommunist transitions are over. Across Eastern Europe, the transitions yielded much greater variety in political and economic institutional outcomes than was first anticipated. Although some postcommunist countries reached consolidated democracy, others deviated into new forms of authoritarianism, and still others lingered in hybrid-regime limbo. Socialism's command economy was successfully dismantled, but unexpected and distorted forms of capitalism arose in its place, often of a thuggish character, more freebooter than free market. And, finally, the transitions gave rise to very different types of postcommunist states, bearing little likeness to the ideal liberal state. Indeed, the major flaw in the neoliberal blueprint for the postcommunist transition was its assumption about the nature of state and society. From a neoliberal perspective, state and society were depicted as autonomous entities, in which society was seen as an aggregate of individuals with competing interests, while the state is composed of politically neutral institutions charged with private conflict resolution and public safety.

Postcommunist state building was unique in comparison with previous historical experience in that the flow of power resources ran from state to society, rather than in the opposite direction. The postcommunist state was bequeathed a rich inheritance of coercive and economic resources. Thus, the big question was where would the new line be drawn that staked out claims to coercion and capital between state and society? Early scholarship on the postcommunist transitions was strongly influenced by the underlying, and often unstated, neoliberal assumption of societal autonomy from the state. But society could not achieve this condition until it was able to consolidate its own claims on power resources, independent from and protected from the state. Because of this, the particular ways in which coercion and capital were reconfigured, more than anything else, shaped postcommunism's variant institutional outcomes.

This book has focused on the emergence of two different postcommunist states: a "contractual" state in Poland and a "predatory" state" in Russia. The Polish state evolved with greater checks on political power, internally through institutional checks and balances and externally through legal mechanisms that protect society's nascent autonomy. In Poland, the power resources of the old communist state were redistributed, and the state-society boundaries over coercion and capital were clearly marked. Coercion was tamed. The state's coercive resources were largely depoliticized and subordinated to institutional checks and civilian political control. As a result, capital was transformed. Economic resources were transformed into legally protected private property and new sources of entrepreneurial wealth were created. The state's new revenue claims on private wealth were recognized and legitimated. The emergence of the "contractual" state in Poland was facilitated by recurring political phenomenon of "elite consensus." It's not as if Polish politics in the 1990s was especially amicable; it wasn't. Even among ideological allies and erstwhile friends, political competition was divisive, often bitterly so. But at critical junctures in the Polish transition, these divisions were bridged by elite consensus.

By contrast, the Russian state evolved with fewer constraints on political power, internally through the rise of strong executives and externally through weak legal mechanisms that make society more vulnerable to political predation. The Russian state continued to have unchecked access to coercive resources. Coercion remained in the service of politics, while civilian control and legal constraints were ineffective and weak. As a result, capital remained vulnerable to state predation. The boundary line between public and private, and between state and society, was never clearly defined. Some economic resources were transformed into private property, but the most valued assets were made into economic concessions, which the state never fully relinquished its claim to. The Russian state struck a schizophrenic pose(s) on the use of coercion. State leaders at times railed against overly zealous tax inspectors and brought charges against conspicuously corrupt collectors, but more often acted oblivious to such behavior. The boundary line staking out the limits of coercion was ever shifting, and the state found it difficult to adhere to its own rules. State leaders could never come to agree on where the line should be drawn, or perhaps they never wanted to. Societal elites, meanwhile, remained divided among themselves, and they were incapable of defending their autonomy and claims on power resources. In the end, coercion was not subjected to institutional constraint, but to political convenience.

These institutional outcomes were not preordained, but rather they were the accumulated result of multiple contests among state actors, and between state and societal actors. In this regard, taxation was one of the principal arenas in which the battles over coercion and capital were fought and ultimately resolved. To try to explain the divergent state-building outcomes in Poland and Russia, this book has employed a "fiscal sociology" approach. It sought to uncover the economic and political constraints within which actors worked to realize their claims on economic resources in the building of a new tax system, and, in so doing, imparted a distinguishing character on the postcommunist state. I have systematically investigated the initial conditions, the politics of revenue bargaining, the norms of behavior in the transitional tax regimes, the development state fiscal capacity, and the reconfiguration of state-society relations. The occurrences that took place along the road to building a new tax system contributed to the emergence of Poland's "contractual" and Russia's "predatory" postcommunist states.

Initial Conditions At the outset of the postcommunist transition, Poland and Russia shared similar institutional and policy inheritances from the old regime. But more important for their subsequent trajectory, they differed fundamentally in their organization of capital and coercion. The initial conditions are the inheritance of the old regime. They constrain political maneuvering and policymaking early on. They are by no means insurmountable, imposing an inevitable transition destiny of democracy or despotism. But their influence is weighty and needs to be accounted for, especially regarding the strategic choices of political actors in the formative first phase of the postcommunist states. The uniqueness of postcommunist state building again is that the state is already in possession of a vast array of economic, coercive, and bureaucratic-legal resources at the start of the process. This condition is shared by all postcommunist states, but not in the same manner. Variations in economic and political structures at the time of the collapse of the old regime had a decisive influence on the construction of different tax regimes by postcommunist state builders.

Regarding capital, the postcommunist states started out revenue-dependent on a relatively small number of very large enterprises. The command economy of the old regime concentrated economic activity in industrial complexes in order to facilitate the management of its monopoly on economic resources. But this narrow revenue base posed a formidable challenge to postcommunist state builders: first, the necessity of expanding the base through the cultivation of new revenue sources; and, second, the need to refurbish the inherited administrative apparatus of tax collection, which was designed to serve the narrow revenue base of the command economy. But within this general structural constraint, particular variations existed concerning the location of revenue in the transition economies. In Poland, capital was dispersed and generated by commerce. The revenue base lacked reliable big income-generating enterprises, although it did include an already established and growing private sector of small businesses. By contrast, in Russia capital was concentrated and generated by commodities. The revenue base lacked a developing small-business private sector, but did contain very lucrative income sources in the energy and metallurgy export sectors. The extractive attention of state builders is drawn inevitably to those who generate wealth, and here is where one will find the conflicts and compromises that gave shape to transitional tax regimes.

Regarding coercion, although the particular way in which coercion is employed in postcommunist states was sorted out as part of the politics of the transition phase, this particular institutional outcome was strongly influenced by developments during the breakdown phase. Notable here is whether old regime elites or new counterelites, who each bring different experiences and inclinations about coercion, end up occupying positions of power in the postcommunist state. As a result, these variant elite structures affected how the coercive resources of the state were reconfigured in the new regime. In places where old regime elites prevailed, as in Russia, state coercive resources tended to be placed under executive control with weak political-institutional checks; in places where counterelites prevailed, as in Poland, state coercive resources tended to be subjected to parliamentary control with stronger institutional checks. Variant outcomes in the organization of coercion, in turn, influenced the types of compliance strategies most likely to be employed in the new tax systems.

Politics of Revenue Bargains   The organization of capital and coercion, in turn, directly influenced the politics of tax reform, giving rise to two different types of revenue bargains: Poland's "state-labor" revenue bargain and Russia's "state-elite" revenue bargain. Communist societies were among the most heavily taxed in the world, but the burden was hidden in the command economy. It would not be so easy, however, to conceal tax burdens in the transition economy, where state budgets and societal wealth were publicly scrutinized and debated. The revenue claims made by postcommunist states often encountered resistance from society. This resistance led state leaders to negotiate, in ad hoc and piecemeal fashion, revenue bargains with those societal actors who had access to wealth. The revenue bargains brought together three sets of interests: the economic interests of societal actors, the electoral interests of political actors, and the fiscal interests of the state. Most postcommunist states successfully enacted at least one major tax reform, based on a model of the mature capitalist states, early in the transition. A few others managed to implement a second major tax reform, based on a model of a low-rate flat-tax system, during the second transition decade. The success or failure of major tax reform attempts depended largely on the political constraints of postcommunist revenue bargains.

Because wealth was dispersed, the Polish state was forced to target worker households for revenue. In the 1990s, Poland pieced together a "state-labor" revenue bargain, by which public-sector wage earners were brought into the revenue net in exchange for social protection. In Russia, state leaders were forced to bargain with economic and regional elite actors, who made rival claims to concentrated high-yielding income sources. Russia's "state-elite" revenue bargain rested on an exchange of economic resources for political support. In both cases, revenue bargains eventually had a negative effect on the fiscal interests of the state. Enacting further tax reform, however, was not so easy. The Polish "state-labor" revenue bargain proved resilient to repeated attempts to undermine it by free market liberals when they controlled the Finance Ministry. In the end only the prospects of EU membership forced Polish elites to compromise and enact a partial tax reform, which still maintained most policy features of the revenue bargain. By contrast, in the early 2000s Russia enacted a second major reform, known as the "Russian Tax Revolution." Under a new president, Russia used coercion to break free of the political constraints of the "state-elite" revenue bargain and reassert the fiscal interests of the central state. Those who resisted were forcibly divested of the economic resources they acquired during the 1990s.

Making Transitional Tax Regimes In addition to tax-policy-compromising revenue bargains, transitional tax regimes entailed the means of extraction and the strategies of compliance devised by postcommunist states. In this case, Poland developed a tax regime based on "legalistic consent," while Russia built a tax regime based on "bureaucratic coercion." The revenue bargains that were formed in the early 1990s influenced the divergent shape of transitional tax regimes. In particular, revenue-bargain actors had an interest in particular means of extraction and patterns of compliance.

Regarding the means of extraction, the organization of state finances in general indicates whether the central state presides over a horizontally coherent and vertically coordinated system of revenue extraction. In Poland, the structure of state finances in the early transition was coherent and coordinated, in stark contrast to the structure of state finances in Russia. In the second decade, however, Poland moved to partially decentralize state finances, while Russia moved in an opposite, recentralizing direction. The tax administration is especially relevant as the state agency that directly interacts with society in the extraction process. The capacity and demeanor of the tax administration has enormous influence over the behavior of state and society in tax collection. Both Poland and Russia struggled throughout the transition to strengthen administrative capacity and develop a professional culture, with incremental success. Finally, the role of coercion in tax collection is a key component determining the character of a state's means of extraction. In Poland, coercion was institutionally constrained and played only a small role in tax collection; in Russia, coercion was never fully constrained and ended up playing a major role in tax collection.

The Polish and Russian transitional tax regimes were most notably distinguished from one another by contrasting state compliance strategies. Polish society responded quickly to macrostructural reform, to the opportunities of market capitalism as well as to the constraints of tax collection. As a result, the revenue base went from being highly concentrated to widely dispersed, from large enterprises to wage-earner households and petty capitalist entrepreneurs. The challenge for the postcommunist state was to locate and claim wealth from these small and numerous economic actors. The practical and legal limits on the tax administration meant that the state needed to cultivate at least some degree of voluntary compliance in society. And it succeeded. With the income generated from new revenue sources, the Polish state strengthened its fiscal capacity, becoming more resilient to the lingering threat of fiscal crisis. Polish society, meanwhile, learned quickly to work the new tax regime in wily ways to lighten its burden. Yet when compared to other postcommunist countries, the level of outright evasion in Poland was relatively low. Poland developed a tax regime based on "legalistic consent," a minimalist type of quasi-voluntary compliance. In principle, Polish society accepted its newly assigned status as taxpayers as well as the state's new revenue claims. In practice, however, Polish society tended to avoid complying in full and contrived a variety of formal and informal tactics to reduce its tax burden. Polish taxpayers big and small readily took advantage of tax law loopholes and legal checks on the state bureaucracy. As a result, the new targets of state tax collection—wage earners and petty capitalists—managed to hang on to a greater share of their wealth, while still paying something to the state. It was enough.

For Russia in the early part of the decade, coercion was not effectively incorporated into the new state system of revenue extraction. Tax claims were routinely ignored without a credible threat of sanction. By mid-decade, however, the state finally redirected its coercive talent to the task of tax collection. In particular, the state began to use coercion more readily against the new small-business sector. But the large corporate taxpayers, on whom the state was dependent for income, mostly remained insulated from coercive pressure to fulfill their tax obligations, protected by central and regional political patrons. Only after the reelection of Yeltsin in 1996 did the government attempt to deploy coercion against the largest tax delinquents in the corporate sector. But for all of the coercive potential inherent in the postcommunist state, the results of these initial efforts to use coercion to alter the state-elite revenue bargain were notably futile. But this all changed following the 1998 financial collapse and the 2000 presidential election. Putin was much less inhibited than his predecessor in using the coercive resources entrusted to central executive power. Because wealth was concentrated, the state did not have to negotiate with the new economic and regional elites; it could simply threaten them with the use of force. In the 2000s, the coercive and bureaucratic-administrative power resources of the state were often the most prominent feature of the revenue extraction process. The legal constraints on the power of state bureaucrats to encroach on society's wealth were vigorously enforced in Poland, but only selectively so in Russia. Instead, Russia's transitional tax regime was based on "bureaucratic coercion," which, in the words of the tax police chief, meant simply that "people must learn to be afraid of us."

Building Fiscal Capacity   Postcommunist tax regimes directly influenced state fiscal capacity. Here again postcommunist Poland and Russia provide contrasting cases, with similar starting points and different outcomes. The Polish state crafted a revenue bargain with wage-earning households and a tax regime based on "legalistic consent." In so doing, it broke out of the inherited constraint of a narrow base. By the mid-1990s, income was drawn increasingly from new sources, at sufficient volume and at reliable intervals. Consequently, the state was able to better manage credit and currency. The Russian state, meanwhile, crafted an elite revenue bargain and a tax regime based on "bureaucratic coercion." It remained fiscally dependent on large manufacturing and commodity exports in general and the energy sector in particular. By mid-decade, even these usually reliable sources of income could not meet the most basic fiscal needs. The state was forced to borrow more than it was capable of paying back and fiscal capacity was undermined. When the international financial crisis of 1998 reached Eastern Europe, Poland demonstrated sufficient fiscal capacity to withstand the financial shock, and achieved limited growth; by contrast, the international crisis exposed Russia's weak fiscal capacity, and the postcommunist state was forced to declare itself bankrupt.

In 2008, a second international financial crisis hit Eastern Europe, originating in the mature capitalist states. Like in 1998, Poland proved resilient; unlike 1998, Russia did as well. In the 2000s, Poland's transitional tax regime continued to provide a firm foundation for state fiscal capacity. The Polish state extracted revenue mainly from the domestic economy, which was sustained by consumption. Finance Minister Rostowski resisted urgent demands for an aggressive and expensive state intervention. State finances were stretched and the budget deficit grew, but in 2009 Poland's economy was the lone case of positive growth in Europe. In Russia, the 2008 capital crisis once again exposed the state's fiscal vulnerability to energy price decreases. Unlike 1998, however, Russian state finances survived. After nearly a decade of windfall petroleum profits and Finance Minister Kudrin's frugal management of tax revenues, state fiscal capacity was sufficiently strengthened to withstand the worst effects. It was enough to keep the economy going until late 2009, when the price of oil began to rise again and the economy showed signs of renewed growth.

Reconfiguring State-Society Relations   Postcommunist state building was unique in that the process entailed discarding, rather than accumulating, power resources. Indeed, the experience might better be called society building, instead of state building. In this regard, the accumulated results of the many battles that took place over taxation had an indelible impact in shaping postcommunist state-society relationships. More specifically, the process of institutional reconfiguration of coercion and capital led to "civil society" in Poland and to "dependent society" in Russia.

The limits on coercion were more clearly delineated through state-society battles over taxation. In Poland, an elite consensus formed very early, according to which society would be protected from state coercion. Consistent with this, the rules governing the use of coercion in tax collection were generally well defined and routinely enforced. As a consequence, tax avoidance was not criminalized; instead, state coercion in tax collection was tamed by firmly erected legal protections for society. In Russia, by contrast, the rules regarding coercion were enforced only sometimes, and certainly not if political authority intervened. Russia's postcommunist elites were divided among themselves, and they could never come to an agreement on the reconfiguration of power and wealth between state and society. This was clearly shown in the new tax regime, where tax avoidance was criminalized as state prerogative prevailed over the loosely grounded legal protections of the private realm. In Poland, state coercion was restrained and channeled into the legal system; in Russia, state coercion was unleashed and resided in the police and bureaucratic apparatus.

The norms of coercion, in turn, had a direct effect on the way in which capital and society was reorganized in the postcommunist transitions. In Poland, the tax system contributed directly to the consolidation of "social-market capitalism," an economy that embraces both free markets and social protections. In Russia, the tax system led directly to the consolidation of "concessions capitalism," a two-tiered economy in which, on one level, the state continues to own the most lucrative economic assets and, on the other level, the state espouses private property and entrepreneurship. The Russian state preempted the establishment of any institutions that might become an autonomous power base. The emergence of civil society required an independent basis of elite status, civic association, and moral authority. In postcommunist Eastern Europe, Poland was noteworthy for the reestablishment of civil society. Taxation helped enable Polish elites to maintain sources of wealth and status independent from the state, to bolster the capacity for self-organization of civic associations, and to reinforce the autonomy of the Church. But none of these developed in Russia, where the state used taxation to keep society weak. Most notably, the bureaucratic-coercive tax regime undermined the institutions that would protect private wealth. As a result, Russia's postcommunist elites remained dependent on the state; their roots in postcommunist society were neither wide nor deep. The social bases of civil society simply did not exist. Ultimately, the success or failure in constructing effective checks on coercive power and in formalizing private property rights, which was largely determined in the political battles over taxation, stand out as perhaps the most decisive developments in postcommunist state building.

Notes

INTRODUCTION

1. Edmund Burke, *Reflections on the Revolution in France* (New York: Anchor Books, 1973 ed.), 244.

2. The "realist" view of the state, associated with Niccolò Machiavelli and Max Weber, is distinguished from the "liberal" view, associated with Adam Smith, as well as the Marxist view, associated with Karl Marx and Friedrich Engels, and the "organic" view, associated with Georg Wilhelm Friedrich Hegel. For a sampling of classic writings on the state, see David Held, ed., *States and Societies* (New York: New York University Press, 1983).

3. Complementing coercion and capital are bureaucratic-administrative resources, which are included in this book as a separate unit of analysis, even though this resource is sometimes subsumed under coercion. The modern state is also sustained by ideological resources, most notably variant forms of ethnonationalisms and civic religions, which are expressed as socially binding normative narratives and sacred symbols that legitimate the modern state's claim to rule.

4. Charles Tilly, *Coercion, Capital and European States, AD 900–1992* (Oxford: Blackwell Publishers, 1994 reprint ed.), 17.

5. Charles Tilly, *Formation of Nation-States in Western Europe* (Princeton: Princeton University Press, 1977); Michael Mann, *The Sources of Social Power*, vol. 1 (Cambridge: Cambridge University Press, 1986).

6. Joel Migdal, *Strong Societies and Weak States: State-Society Relations and State Capabilities in the Third World* (Princeton: Princeton University Press, 1988); Karen Barkey, *Bandits and Bureaucrats: The Ottoman Route to State Centralization* (Ithaca: Cornell University Press, 1994); Guenther Roth, "Personal Rulership, Patrimonialism, and Empire-Building in the New States," *World Politics* 20, no. 2 (January 1968): 194–206.

7. This distinctive feature of postcommunist state building is highlighted in Timothy Colton and Stephen Homes, eds., *The State after Communism: Governance in the New Russia* (Lanham, Md.: Rowman and Littlefield, 2006); also, Philip Roeder, "Transitions from Communism: State-Centered Approaches," in *Can Democracy Take Root in Post-Soviet Russia?*, ed. Harry Eckstein, Frederic J. Fleron Jr., Erik P. Hoffmann, and William M. Reisinger (Lanham, Md.: Rowman and Littlefield, 1998).

8. The "recombinant" institutional character of postcommunism is well described in regard to the economic transformation in David Stark and Laszlo Bruszt, *Postsocialist Pathways* (New York: Cambridge University Press, 1998).

9. Gianfranco Poggi, *The Development of the Modern State: A Sociological Introduction* (Stanford: Stanford University Press, 1978); Mancur Olson, *Power and Prosperity* (New York: Basic Books, 2000); and Robert Bates, *Prosperity and Violence: The Political Economy of Development* (New York: Norton, 2001).

10. Margaret Levi, "The Predatory Theory of Rule," *Politics and Society* 10, no. 4 (December 1981): 431–65; Peter Evans, "Predatory, Developmental, and Other Apparatuses: A Comparative Political Economy on the Third World State," *Sociological Forum* 4, no. 4 (1989): 561–87; Robert Bates, *When Things Fell Apart: State Failure in Late-Century*

Africa (New York: Cambridge University Press, 2008); Larry Diamond, "Democratic Rollback: The Return of the Predatory State," *Foreign Affairs* (March–April 2008).

1. TOWARD A FISCAL SOCIOLOGY OF THE POSTCOMMUNIST STATE

1. A notable exception to these early trends was Alice Amsden, Jacek Kochanowicz, and Lance Taylor, *The Market Meets Its Match* (Cambridge: Harvard University Press, 1994). The state also went missing in the early comparative transitions literature, although it was incorporated into analysis after considering the postcommunist cases. Guillermo O'Donnell, "On the State, Democratization and Some Conceptual Problems: A Latin American View with Glances at Some Postcommunist Countries," *World Development* 21, no. 8 (1993): 1355–69; and Juan Linz and Alfred Stepan, *Problems of Democratic Transition and Consolidation: Southern Europe, South America, Eastern Europe* (Baltimore: Johns Hopkins University Press, 1996).

2. Robert Plant, *The Neo-Liberal State* (Oxford: Oxford University Press, 2010); David Held, *Political Theory and the Modern State* (Stanford: Stanford University Press, 1989); and Martin Carnoy, *The State and Political Theory* (Princeton: Princeton University Press, 1984).

3. Keith Darden, *Economic Liberalism and Its Rivals: Formation of International Institutions among Post-Communist States* (Cambridge: Cambridge University Press, 2009).

4. Anders Aslund and Richard Layard, eds., *Changing the Economic System in Russia* (New York: St. Martin's Press, 1993).

5. Jeffrey Sachs, *Poland's Jump to the Market Economy* (Cambridge: MIT Press, 1993), 3.

6. Oliver Blanchard, *The Economics of Post-Communist Transition* (Oxford: Clarendon Press, 1997), 1–3.

7. Anders Aslund, *Building Capitalism: Transformation of the Soviet Bloc* (Cambridge: Cambridge University Press, 2001).

8. Richard Ericson, "Economics and the Russian Transition," *Slavic Review* 57, no. 3 (Fall 1998); Joseph Stiglitz, *Globalization and Its Discontents* (New York: Norton and Sons, 2002).

9. Marshall Goldman, *Lost Opportunity: What Has Made Economic Reform in Russia So Difficult?* (New York: Norton, 1996).

10. Janine Wedel, *Collision and Collusion: The Strange Case of Western Aid to Eastern Europe* (New York: Palgrave Macmillan, 1998).

11. Sachs, *Poland's Jump to the Market Economy*, xiii.

12. Some economists interested in the postcommunist transition were clearly cognizant of coercion. See Mancur Olson, "Dictatorship, Democracy, and Development," *American Political Science Review* 87, no. 3 (September 1993): 567–76. But Olson's "rational actor" explanation for the historical reconciliation of coercion and capital in the form of the "stationary bandit" was not included in the neoliberal reform blueprints devised by international financial institutions or their attendant advisers.

13. Two excellent studies that feature the adaptation of communist coercion to the transition economy are Alena Ledeneva, *How Russia Really Works* (Ithaca: Cornell University Press, 2006), and Vadim Volkov, *Violent Entrepreneurs: The Use of Force in the Making of Russian Capitalism* (Ithaca: Cornell University Press, 2002).

14. Thomas Schelling, "Economics and Criminal Enterprise," *Public Interest* 7 (Spring 1967): 61–78; Milton and Rose Friedman, *Free to Choose: A Personal Statement* (New York: Harcourt, 1980).

15. At the forefront of this scholarly reaction was Stephen Homes, "Cultural Legacies or State Collapse," in *Postcommunism: Four Perspectives*, ed. Michael Mandelbaum (New York: Council on Foreign Relations, 1996).

16. This book employs concepts common in comparative theory on the state. The concepts of state "despotic" power, meaning policymaking, and state "infrastructural" power, meaning policy implementation, are borrowed from Michael Mann, "The Autonomous Power of the State," in *States in History*, ed. John Hall (Oxford: Basil Blackwell, 1986). The imprecise concepts of "strong" and "weak" are used as a basic indicator for comparing states and evaluating state-society relations. A strong state is likely to possess institutional coherence, professional expertise, administrative competence, and decision-making autonomy. It is capable of making policy and implementing policy without interference from nonstate actors. A strong society is likely to exhibit the capacity for self-organization and collective action. In a strong society, the state does not monopolize access to economic, ideological, and status resources. For further discussion of these concepts, see Migdal, *Strong Societies and Weak States* Joel Migdal, Atul Kohli, and Vivienne Shue, eds., *State Power and Social Forces: Domination and Transformation in the Third World.* (New York: Cambridge University Press, 1994); and Peter Evans, *Embedded Autonomy: States and Industrial Transformation* (Princeton: Princeton University Press, 1995). In evaluating state capacity, comparative theory tends to employ a "functionalist" approach in that the focus is on the "ends" of state policy. For a critique of this approach, which draws attention to the "means" of state policy, see Robert Jackman, *Power without Force: The Political Capacity of Nation-States* (Ann Arbor: University of Michigan Press, 1993).

17. See Joel Hellman, Geraint Jones, and Daniel Kaufman, "Seize the Day, Seize the State," *World Bank: Policy Research Working Paper* no. 2444 (2000); Kathryn Stoner-Weiss, *Resisting the State: Reform and Retrenchment in Post-Soviet Russia* (New York: Cambridge University Press; 2006); Vanelin Ganev, *Preying on the State* (Ithaca: Cornell University Press, 2007).

18. The incapable state is described in Cynthia Roberts and Thomas Sherlock, "Bringing the Russian State Back In: Explanations of the Derailed Transition to Market Democracy," *Comparative Politics* 31, no. 4 (July 1999): 477–98; Valerie Sperling, ed., *Building the Russian State: Institutional Crisis and the Quest for Democratic Governance* (Boulder, Colo.: Westview Press, 2000); and Gerald M. Easter, "Politics of Revenue Extraction in Post-Communist States: Poland and Russia Compared," *Politics and Society* 30, no. 4 (2002): 599–627.

19. See, for example, Joseph Blasi, Maya Kroumova, and Douglas Kruse, *Kremlin Capitalism: The Privatization of the Russian Economy* (Ithaca: Cornell University Press, 1997); Alena Ledeneva, *Russia's Economy of Favors* (New York: Cambridge University Press, 1998); and Stefanie Harter and Gerald Easter, eds., *Shaping the Economic Space in Russia* (Aldershot, England: Ashgate Publishers, 2000).

20. See Timothy Frye and Andrei Schleifer, "The Invisible Hand and the Grabbing Hand," *American Economic Review: Proceedings and Papers*, vol. 87 (1997): 354–58; Stefan Hedlund, *Russia's Market Economy: A Bad Case of Predatory Capitalism* (London: Routledge, 1999); Conor O'Dwyer, *Runaway State Building: Patronage Politics and Democratic Development* (Baltimore: Johns Hopkins University Press, 2006).

21. For predators, bandits, and racketeers, see Margaret Levi, "The Predatory Theory of Rule," *Politics and Society* 10, no. 4 (2001): 431–65; Mancur Olson. "Dictatorship, Democracy, and Development," *American Political Science Review* 87, no. 3 (September 1993): 567–76; Charles Tilly, "State-Making and War-Making as a Protection Racket," in *Bringing the State Back In*, ed. Peter Evans, Dietrich Reuschmeyer, and Theda Skocpol (New York: Cambridge University Press, 1986).

22. Tilly, *Coercion, Capital and European States.*

23. See, for example, the excellent case studies in David Newbury, *Tax and Benefit Reform in Central and Eastern Europe* (London: Centre for Economic Policy Research, 1995); Jozef van Brabant, *The Political Economy of Transition: Coming to Grips with History and Methodology* (London: Routledge, 1998), 93.

24. *Komsomolskaia Pravda*, 25 August 1998.

25. Thane Gustafson, *Capitalism Russian-Style* (New York: Cambridge University Press, 1999), 193.

26. As an example of this earlier literature, see Walter Bagehot's classic study, *The English Constitution* (New York: Oxford University Press, 2001 [1867]).

27. Tilly's 1975 edited volume on West European state building, *The Formation of National States in Western Europe*, was an influential forerunner of the "return to the state" in political science. It included two chapters devoted to taxation and state building: Gabriel Ardant, "Financial Policy and Economic Infrastructure of Modern States and Nations," and Rudolf Braun, "Taxation, Socio-political Structure, and State-Building: Great Britain and Brandenburg-Prussia," but these European historians did not have an immediate impact on American comparativists.

28. Margaret Levi, *Of Rule and Revenue* (Berkeley: University of California Press, 1988).

29. For democracy, see Robert Bates and Donald Lien, "A Note on Taxation, Development, and Representative Government," *Politics and Society* 14, no. 1 (1985): 53–70. For the resources curse, see Terry Karl, *The Paradox of Plenty: Oil Booms and Petro-States* (Berkeley: University of California Press, 1997); also, a good review of this literature is Michael Ross, "The Political Economy of the Resource Curse," *World Politics* 5, no. 2 (January 1999): 297–322.

30. Scott Gehlbach, *Representation through Taxation: Taxability and the Political Economy of Postcommunism* (Cambridge: Cambridge University Press, 2008).

31. Sven Steinmo, *Taxation and Democracy: Swedish, British, and American Approaches to Financing the Modern State* (New Haven: Yale University Press, 1993), 7.

32. For domestic politics, see Steinmo, *Taxation and Democracy*, and Sven Steinmo and Caroline Tolbert, "Do Institutions Really Matter? Taxation and Industrial Democracies," *Comparative Political Studies* 31, no. 2 (1998): 165–87; also see the review by Andrew Gould, "Democracy and Taxation," *Annual Review of Political Science*, vol. 5 (2002): 87–110. For regime types, see Mancur Olson, *Power and Prosperity: Outgrowing Communist and Capitalist Dictatorships* (New York: Basic Books, 2000); a critique of Olson is found in Jose Cheibub, "Political Regimes and the Extractive Capacity of Governments: Taxation in Democracies and Dictatorships," *World Politics* 50, no. 3 (1998): 349–76. For international forces, see the review and critique by Mark Hallerberg and Scott Basinger, "Internationalization and Changes in Tax Policy in OECD Countries: The Importance of Domestic Veto Players," *Comparative Political Studies* 31, no. 3 (June 1998): 321–52.

33. See, respectively, Anna Grzymala-Busse, *Reinventing Leviathan: The Politics of Administrative Reform in Developing Countries* (New York: Cambridge University Press, 2007); Daniel Treisman, "Russia's Tax Crisis: Explaining Falling Revenues in a Transitional Economy," *Economics and Politics* 11, no. 2 (July 1999): 145–69, Andre Schleifer and Daniel Treisman, *Without a Map: Political Tactics and Economic Reform in Russia* (Cambridge: MIT Press, 2000); and Hilary Appel, *Tax Politics in Eastern Europe* (Ann Arbor: University of Michigan Press, 2011).

34. Evan Lieberman, *Race and Regionalism in the Politics of Taxation in Brazil and South Africa* (New York: Cambridge University Press, 2003). Other works that take a cultural approach include Carolyn Webber and Aaron Wildavsky, *A History of Taxation and Expenditure in the Western World* (New York: Simon and Schuster, 1986).

35. John Scholz and Neil Pinney, "Duty, Fear, and Tax Compliance: The Heuristic Basis of Citizenship Behavior," *American Journal of Political Science* 39, no. 2 (May 1995): 490–512. Benno Torgler stands at the forefront of an extensive examination of the social-cultural influences on "tax morale," including the findings that large numbers of practicing Protestants and ethnic homogeneity correlate positively with higher levels of tax

compliance. Benno Torgler, *Tax Compliance and Tax Morale* (Cheltenham, U.K.: Edward Elgar, 2007).

36. Marc Berenson, "Less Fear, Little Trust: Deciphering the Whys of Ukrainian Tax Compliance," in *Orange Revolution and Aftermath: Mobilization, Apathy, and the State in Ukraine*, ed. P. D'Anieri (Baltimore: Johns Hopkins University Press, 2010). Also see the chapters on Eastern Europe by Benno Torgler, Katarina Ott, Jan Hanousek, and Filip Palda in Nicolas Hayoz and Simon Hug, eds., *Tax Evasion, Trust, and State Capacities* (Bern: Peter Lang, 2007).

37. The second wave of postcommunist scholarship was more interested in institutions than the first, yet the influence of neoliberal economics on the study of postcommunist politics remained strong. In this regard, the issue of taxation highlights the way in which scholarship on Eastern Europe fundamentally diverged from scholarship on China, where research on taxation instinctively sought out political explanations. Thomas P. Bernstein and Xiaobo Lu, *Taxation without Representation in Contemporary Rural China* (New York: Cambridge University Press, 2008); Victor Shih, *Factions and Finance in China* (New York: Cambridge University Press, 2009).

38. As an exception, coercion has been a consistent theme in the political economy approach of Timothy Frye; for example, see "Credible Commitment and Property Rights: Evidence from Russia," *American Political Science Review* 98. no. 3 (August 2004): 453–66.

39. Tilly, "State-Making and War-Making as a Protection Racket"; Tilly, *Coercion, Capital, and European States*.

40. Ardant, "Financial Policy and Economic Infrastructure of Modern States and Nations," 174.

41. Philip Hoffman and Kathy Norberg, eds., *Fiscal Crises, Liberty, and Representative Government, 1450–1789* (Stanford: Stanford University Press, 2004); Richard Bonney, ed., *The Rise of the Fiscal State in Europe, 1200–1815* (Oxford: Oxford University Press, 1999); Thomas Ertman, *Birth of the Leviathan: Building States and Regimes in Medieval and Early Modern Europe* (New York: Cambridge University Press, 1997); John Brewer, *The Sinews of Power: War, Money, and the English State* (Cambridge: Harvard University Press, 1988); Sheldon Pollack, *War, Revenue, and State Building: Financing the Development of the American State* (Ithaca: Cornell University Press, 2009).

42. Much of Schumpeter's work was translated and incorporated into Anglo-American social science; see the collection of essays *Capitalism, Socialism, and Democracy* (New York: Harper and Row, 1976, 3rd ed.). Schumpeter is still best known for the concepts of "business cycle" and "creative destruction" in reference to modern capitalism. Very little of Goldscheid's extensive work on the sociology of taxation has been translated. See his article "Some Controversial Questions in the Theory of Taxation," in *Classics in the Theory of Public Finance*, ed. R. A. Musgrave and A. T. Peacock (London: Macmillan Press, 1958).

43. Several articles that do a good job of dissecting and summarizing the main points of Schumpeter's fiscal sociology in relation to the modern state are John Campbell, "The State and Fiscal Sociology," *Annual Review of Sociology*, vol. 19 (1993): 163–85; Jürgen Backhaus, "Fiscal Sociology: What For?" *American Journal of Economics and Sociology*, vol. 61 (2002): 55–78; Mick Moore, "Revenues, State Formation, and the Quality of Governance in Developing Countries," *International Political Science Review* 25, no. 3 (2004): 297–319; and Alexander Ebner, "Institutions, Entrepreneurship, and the Rationale of Government: An Outline of the Schumpeterian Theory of the State," *Journal of Economic Behavior and Organization*, vol. 59 (2006): 497–515.

44. Joseph Schumpeter, "The Crisis of the Tax State," *International Economic Papers* vol. 4 (1954): 6.

45. Ibid., 16.

46. For a sympathetic discussion of the limits of Schumpeter's analysis to the twentieth-century tax state, see R. A. Musgrave, "Schumpeter's Crisis of the Tax State: An Essay in Fiscal Sociology," *Journal of Evolutionary Economics* 2, no. 2 (1992): 89–113.

47. The field of public finance was influenced by German-born Richard Musgrave, who was a student of Schumpeter's. Musgrave stressed the social limits of the market and subsequent need for the state to play a corrective role through fiscal policy. His seminal text was *A Theory of Public Finance*, first published in 1959. The rival to this approach was public choice theory, associated with James Buchanan, which saw the state as a negative influence on economic activity and advocated a restrained fiscal policy to curb its distorting interventions. Their competing views about the state and taxation are nicely summarized and debated in James Buchanan and Richard Musgrave, *Public Finance and Public Choice: Two Contrasting Visions of the State* (Cambridge: MIT Press, 1999).

48. See, for example, the collection of essays and retrospectives in Malcolm Gillis, ed., *Tax Reform in Developing Countries* (Durham, N.C.: Duke University Press, 1989). Two classics from this literature include Carl S. Shoup, John Due, and Lyle Fitch, *The Fiscal System of Venezuela* (Baltimore: Johns Hopkins University Press, 1959), and Richard M. Bird, *Taxation and Development: Lessons from Colombian Experience* (Cambridge: Harvard University Press, 1970).

49. James O'Connor, *The Fiscal Crisis of the State* (New York: St. Martin's, 1973); Fred Block, "The Fiscal Crisis of the Capitalist State," *Annual Review of Sociology* vol. 7 (August 1981): 1–27.

50. David Jacobs and Don Waldman, "Toward a Fiscal Sociology: Determinants of Tax Regressivity in the American State," *Social Science Quarterly*, vol. 64 (1983): 550–65.

51. Campbell, "State and Fiscal Sociology," 163.

52. Isaac Martin, Ajay Mehrota, and Monica Prasad, eds., *The New Fiscal Sociology: Taxation in Comparative and Historical Perspective* (New York: Cambridge University Press, 2009); Deborah Brautigam, Odd-Helge Fjeldstad, and Mick Moore, *Taxation and State-Building in Developing Countries* (Cambridge: Cambridge University Press, 2008); Richard Wagner, "States and the Crafting of Souls: Mind, Society, and Fiscal Sociology," *Journal of Economic Behavior and Organization*, vol. 59 (April 2006): 516–24.

53. Moore, "Revenues, State Formation, and the Quality of Governance," 298.

54. Pioneering work in this area was done by sociologist John Campbell, "An Institutional Analysis of Fiscal Reform in Postcommunist Europe," *Theory and Society*, vol. 25 (1996): 45–84.

55. Three variations in elite composition occurred during the transition process: (1) regime breakdown from below, in which society was organized, putting pressure on the regime from below, and counterelites came to power, taking responsibility for the power resources of the state; (2) regime breakdown from above, in which old regime elites briefly shared power with counterelites before eventually reconsolidating their dominant place in the state; and (3) regime breakdown from without, in which old regime elites were able to maintain their access to power resources without significant challenge from counterelites. See Gerald M. Easter, "Preference for Presidentialism: Regime Change in Russia and the NIS," *World Politics* 49, no. 2 (January 1997): 184–211.

2. THE FISCAL CRISIS OF THE OLD REGIME

1. See the excellent collection of essays in Hoffman and Norberg, eds., *Fiscal Crises, Liberty, and Representative Government*; Bonney, ed., *The Rise of the Fiscal State in Europe*

2. Lawrence Stone, *The Causes of the English Revolution* (New York: Harper Torchbook, 1972), and Michael Kwass, *Privilege and the Politics of Taxation in Eighteenth Century France* (Cambridge: Cambridge University Press, 2000).

3. Marc Bloch, *Feudal Society*, vol. 1 (Chicago: University of Chicago Press, 1961), 241.

4. For a good discussion of the recurring patterns of social organization in Soviet and tsarist Russia, see Robert Tucker, *Stalinism: Essays in Historical Interpretation* (New York: Norton, 1978).

5. "The Eighteenth Brumaire of Louis Napoleon," cited in Robert Tucker, ed., *The Marx- Engels Reader* (New York: Norton, 1978, 2nd ed.), 612.

6. Karl Marx, *Capital*, vol. 1 (New York: Vintage Press, 1977), 921, 922.

7. Rudolf Hilferding, *Finance Capital* (London: Routledge and Kegan Paul, 1985), chap. 23, "Finance Capital and Classes."

8. Rosa Luxemburg, *The Accumulation of Capital* (New York: Monthly Review Books, 1968), chap. 32.

9. N. Bukharin and E. Preobrazhensky, *The ABC of Communism* (Ann Arbor: University of Michigan Press, 1966), 337.

10. Janet Martin, *Medieval Russia, 900–1584* (New York: Cambridge University Press, 1995).

11. Jerome Blum, *Lord and Peasant in Russia* (Princeton: Princeton University Press, 1961), 605.

12. Olga Crisp, *Studies in the Russian Economy before 1914* (London: Macmillan, 1976), 9, 10, 80.

13. Robert Gorlin, "Problems of Tax Reform in Imperial Russia," *Journal of Modern History* 49, no. 2 (June 1977): 246–65.

14. Late imperial Russia's modernization drive was also hurried along by an injection of foreign capital, which brought a crippling debt. Theodore von Laue, *Sergei Witte and the Industrialization of Russia* (New York: Columbia University Press, 1963).

15. Alfred Rieber, *Merchants and Entrepreneurs in Imperial Russia* (Chapel Hill, N.C.: University of North Carolina Press, 1982).

16. Stefan Plaggenborg, "Tax Policy and the Question of Peasant Poverty in Tsarist Russia," *Cahiers du monde russe* 36, nos. 1–2 (January–June 1995): 53–70.

17. Crisp, *Studies in Russian Economy*, 27.

18. Patricia Herlihy, *The Alcoholic Empire: Vodka and Politics in Late Imperial Russia* (New York: Oxford University Press, 2002), chap. 8.

19. Yanni Kotsonis, "Face to Face: The State, the Individual and the Citizen in Russian Taxation, 1863–1917," *Slavic Review* 63, no. 2 (Summer 2004): 228.

20. A. I. Tolkushkin, *Istoriia nalogov v Rossii* (Moscow: Iurist, 2001), 197.

21. V. I. Lenin, "Immediate Tasks of Soviet Government" (April 1918), in *The Lenin Anthology*, ed. Robert Tucker (New York: Norton, 1977), 445.

22. E. H. Carr, *The Bolshevik Revolution, 1917–1923*, vol. 2 (New York: Norton and Co., 1985), 247–48.

23. Maurice Dobb, *Soviet Economic Development since 1917* (New York: International Publishers, 1948), 101.

24. Carr, *Bolshevik Revolution*, vol. 2, 260.

25. V. I. Lenin, "The Tax-in-Kind," quoted in Alexander Erlich, *The Soviet Industrialization Debate* (Cambridge: Harvard University Press, 1960), 6.

26. The NEP also brought the reinstatement of the "self-tax" system (*samoblozhenie*), which gave peasant villages fiscal autonomy over local finances, cutting the state out of the matter. E. H. Carr, *Foundations of the Planned Economy*, vol. 2 (London: Macmillan, 1971), 464–66.

27. Dobb, *Soviet Economic Development*, 141.

28. Alan Ball, *Russia's Last Capitalists: The Nepmen, 1921–1929* (Berkeley: University of California Press, 1987).

29. A most interesting firsthand account of the early Bolshevik tax administration is found in the memoirs of Soviet finance minister A. G. Zverev: *Zapiski ministra* (Moscow: Politizdat, 1973), 79.

30. Moshe Lewin, *The Making of the Soviet System* (New York: Pantheon Books, 1985).

31. Franklyn Holzman, *Soviet Taxation* (Cambridge: Harvard University Press, 1955), 114, 115.

32. Tolkushkin, *Istoriia nalogov*, 205.

33. Moshe Lewin, *Russian Peasants and Soviet Power* (New York; Norton, 1975), 516.

34. The pro-NEP side was represented by the "Rightists," including Nikolai Bukharin; the anti-NEP side was represented by the "Leftists," including Evgeny Preobrazhensky. For good summations of the economics and the politics of the debate, see Alexander Erlich, *The Soviet Industrialization Debate* (Cambridge: Harvard University Press, 1960), and Stephen Cohen, *Bukharin and the Bolshevik Revolution: A Political Biography, 1888–1938* (New York: Knopf, 1973).

35. R. W. Davies, *The Soviet Economy in Turmoil, 1929–1930* (Cambridge: Harvard University Press, 1989), 97–99; Carr, *Foundations of the Planned Economy*, 466, 467; Ball, *Russia's Last Capitalists*, 140–45.

36. William Conyngham, *Industrial Management in the Soviet Union: The Role of the CPSU in Industrial Decision-Making, 1917–1970* (Stanford: Hoover Institution Press, 1973).

37. A nice summary of the 1930 tax reform is found in Holzman, *Soviet Taxation*, 118–22. Turnover and profits taxes provided the vast majority of income from the state sector. Other sources of revenue from the state sector included a corporate income tax on cooperatives and miscellaneous administrative and user fees.

38. Dobb, *Soviet Economic Development*, 385. The turnover tax alone accounted for two-thirds of all taxes collected at this time.

39. Stephen Wegren, *Agriculture and the State in Soviet and Post-Soviet Russia* (Pittsburgh, Penn.: University of Pittsburgh Press, 1998). The term "urban bias," however, should not imply that urban households got off easy with the tax burden, because they did not.

40. For the politics behind this adjustment, see Gerald M. Easter, *Reconstructing the State: Personal Networks and Elite Identity in Soviet Russia* (New York: Cambridge University Press, 2000), chap. 6.

41. Lewin, *Making of the Soviet System*, 142–77.

42. Holzman, *Soviet Taxation*, 179 (table 29).

43. Alec Nove, *An Economic History of the USSR* (New York: Penguin Books, 1982 rev. ed.), 253.

44. Zverev, *Zapiski ministra*, 198.

45. Tolkushkin, *Istoriia nalogov*, 252.

46. Holzman, *Soviet Taxation*, 200–206 (table 45).

47. Ibid., 229 (table 49), 252 (table 52).

48. Roman Szporluk, *Russia, Ukraine and the Breakup of the Soviet Union* (Stanford: Hoover Institution Press, 2000).

49. For good political overviews of these events, see Joseph Rothschild and Nancy M. Wingfield, *Return to Diversity: A Political History of East Central Europe since World War II* (New York: Oxford University Press, 1989); Michael Bernhard, *The Origins of Democratization in Poland* (New York: Columbia University Press, 1993); and Grzegorz Ekiert, *The State against Society: Political Crises and Their Aftermath in East Central Europe* (Princeton: Princeton University Press, 1996). For an economic overview, see Ben Slay, *The Polish Economy* (Princeton: Princeton University Press, 1994).

50. Slay, *Polish Economy*, 16.

51. John Montias, *Central Planning in Poland* (New Haven: Yale University Press, 1962), 52–55. Poland's postwar economic debates resembled those in Soviet Russia during the 1920s. The more moderate socialist position was represented by Czeslaw Bobrowski in the Central Planning Office, while the more radical position was represented by Hilary Minc in the Industry and Trade Ministry. The new finance minister, Tadeusz Dietrich, was an ally of Hilary Minc and the pro-Soviet industrializationists.

52. Montias, *Central Planning in Poland*, 55.

53. Ibid., 132.

54. Ibid., 63, 195, 206.

55. Batara Simatupang, *The Polish Economic Crisis* (London: Routledge, 1994), 134–35.

56. Ibid.

57. Montias, *Central Planning in Poland*, 156–57. Michal Kalecki was one of the twentieth century's most respected socialist economists. He moved to the West after World War II but still consulted with Poland's communist government.

58. Ibid., 313. The United States loaned Poland $93 million.

59. The *Dziady* was an ancient Slavic custom, where a large feast was held to commemorate deceased ancestors. Mickiewicz's epic poem by the same name gave the celebration added political significance for its nationalist inspiration at the time of Poland's partition among Central Eastern Europe's despotic empires.

60. Simatupang, *Polish Economic Crisis*, 157–59.

61. Kazimierz Poznanski, *Poland's Protracted Transition* (Cambridge: Cambridge University Press, 1996), 5 (table 1.1); Simatupang, *Polish Economic Crisis*, 54, 56; *Rocznik statystyczny handlu zagranicznego 1983* (Warsaw: GUS, 1983), 73.

62. Mario Nuti, "Hidden and Repressed Inflation in Soviet-Type Economies," *Contributions to Political Economy*, vol. 5 (1986): 37–82.

63. Slay, *Polish Economy*, chap. 1.

64. Poznanski, *Poland's Protracted Transition*, 25–29.

65. Robert Thurston and Bernd Bonwetsch, eds., *The People's War: Responses to World War II in the Soviet Union* (Urbana-Champagne: University of Illinois Press, 2000); Amir Weiner, *Making Sense of War: The Second World War and the Fate of the Bolshevik Revolution* (Princeton: Princeton University Press, 2000).

66. Nove, *Economic History of the USSR*, 325–27, 348–50. In 1956, tax exemptions were expanded for low income households, and in 1957 wartime taxes on single women and childless couples were eliminated.

67. Zverev, *Zapiski ministra*, 251.

68. J. A. Newth, "Income Distribution in the USSR," *Soviet Studies* 12, no. 2 (October 1960): 193–96.

69. Linda Cook, *The Soviet Social Contract and Why It Failed* (Cambridge: Harvard University Press, 1993).

70. The notion of the "human factor" that animated Gorbachev's vision of reform socialism was described in an influential article in the party's main theoretical journal by the Novosibirsk sociologist and Gorbachev adviser, Tatyana Zaslavskaya; *Kommunist,* no. 3 (1987): 97–108.

71. For good overviews and analysis of Gorbachev's reform agenda, see Moshe Lewin, *The Gorbachev Phenomenon* (Berkeley: University of California Press, 1991, expanded ed.); Archie Brown, *The Gorbachev Factor* (Oxford: Oxford University Press, 1997); William Green Miller, ed., *Toward a More Civil Society: The USSR under Mikhail S. Gorbachev* (New York: Harper, 1989).

72. Remarks made at June 1987 Plenum of CPSU. For Gorbachev's economic reform agenda, see Ed Hewett, *Reforming the Soviet Economy* (Washington, D.C.: Brookings Institution Press, 1988).

73. This figure came from Gorbachev himself. CIA: "USSR: Sharply Higher Deficits Threaten Perestroika: A Research Paper" (CIA: Sov-88-10043U; September 1988), 7.

74. Ibid, 9, 12.

75. Stephen Crowley, *Hot Coal, Cold Steel: Russian and Ukrainian Workers from the End of the Soviet Union to the Post-Communist Transformations* (Ann Arbor: University of Michigan Press, 1997), chap. 2.

76. CIA: "USSR: Sharply Higher Deficits Threaten Perestroika," x; and R. Kaufman and J. Hardt, eds., *The Former Soviet Union in Transition: US Congress, Joint Economic Commission* (Armonk, N.Y.: M. E. Sharpe, 1993), 47 (table 5).

77. Martin Gilman, *No Precedent, No Plan: Inside Russia's 1998 Default* (Cambridge: MIT Press, 2010), 11.

78. D. Chernik, A. Pochinok and V. Morozov, *Osnovy nalogovoi sistemy*, 2nd ed. (Moscow: Iuniti, 2000), 156.

79. *New York Times*, 18 March 1991, 10.

80. The Soviet state center also made a feeble attempt to use coercion to try to suppress the nationalist upsurge. In January 1991, Gorbachev issued a decree giving the KGB broad powers to investigate "economic sabotage." The KGB's elite Alpha unit staged an ill-conceived and poorly executed coup against the nationalist-controlled Lithuanian parliament, which only showed the ineptness of the state center and accelerated the process of territorial disintegration.

81. *Izvestiia*, 22 May 1991, 2.

82. V. M. Rodionov, ed., *Finansy* (Moscow: Finansy i statistiki, 1992), 273.

83. *Izvestiia*, 26 July 1991, 2.

84. A notable exception on this point is Anders Aslund, who quite accurately equated Gorbachev's handling of state finances with Edward Gierek's performance in Poland. See Aslund, *Gorbachev's Struggle for Economic Reform* (Ithaca: Cornell University Press, 1991), 222; also see Vladimir Mau and Irina Starodubrovskaya, *The Challenge of Revolution: Contemporary Russia in Historical Perspective* (Oxford: Oxford University Press, 2001).

85. Poznanski, *Poland's Protracted Transition*, 84.

86. Ibid., 91 (table 4.1).

87. Slay, *Polish Economy*, 52, 53 (table 2.1).

88. Poznanski, *Poland's Protracted Transition*, 89.

89. Slay, *Polish Economy*, 53 (table 2.1).

90. Britain's Margaret Thatcher visited Poland in 1988, and affirmed to Jaruzelski that in the absence of political liberalization, there would be no financial assistance or debt relief from the West.

91. *Economist*, 3 December 1988, 52.

92. In this scheme, most powers were allocated to the lower house, the Sejm, which had 460 seats, of which two-thirds were set aside for the communist party and its allies; the less powerful upper house, the Senate, had 100 seats, which were all openly contested.

93. *Guardian*, 1 August 1989.

94. *New York Times*, 26 May 1988.

95. John Tedstrom, "Problem of Fiscal Policy Reform during the Transition: A Baltic Case Study," in *Former Soviet Union in Transition*, ed. John P. Hardt and Richard F. Kaufman, 220–21 (Washington, D.C.: Joint Economic Committee, Congress of the United States, 1993).

96. Ibid.

97. James Duran, "Russian Fiscal and Monetary Stabilization," in *Former Soviet Union in Transition*, ed. Hardt and Kaufman, 201.

98. In late 1990, Yeltsin reached agreements with Sakha-Yakutia over the division of spoils from the region's diamond industry and, in April 1991, with Tatarstan over oil revenues. *Times* (London), 31 December 1990; *Guardian*, 20 April 1991.

99. Piroska Nagy, "The Fiscal Component of the First Russian Stabilization Effort, 1992–93." In *Fiscal Policy and Economic Reform*, ed. Mario Blejer and Teresa Ter-Minassian, 224–25 (London: Routledge, 1997).

100. *Rossiiskaia gazeta*, 10 January 1991.

101. *Financial Times*, 29 July 1991, 7.

102. Mikhail Gorbachev, *Memoirs* (New York: Doubleday, 1995), 382.

103. The tax compromise was the last and most contentious issue to be negotiated between the center and the republics in the New Union Treaty, found in "Article Nine: On Union Taxes and Levies." Gorbachev, *Memoirs*, 628.

104. Duran, "Russian Fiscal and Monetary Stabilization," 201.

105. *Rossiiskaia gazeta*, 1 November 1991.

106. Aslund, *Gorbachev's Struggle*, 204.

107. *New York Times*, 22 November 1991.

108. *Rossiiskaia gazeta*, 30 November 1991.

109. Boris Yeltsin, *The Struggle for Russia* (New York: Times Books, 1994), 120–21.

110. The term "fiscal trap" was used by Janos Kornai, *Highways and Byways: Studies on Reform and Post-Communist Transition* (Cambridge: MIT Press, 1995), chap. 5.

111. Vito Tanzi, "Inflation, Lags in Collection, and the Real Value of Tax Revenue," *IMF Staff Papers*, vol. 24 (March 1977).

3. POLITICS OF TAX REFORM

1. The IMF *Tax Policy Handbook* summed up nicely how the particular policy features would fundamentally restructure the inherited system of revenue extraction in the postcommunist states: VAT, PIT, CIT, and customs reforms. P. Shome, ed., *Tax Policy Handbook* (Washington, D.C.: International Monetary Fund, 1995).

2. The IMF was much less enthusiastic about flat-tax reform among postcommunist states. It mobilized resources to counter the claims of free-market, flat-tax advocates. Anna Ivanova, Michael Keen, and Alexander Klemm, "The Russian Flat Tax Reform," *IMF Working Paper*, no. 16 (January 2005).

3. Leszek Balcerowicz, "The Interplay between Economic and Political Transition," in *Lessons from the Economic Transition: Central and Eastern Europe in the 1990s*, ed. Salvatore Zecchini (Dordrecht, the Netherlands: Kluwer Academic Publishers, OECD, 1997), 160.

4. Leszek Balcerowicz, *Socialism, Capitalism, Transformation* (Budapest: Central European University Press, 1995), 340–53.

5. The team included Marek Dambrowski, an original participant of the 1970s informal circle, who was named deputy finance minister and oversaw fiscal policy; Jerzy Kozminski, a former student of Balcerowicz, who served as the political liaison with the legislature; and, Stefan Kawalec, a former member of the Student Committee of Solidarity and Balcerowicz associate, who assumed responsibility for finance and banking issues. Dariusz Rosati, *Polski droga do rynku* (Warsaw: Polskie wydawnictwo ekonomyczne, 1998), 37–43.

6. Balcerowicz, *Socialism, Capitalism, Transformation*, 342.

7. For a more detailed overview of the new tax code, see I. Bolkowiak, D. Lubick, and H. Sochaska-Krysiak, "An Evaluation of Tax Reform in Poland," *PPRG Discussion Paper*

no. 5 (Warsaw: Policy Research Group [PPRG], 1991); *OECD Economic Surveys: Poland* (Paris: OECD, 1994), 171–74; and, Marek Belka, Anna Krajewska, Stefan Krajewski, and Anibal Santos, "Poland: Country Overview Study," *Eastern European Economics* 30, no. 1 (Fall 1991): 27–28.

8. Three types of SMEs based on the size of the work staff were recognized: Micro (1–10 employees), Small (11–49 employees), and Medium (50–249 employees).

9. Alan Tait and Nuri Erbas, "Excess Wage Tax," in *Fiscal Policy and Economic Reform*, ed. Mario Blejer and Teresa Ter-Minnisian (London: Routledge, 1997), 181–222.

10. *OECD Economic Surveys: Poland* (Paris: OECD, 1992), 163.

11. The dividend tax was determined by taking into account a firm's founding capital, annual budgetary outlays, and annual profits.

12. Belka, Krajewska, and Santos, "Poland," 28.

13. Mark Kramer, "Polish Workers and the Post-Communist Transition, 1989–93," *Europe-Asia Studies* 47 (June 1995), 669-712; Slay, *Polish Economy*, 157–58; Grzegorz Ekiert and Jan Kubik, *Rebellious Civil Society: Popular Protest and Democratic Consolidation in Poland, 1989-1993* (Ann Arbor: University of Michigan Press, 2001), 118.

14. Grzegorz Ekiert, "Legacies of Struggle and Defeat," in *Transition to Democracy in Poland*, ed. Richard Staar, 2nd ed. (New York: St. Martin's Press, 1998), 40.

15. *Rocznyk Statystyczny, 1992* (Warsaw: GUS, 1992); *Rocznyk Statystyczny, 1993* (Warsaw: GUS, 1993); *Rocznyk Statystyczny, 1995* (Warsaw: GUS, 1995).

16. "Polish Economy and Politics since the Solidarity Takeover," *PPRG Discussion Papers* no. 6 (Warsaw: Policy Research Group, 1991), 8.

17. For an excellent analysis of the revival of protest and its incorporation into the new democratic political system, see Ekiert and Kubik, *Rebellious Civil Society*.

18. *Rzeczpospolita*, 16 February 1991. This antitax demonstration was organized by the All-Poland Trade Union Alliance (OPZZ).

19. Kramer, "Polish Workers."

20. David Ost, *The Defeat of Solidarity: Anger and Politics in Postcommunist Europe* (Ithaca: Cornell University Press, 2005), 154.

21. *Rzeczpospolita*, 16 February 1991; Ekiert and Kubik, *Rebellious Civil Society*, 118–19.

22. Polish News Bulletin, 21 May 1991.

23. Protesting farmers in Slupsk and Rzepin, for example, cited the *popiwek* in lists of grievances: Polish News Bulletin, 15 February 1991 and 11 March 1991. Later, in August, the small farmers union (NSZZ Rural Solidarity) organized the tax-in-kind collective protest against the low prices that state wholesalers were paying for farm products. Polish News Bulletin, 8 August 1991.

24. Saul Estrin, Mark Schaffer, and I. J. Singh, "The Provision of Social Benefits in State-Owned, Privatized and Private Firms in Poland," in *Enterprise and Social Benefits after Communism*, ed. Martin Rein, Barry L. Friedman, and Andreas Worgotter (Cambridge: Cambridge University Press, 1997), 46 (table 2.13).

25. Belka, Krajewska, and Santos, "Poland," 55; Slay, *Polish Economy*, 157–58.

26. Balcerowicz, *Socialism, Capitalism, Transformation*, 356–57.

27. *OECD Economic Surveys: Poland* (Paris: OECD, 1994), 63.

28. Polish News Bulletin, 17 June 1991.

29. *Wybory 1991: Programy Partii i Ugrupowan Politychnych* (Warsaw: Institute of Political Studies of the Polish Academy of Science, 2001), 97, 115, 140, 161, 181, 184, 237, 247, 268, 270. The party/blocs finishing with more than 3% included Solidarity Electoral Action: 33.8%; Democratic Left Alliance: 27.1%; Freedom Union: 13.4%; Polish People's Party: 7.3%; Movement for Reconstruction of Poland: 5.6%: Labor Union: 4.7. Balcerowicz's political bloc, the Freedom Union, was the exception.

30. Gaidar's paternal grandfather was Arkady Gaidar, who served in the Red Army during the Civil War and later wrote patriotic tales about the Bolshevik front lines. His maternal grandfather was Pavel Bazhov, who penned popular fairy tales about the magical Ural Mountains. His father was Admiral Timur Gaidar, who encouraged his son to lead the economic reform.

31. Yegor Gaidar, *Dni porazhenii i pobed* (Moscow: Vagrus, 1996), 23–27.

32. D. G. Chernik, ed., *Nalogi: Uchebnoe posobie* (Moscow: Finansy i statistiki, 1998), 49–53.

33. Maciej Grabowski and Stephen Smith, "The Taxation of Entrepreneurial Income in a Transition Economy: Issues Raised by the Experience of Poland," in *Tax and Benefit Reform in Central and Eastern Europe*, ed. David Newbury, 106–13 (London: Centre for Economic Policy Research, 1995).

34. Gaidar, *Dni porazhenii*, 100.

35. The largest regional contributors to the state budget were accorded "donor" status. The list included about a dozen regions, although the list changed a bit from year to year. The regions that most often were assigned donor status included Moscow city, Moscow Oblast, St. Petersburg city, Sverdlovsk, Perm, Chelyabinsk, Samara, Nizhnyi Novgorod, Krasnoyarsk, Yaroslavl, Tyumen (more specifically the two smaller oil-producing administrative districts on the territory of Tyumen, Khanti-Mansi and Yamalo-Nenets), Tatarstan, and Bashkhortostan.

36. Boris Yeltsin, *The Midnight Diaries* (New York: Public Relations, 2000), 229.

37. Gerald M. Easter, "Redefining Centre-Regional Relations in the Russian Federation: Sverdlovsk *Oblast*," *Europe-Asia Studies* 49, no. 4 (June 1997): 617–36.

38. Leonid Smyrnygin, "Typologies of Conflicts in Modern Russia," and Aleksei Lazrov, "Budgetary Federalism," in *Conflict and Consensus in Ethno-Territorial and Center-Regional Relations in Russia*, ed. Jeremy Azrael and Emil Payin (Santa Monica, Calif.: RAND, 1998), chaps. 1 and 2.

39. Boris Fedorov, *10 bezumnykh let* (Moscow: Soversheno sekretno, 1999).

40. *Vlast*, 26 May 1998, 41.

41. Juliet Johnson, *A Fistful of Rubles: The Rise and Fall of the Russian Banking System* (Ithaca: Cornell University Press, 2000).

42. Gaidar, *Dni porazhenii*, 99.

43. For a good analysis of the unraveling of Russia's democratic movement, see Michael Urban, Vyacheslav Igrunov, and Sergei Mitrokin, *Rebirth of Politics in Russia* (New York: Cambridge University Press, 1997).

44. Insightful works that cover the political fragmentation and realignments of Poland's early transition include Ost, *Defeat of Solidarity*; Anna Grzymala-Busse, *Redeeming the Past: The Regeneration of Communist Parties in East Central Europe* (New York: Cambridge University Press, 2002); and Raymond Taras, *Consolidating Democracy in Poland* (Boulder, Colo.: Westview Press, 1995).

45. Jerzy Wiatr, "Executive-Legislative Relations in Crisis: Poland's Experience, 1989–1993," in *Institutional Design in New Democracies: Eastern Europe and Latin America*, ed. Arend Lijphardt and Carlos Waisman (Boulder, Colo.: Westview, 1996).

46. *OECD Economic Surveys: Poland* (Paris: OECD, 1994), 63.

47. Ibid., 64. This practice was strikingly similar to the manner by which enterprise managers and tax officials negotiated tax bills in the old command economy.

48. The four parties were the Polish Peasants Party, the Democratic Left Alliance, the Non-Party Pro-reform Bloc, and the Union of Labor. Inka Sklodowska, ed., *Wybory 1993: Partie i ich programy* (Warsaw: Institute of Political Studies at Polish Academy of Science, 2001), 91, 93, 120, 308, 357.

49. *OECD Economic Surveys: Poland* (Paris: OECD, 1994), 63–64.

50. Grzegorz Kolodko, *From Shock to Therapy: The Political Economy of Postsocialist Transformation* (Oxford: Oxford University Press, 2000), 213, 214.

51. *OECD Economic Surveys: Poland: 2000–2001* (Paris, OECD, 2001), 80–83, 90. In 1992, public sector employment accounted for 42% of the workforce; in 1996, it was down to 38%. The privatization process picked up pace again in the later 1990s.

52. Agnieszka Parlinska, "Legal Aspects of Polish Tax and Social Security in Agriculture," *Aestimum*, vol. 53 (December 2008): 75–87.

53. Poznanski, *Poland's Protracted Transition*, 270.

54. Francis Millard, *Polish Politics and Society* (London: Routledge, 1999), 114–16.

55. Aleks Szczerbiak, *Poles Together? The Emergence and Development of Political Parties in Post-Communist Poland* (Budapest: CEU Press, 2001), 130, table 4.

56. The remarks were made by T. Zezioranski in an opinion piece in *Zycie Gospodarcze*, no. 16 (21 April 1991).

57. In 1994, the wages of public sector workers were increased in January by 9% and in June by 13%. In 1995, wages rose in January by 10.5%, in July by 17%, and in October by 14.5%. In July 1996, public sector wages were boosted by 20%. *OECD Economic Surveys: Poland* (Paris: OECD, 1997), 163–69.

58. Boris Fedorov, *Pytaias' poniat' Rossii* (St. Petersburg: Limbus, 2000), 112. *Rossiiskaia gazeta*, 5 November 2001. *Saint Petersburg Times*, 9–14 November 1994; *RFE/RL*, no. 27 (7 February 1997).

59. A government commission estimated that over $2 billion in revenue was lost to the budget in 1996 via customs-determined exemptions. As an example of the tax administration's penchant for applying higher rates, in 1997 the Ministry of Finance authorized an exemption on the 15% profits tax on treasury bills. Through a loophole in the legislation, the tax administration not only still tried to collect the tax but raised the rate to 43%. *Kommersant*, 15 February 1997; *Segodnia*, 19 February 1997; *Saint Petersburg Times*, January 27–February 2, 1997.

60. Yeltsin, *Midnight Diaries*, 215–16.

61. Presidential Decree no. 2268 (1993): D. G. Chernik, A. P. Pochinok, and V. P. Morozov, *Osnovy nalogovoi sistemy* (Moscow: Iuniti, 1998), 197.

62. D. G. Chernik, A. P. Pochinok, and V. P. Morozov, *Osnovy nalogovoi sistemy*, 2nd ed. (Moscow: Iuniti, 2000), 202.

63. Lev Freinkman, Daniel Treisman, and Stepan Titov, "Subnational Budgeting in Russia," *World Bank Technical Paper*, no. 452 (1999): 32.

64. "Dogovor mezhdu Rossiikoi Federatsei ii Sverdlovskoi oblast'iu"(Article 12). *Oblastnaia gazeta*, 24 January 1996 and 8 February 1996.

65. *Russian Economy: Trends and Outlooks, 2002* (Moscow: Institute for the Economy in Transition, 2003), 60–61.

66. Nagy, "The Fiscal Component of the First Russian Stabilization Effort," 239.

67. *OECD Economic Surveys: Russian Federation, 1995* (Paris: OECD, 1995), 46.

68. *Saint Petersburg Times*, 23–29 August 1994, May 26–June 2, 1996, 6–12 January 1997, 24–30 March 1997.

69. *Nalogovyi vestnik*, no 1 (1997), 62.

70. Fedorov, *Pytias poiat rossiiu*, 79–84.

71. As part of "loans for shares," Potanin's Uneximbank secured 38% of Norilsk Nikel in 1995 for $170 million ($140 million short of the government's asking price). *Moscow Times*, 1 September 2003.

72. *Rossiiskaia gazeta*, 7 August 1998; *Delovoi kvartal*, 5 February 1998, 6.

73. Gilman, *No Precedent, No Plan*.

74. Regional vote totals: Vladimir Gelman and Grigorii Golosov, eds., *Elections in Russia, 1993–1996* (Berlin: Edition Sigma, 1999), 273, table 7; Lazrov, "Budgetary Federalism," 27, table 3.1.

75. The percentage of tax income covering the state budget rose from 77% in 1991 to 84% in 1995, but then declined to 82% in 1997. *Poland: International Economic Report, 1997/1998* (Warsaw: World Economy Research Institute, 1998), 113.

76. Patrick Lenain and Leszek Bartoszuk, "The Polish Tax Reform," *OECD: Economic Department Working Papers*, no. 234 (March 2000), 7, 8.

77. Ibid., 8.

78. Ibid., 7, 22, table 2.

79. *Warsaw Voice*, 5 November 1995; *Warsaw Voice*, 5 January 1997.

80. *Wybory 1997: Partie i ich programy:* (Warsaw: Institute of Political Studies, Polish Academy of Science, 2004), 76–78, 120–22, 169, 171, 228–29.

81. Ibid., 106.

82. *Business and Economic Outlook: 1998* (Warsaw: Warsaw Voice, 1998), 6, 7.

83. Balcerowicz's chief assistants were born in the 1970s and graduated from the Warsaw School of Economics. They included Pawel Zarozny, in charge of tax reform; Ryszard Petru, in charge of pension reform; and Jakub Karnkowski, a former student of Balcerowicz and his personal assistant. *Business and Economic Outlook: 1998*, 15, 16.

84. *OECD Economic Surveys: Poland: 2000* (Paris: OECD, 2001), 107.

85. Ibid., 93–114.

86. *Warsaw Voice*, 13 September 1998.

87. *Warsaw Voice*, 6 September 1998; *Warsaw Voice*, 20 September 1998.

88. *Warsaw Voice*, 14 November 1999.

89. *Warsaw Voice*, 5 December 1999.

90. *OECD Economic Surveys: Poland: 2000–2001*, 107.

91. *Central Europe Review* 2, no. 20 (22 May 2000).

92. Fedorov, *10 bezumnykh let*, 188, 189.

93. Ibid. Sergei Alekshenko was the new committee's head who made this declaration.

94. Earlier, Shatalov served in the Supreme Soviet's committee for budget and tax policy; from November 1997 to 2000, Shatalov worked in the private sector as a tax consultant.

95. *Nezavisimaia gazeta*, 13 May 1995.

96. *Nezavisimaia gazeta*, 23 October 1996; *Rossiiskaia gazeta*, 17 July 1997; *Saint Petersburg Times*, 21–27 April 1997.

97. *Nalogovyi vestnik*, no. 3 (1997).

98. *Russian Reform Monitor*, no. 105 (23 February 1996).

99. Yegor Gaidar, ed., *The Economics of Transition* (Cambridge: MIT Press, 2003), 197.

100. *Russian Reform Monitor*, no. 121 (11 April 1996).

101. Gilman, *No Precedent, No Plan*, chaps. 1, 2.

102. *Moscow Times*, 26 November 1997.

103. *Komsomolskaia Pravda*, 1 August 1998.

104. Laszlo Bokros, "Experience and Perspectives of Financial Sector Development in Central and Eastern Europe," *CASE-CEU Working Papers*, no. 38 (Warsaw: CASE-CEU, 2001), 6.

105. The circumstances that led to low contestation varied according to the particulars of a country's domestic politics. First, there was the case of democratic institutions, wherein free-market finance ministers were insulated from political opposition (Estonia). Second, there was the case of semiauthoritarian institutions, wherein strong executives managed to dictate policy changes to the legislature through hegemonic parties (Russia,

Ukraine). Third, there was the case of institutional change, whereby semiauthoritarian regimes were uprooted either by popular demonstrations (Serbia, Georgia) or by transformative elections (Slovakia, Romania), creating short-lived conditions similar to "extraordinary politics." Only the Czech Republic passed a flat-tax reform (by two votes) in a condition of "high contestation." The Czech flat tax was applied to "super gross" personal income, that is, PIT based on gross income and additional wage benefits. The rate was set at 15%, but with the expanded income items, it is closer to 23%. *Policy Brief: Economic Survey of the Czech Republic, 2008* (Paris: OECD, April 2008), 5.

106. *Warsaw Voice*, 21 May 2000.

107. A summary of the European Commission's commitment to the accession process and the first annual progress report can be found in "Report on Progress toward Accession by Candidate Countries," European Commission, *Composite Paper* (1999). Available in European Commission on-line archive: http://ec.europa.eu/enlargement/archives/pdf/key_documents/1998/composite_en.pdf.

108. European Commission on-line archive for taxation reports on the accession candidate countries is found at http://europa.eu/scadplus/leg/en/s10000.htm#FISCADH.

109. For a good discussion of the lack of fit in VAT regimes between East and West, see Michael Keen and Stephen Smith, "The Future of the Value Added Tax in the European Union," *Economic Policy* 11, no. 23 (October 1996): 373–420.

110. According to EU rules, individual states retain the right to determine their own direct taxation policies on corporate and personal income. However, a normative check was devised for direct taxation: The Code of Conduct for Business Taxation, adopted in December 1997, which monitors "harmful" tax practices: http://ec.europa.eu/taxation_customs/resources/documents/primarolo_en.pdf.

111. Wojtek Kosc, "EC 2000 Progress Report on Poland," *Central European Review* 2, no. 39 (November 2000); Mark Schaffer, "Government Subsidies to Enterprises in Central and Eastern Europe: Budgetary Subsidies and Tax Arrears," *CEPR Discussion Papers*, no. 1144 (London: Centre for Economic Policy Research, 1995).

112. See Mihaly Hogye, "Comparative Approaches to Tax Administration Reform in Central and Eastern Europe," in *Local and Regional Tax Administration in Transition Countries*, ed. M. Hogye, 50–80 (New York: Open Society: Local Government and Public Service Reform Institute, 2000).

113. *Business and Economic Outlook: 1998*, 8.

114. *European Commission: Regular Report on Poland's Progress toward Accession* (1998), 28.

115. *Warsaw Voice*, 7 January 2001.

116. *Warsaw Voice*, 7 March 2003.

117. See the "Summaries of Legislation: Taxation" for Poland. Available from the EU on-line archive: http://europa.eu/scadplus/leg/en/lvb/e10106.htm.

118. Ibid.

119. Ibid.

120. *Warsaw Voice*, 29 June 2005. In the sixteenth and seventeenth centuries, the aristocrat-dominated Sejm operated by *liberum veto*, a principle of unanimous voting that allowed any disgruntled viscount to block legislation.

121. *International Herald Tribune*, 1 February 2006.

122. *Financial Times*, 2 February 2006.

123. Lenain and Bartoszuk, "The Polish Tax Reform," 30, figure 4.

124. *Wybory 2001: Partie i ich programy* (Warsaw: Institute of Polish Studies, Academy of Sciences, 2002). Although all major political blocs called for lowering the tax burden, they disagreed over which enterprises should receive tax relief. Of the seven parties that

made it into the Sejm, six (DLA, Solidarity bloc, Polish Peasants Party, Law and Justice, Self-Defense of Poland, and League of Polish Families) explicitly tied tax relief to job creation, and hence the protection of labor. Only the Civic Platform, the alternative free-market liberal-democratic party, espoused unconditional tax reform in general, and the flat tax in particular.

125. M. Jakubiak and M. Markiewicz, "Capital Mobility and Tax Competition in the EU Enlargement," *CASE: Working Paper* (June 2005), table 1.

126. *Warsaw Voice*, 7 March 2003.

127. Wieslaw Ciesielski, "Tax Administration and Tax System in Poland," *Tax Information Bulletin* (Warsaw: Ministerstwo finansow, 2004). 5.

128. Tax-News.com (Brussels: 25 April 2002); http://www.tax-news.com/asp/story.asp?storyname = 8002.

129. *Warsaw Business Journal*, 22 July 2005.

130. *Warsaw Voice*, 20 September 1998.

131. Evgeny Primakov, *Vosem mesiatsev plius* (Moscow: Mysl, 2002), 39.

132. *Komsomolskaia pravda*, 25 September 2003.

133. Yeltsin, *Midnight Diaries*, chap. 1.

134. Unity, which did well in the popular vote, had seventy-four seats, while Fatherland, which did well in single-candidate districts, had sixty-five seats. The Communists, with 110 seats, had the largest bloc in the new Duma.

135. In his first term, this tactic was tried against former Kremlin insiders, business tycoons Valdimir Gusinsky and Boris Berezovsky, who fell into disfavor and were forced into exile. It was also used to impress regional mavericks, for example in 2001 when a wave of corruption and tax fraud investigations crashed down on the Far Eastern Primorskii shore, causing powerful regional governor Yevgeny Nazdratenko to relinquish his post. *RFE/RL Security Watch*, 28 August 2000; *RFE/RL Crime and Corruption Watch*, 7 March 2002.

136. *Izvestiia*, 11 October 2001.

137. In 2001, Finance Minister Kudrin began to chair a special commission that met with industry representatives to set tax rates. *RFE/RL: Newsline*, 7 January 2002. In the same year, the Union of Industrialists and Entrepreneurs established a special committee on tax policy that continues to meet regularly with the government. Through this committee, the Union was made part of the process of tax policymaking by introducing its own reform proposals and responding to government initiatives. *Kommersant*, 20 February 2003; *Moscow Times*, 29 November 2001, 27 February 2002.

138. *RFE/RL: Newsline*, 30 April 2002; *Moscow Tribune*, 17 May 2002.

139. *Saint Petersburg Times*, 12–18 September 1995 and 8–14 July 1996.

140. *Rossiiskaia gazeta*, 31 July 2001.

141. For an overview of the process of tax reform, including the working groups, see T. F. Iutkin, *Nalogi i nalogoblozhenie* (Moscow: Infra-M, 2002), 529–41.

142. Sergei Shatalov, "Tax Reform in Russia: History and Future," lecture delivered at London School of Economics, 10 November 2005; reprinted in *Tax Notes International* 42, no. 9 (29 May 2006): 780.

143. Ibid.

144. Through 1999, the PIT scale included five categories with an upper margin of 35%, but a sixth level of 45% was added in 2000 for income exceeding R300,00 ($100,000), though because of avoidance and privileges the effective rate on personal income was estimated at 13.5%.

145. Prime Minister Kasyanov and Minister of Economic Development and Trade German Gref joined corporate lobbies in calling for more radical VAT reductions.

Gref, for example, told the country's top retailers that the VAT rate should be cut to 13%. *Moscow Times*, 22 January 2004, 5.

146. Shatalov, "Tax Reform in Russia: History and Future," 781.

4. STATE MEETS SOCIETY IN THE TRANSITIONAL TAX REGIME

1. Andzrej Borodo, *Finanse Publicznie: W swietle regulacji prawnych* (Warsaw: Wydawnictwo prawnicze LEX, 2000), 33–59.

2. Ibid., 42–44. Of the twenty-five internal departments of MinFin in 1998, four were dedicated to taxation.

3. One notable exception, however, was the Social and Political Committee, set up in 1994 to fight the growing gray economy. *Polish News Bulletin*, 22 March 1994.

4. From 1992 to 1996, Witold Modzelewski, who had personal ties to Finance Minister Kolodko, was the vice minister for taxes, and then was charged with the founding of the National Fiscal Academy. From 1992 to 1998, Waldemir Manugiewicz, who was a member of the Democratic Left Alliance (SLD), served as a vice minister, overseeing the introduction of the VAT reform, heading the fiscal control department, and serving as undersecretary for taxes.

5. Stanislaw Owsiak, *Finanse Publiczne: Teoria and praktyka* (Warsaw: Wydawnictwo naukowe PWN, 2000), 313, table 28.

6. OECD, "Fiscal Design across Levels of Government: Country Report: Poland" (Paris: OECD, Directorate for Financial, Fiscal and Enterprise Affairs, May 2001), 5–8.

7. The remark was made by Marek Mikusiewicz, the owner of MarcPol retail chain, who was complaining about the widespread smuggling of alcohol. *Gazeta Wyborcza*, 20 April 1993.

8. See remarks by the head of the tax department at this time, Andreij Zelechowski. *Gazeta wyborcza*, 20 August 1993.

9. Polish News Bulletin, 3 September 1992.

10. *Rzeczpospolita*, 7 March 1997, 9.

11. Polish News Bulletin, 12 August 1991.

12. Ibid.

13. Polish News Bulletin, 29 January 1993.

14. Borodo, *Finanse Publicznie*, 82, 83. By 1998, the tax administration had registered twenty-four million taxpayers. The main exception was in the rural economy, where Polish farmers were initially exempted from income tax. The EU accession eventually brought these households into the tax net. *OECD Economic Surveys: Poland, 1998* (Paris, OECD: 1998), 138; Polish News Bulletin, 20 May 1994.

15. The architect of the cadastre reform was the vice minister of finance responsible for taxes, Witold Modzelewski. Polish News Bulletin, 8 June 1994.

16. *Rzeczpospolita*, 13 February 1997, 7.

17. *Gazeta Wyborcza*, 20 August 1994.

18. See interview with Finance Minister Jerzy Osiatynski, Polish News Bulletin, 3 September 1992.

19. See interview with Andreij Zelechowski, MinFin's Tax Department head, in *Gazeta Wyborcza*, 20 August 1993.

20. Centrum Badanii Opinii Spolocznej (CBOS), Public Opinion Survey (April 1998), 3.

21. *Zycie Warsawy*, 2 July 1991.

22. L. Kurowski, E. Ruskowski, and H. Sochacka-Krysiak, *Kontrola finansowa w sektorze publyczym* (Warsaw: Polskie wydawnictwo ekonomiczne, 2000), 274–87.

23. Polish News Bulletin, 15 September 1992.

24. Polish News Bulletin, 4 August 1993.

25. *Puls biznesu*, 25 April 2005, 12.

26. *Guardian*, 8 February 1992, 6; *Economist*, 7 March 1992, 50.

27. Polish News Bulletin, 13 July 2000.

28. *Tax Information Bulletin*, "Tax Administration and Tax System of Poland" (Warsaw: Ministry of Finance, 2004), 25.

29. Ibid., 51. The exact numbers for the year 2003 were 2,568 fiscal audit inspectors, of whom 141 were with the penal fiscal investigation unit.

30. *Economist*, 7 March 1992, 50.

31. *Prawo i gospodarka*, no. 7, 10–11 January 1998, 7.

32. Katarzyna Owsiak and Stanislaw Owsiak, "The Dilemma of Decentralizing the Public Finance System in Poland," *International Journal of Public Administration* 24, no. 2 (2001): 211–24.

33. OECD, "Fiscal Design across Levels of Government," 8–9.

34. "Tax Administration and Tax System of Poland," *Tax Information Bulletin* (Warsaw: Ministry of Finance, 2004), 21. The boards are chaired by the director of the regional tax chamber, and include the heads of the regional tax department, customs service, and fiscal control.

35. OECD, "Fiscal Design across Levels of Government," 5.

36. Polish News Bulletin, 12 March 2003. As a line item, the local subsidies fund annually accounted for roughly 15% of total budgetary expenses. *Rocznik statystychny, 2000* (Warsaw: GUS, 2000), 483, table 2:508.

37. The new territorial division of revenue was announced by the Deputy Finance Minister Jacek Utkiewicz in August 2003. *Parkiet*, 29 August 2003, 7.

38. See summaries of Poland's accession progress reports on tax administration reform at the EU Commission on-line archive: http://europa.eu/legislation_summaries/enlargement/2004_and_2007_enlargement/poland/e10106_en.htm.

39. The power of local tax inspectors to write off a portion of a taxpayer's tax obligation was put into practice by the social-democratic government in the mid-1990s. It was meant to provide tax relief to enterprises in economically depressed regions. Although intended for exceptional cases, the practice became pervasive. It became a scandal when a list was published containing the largest beneficiaries of this practice, including a Lodz distillery that got out of paying twenty-five million zloty in VAT and excise taxes as well as a wealthy individual who got out of paying five million zloty in personal income tax. By giving local tax officials such discretionary power, the opportunities for corruption were greatly increased. See "Why Polish Firms Are Not Afraid of Taxes," Polish News Bulletin, 13 July 2000.

40. *Puls biznesu*, 28 October 2003, 10.

41. "Tax Administration and Tax System of Poland," *Tax Information Bulletin*, 8, 9, 20. As part of this reform, the customs administration was reorganized into fourteen regional offices and sixty-six branch offices. They were given greater responsibility for taxing cross-border trade and for overseeing new EU-sanctioned excise tax warehouses.

42. Ibid., 63–66.

43. *Gazeta wyborcza*, 25 April 2001, 4.

44. The European Commission's approval was conditional on Poland's promise to continue tax administration reform after accession. To demonstrate its good intentions, MinFin published a three-year plan for further tax administration reform. *Puls biznesu*, 28 October 2003, 10.

45. *Wprost*, 14 November 2004, 23.

46. *Puls biznesu*, 2 December 2005, 9.

47. *Polish News Bulletin* (5 September 2007); European Industrial Relations Observatory on-line: https://eurofound.europa.eu/eiro/2008/05/articles/pl0805019i.htm.

48. *Puls biznesu*, 20 October 2004, 6.

49. The group also included representatives of the finance and justice ministries. Polish News Bulletin, 19 December 2000.

50. *Prawo i gospardarki*, 19 April 2001, 4.

51. Polish News Bulletin, 21 June 2000. In a rare success, the Katowice tax office managed to uncover a half-million zloty VAT scam, but only because Interpol first alerted Polish authorities.

52. The 1999 fiscal penal reform established two categories of tax fraud: fiscal offense, subject to fines and possible imprisonment, and petty fiscal offenses, subject to fines only. "Tax Administration and Tax System of Poland," 31, 32.

53. Ibid., 31.

54. Polish New Bulletin, 31 May 2006.

55. The 1999 fiscal penal code reinforced that only a court could determine guilt and that administrative agents could only present evidence. *Rzeczpospolita*, 20 October 1999.

56. Polish News Bulletin, 22 January 2003.

57. Polish News Bulletin, 14 December 2005.

58. Polish News Bulletin, 12 September 2002.

59. *Rzeczpospolita*, 30 December 2002, A1, C1; Polish News Bulletin, 5 May 2004.

60. "Tax Administration and Tax System of Poland," 30, 33.

61. Grzegorz Szczodrowski, *Polski system podatkowy* (Warsaw: Wydawnictwo naukowe PWN, 2007), 97.

62. *Gazeta prawna*, 18 June 2007.

63. *Puls biznesu*, 3 June 2005, 5; *Gazeta prawna*, 13–15 July 2007.

64. *Gazeta prawna*, 13–15 July 2007.

65. *Puls biznesu*, 4 January 2006, 3.

66. Polish News Bulletin, 26 April 2006.

67. *Rzeczpospolita*, 7 February 2007, A1.

68. "Tax Administration and Tax System of Poland," 39–40.

69. Ibid., 40.

70. Fedorov, *10 bezumnykh let*, 194–96.

71. Gerald M. Easter, "The Russian Tax Police," *Post-Soviet Affairs* 18, no. 4 (September–October 2002): 332–62.

72. *Delovoi liudi*, no. 113 (August 2000), 9.

73. IMF, "Russian Federation: Recent Economic Developments," *IMF Staff Country Report*, nos. 99/100 (September 1999), 62.

74. N. G. Ivanova and T. D. Makovnik, *Kazanacheiskaia sistema ispolneniia biudzhetov* (St. Petersburg: Piter, 2001), 34.

75. Ibid., 35.

76. *Rossiiskaia gazeta*, 7 August 1998; *Delovoi kvartal*, 5 February 1998; *Saint Petersburg Times*, March 31–April 6, 1997.

77. William Tompson, "Old Habits Die Hard: Fiscal Imperative, State Regulation and the Role of Russia's Banks," *Europe-Asia Studies* 49, no. 7 (November 1997); A. Yu. Petrov, *Analiz nalogooblozheniia kommercheskikh bankov* (Moscow: REA Plekhanova, 1999), 16–17.

78. *OECD Economic Surveys: Russian Federation, 1997/98* (Paris: OECD, 1997), 59.

79. *Kommersant*, 5 February 1997.

80. *RFE/RL*, no. 31 (13 February 1997).

81. D. G. Chernik, *Nalogi: Uchebnoe posobie*, 91.

82. Richard Highfield and Katheryn Baer, "Tax Administration for Russia," *IMF: Fiscal Affairs Department* (Moscow: April 2000), 3.

83. *Vedomosti*, 1 February 2001.

84. Tolkushkin, *Istoriia nalogov v Rossii*, 302.

85. *Nezavisimaia gazeta*, 14 January 1997.

86. The first limited experiments with market socialism exposed the tax administration's limited capabilities. By January 1990 roughly two hundred thousand quasi-private, profit-driven cooperatives, employing over four million workers, were officially registered and operating in the Soviet Union. Yet the state managed to collect in taxes only 1% of the reported income of the cooperatives. Anthony Jones and William Moskoff, *Ko-ops: The Rebirth of Entrepreneurship in the Soviet Union* (Bloomington: Indiana University Press, 1991), 16, 71.

87. *Nalogovia Politsiia*, no. 20 (October 2001).

88. Kozyrin, A. N., ed., *O federalnykh organakh nalogovoi politsii: S postateinymi materialami* (Moscow: Statut, 2000), 147.

89. *Nalogovia Politsiia*, no. 20 (October 2001).

90. Easter, "The Russian Tax Police," 332–62.

91. Personal interview with author, Yekaterinburg, 22 October 1998.

92. *Nalogovaia politsiia*, no. 19 (October 2001).

93. *Finansy v Rossii: Statisticheskii sbornik* (Moscow: Goskomstat, 1996); *Finansy v Rossii: Statisticheskii sbornik* (Moscow: Goskomstat, 2000); V. F. Soltanganov, *Nalogovaia politsiia: Vchera, segodnia, zavtra* (Moscow: Dashkov, 2000).

94. Soltaganov, *Nalogovaia politsiia*; *Nalogovaia politsiia*, no. 3 (February 2001); *Rossiiskaia gazeta*, 14 March 2002.

95. Soltaganov, *Nalogovaia politsiia*, 158.

96. *Nalogovaia politsiia*, no. 19 (October 2001).

97. *Saint Petersburg Times*, 4 September 1995.

98. MinFin could not completely subordinate customs, however. As late as 2007, MinFin was still trying to sort out a division of labor between the tax administration and customs. *Kommersant*, 14 March 2007.

99. *Kommersant*, 16 February 2007, 1. Anatoly Serdiukov, the hard-line chief of the tax administration, was named the defense minister by Putin, who called for "a more sensible accounting of the huge sums" in the defense budget. In addition, Lyubov Kudelina of the Finance Ministry was made deputy defense minister in charge of fiscal oversight.

100. Darrell Slider and Nikolai Petrov, "Putin and the Regions," in *Putin's Russia*, ed. Dale Herspring, 3rd ed. (Lanham, Md.: Rowman and Littlefield, 2007).

101. *Vlast*, no. 14 (April 2000).

102. Ivanova and Makovnik, *Kazanacheiskaia sistema*, 3; *Finansovaia gazeta*, no. 17 (April 2002).

103. For example, in Perm, *Kommersant*, 15 April 2003, 11; in Altai, *Kommersant*, 17 March 2003, 10.

104. *Rossiiskaia gazeta*, 5 November 2001.

105. Interview with G. Bukaev, *Interfax* (5 March 2002).

106. *Kommersant*, 6 May 2006. This practice was revealed by Mikhail Orlov, head of the State Duma's Expert Council on Taxation.

107. *Kommersant*, 15 February 2003, 5.

108. Shatalov, "Tax Reform in Russia: History and Future," 786, tables 14 and 15.

109. Ibid., 782, table 6.

110. *Moscow Times*, 8 February 2005.

111. A spokesman for the Competitiveness and Entrepreneurship Council noted that the government incorporated less than half of the business group's proposals. *Kommersant*, 25 April 2005.

112. *Kommersant*, 23 November 2005.

113. Supreme Arbitrage Court decrees: 26 June 2009; 28 July 2009 (no. 5172/09); 1 September 2009 (no. 4381/09). *Moscow Times*, 8 December 2009.

114. Marc Berenson, "Rationalizing or Empowering Bureaucrats? Tax Administration Reform in Poland and Russia," *Journal of Communist Studies and Transition Politics* 24, no. 1 (March 2008): 136–55.

115. V. K. Senchagov, *Ekonomicheskaia bezopasnost* (Moscow: Finstatinform, 2002), 58; V. I. Volkovskii, *Nalogovie organy i ekonomicheskaia bezopasnost rossii* (Moscow: Fond podderzhki uchenykh "nauchnaia perspektiva," 2002), 15–17.

116. *Delovie liudi*, no. 113 (August 2000).

117. *Rossiisskaia gazeta*, 14 March 2001.

118. *Izvestiia*, 10 July 2001; *Rossiiskaia gazeta*, 14 March 2001.

119. *Nalogovaia politsiia*, no. 3 (February 2001); *Rossiiskaia gazeta*, 14 March 2002.

120. *Nalogovaia politsiia*, no. 7 (April 2001); *RFE/RL Crime and Corruption Watch*, 7 March 2002.

121. Soltaganov, *Nalogovaya politsiia*, 58, 60.

122. OmskEnergo, 49% owned by Chubais's state electricity monopoly, was charged with "huge tax violations" amounting to more than five hundred million rubles. *Kommersant*, 6 March 2003, 9.

123. The Union of Industrialists and Entrepreneurs, for example, put administrative reform—more restraint and routinization of the work of the state bureaucracy—at the top of its lobbying agenda. *Kommersant*, 27 February 2003, 10.

124. *Izvestiia*, 19 March 2003, 10; *Kommersant*, 8 June 2004. Within the Interior Ministry, the tax police was placed in the Federal Economic and Tax Crimes Service.

125. *Vedemosti*, 9 February 2005, A1; *Moscow Times*, 29 April 2005.

126. Joel Slemrod, ed., *Why People Pay Taxes: Tax Compliance and Enforcement* (Ann Arbor: University of Michigan Press, 1992); J. Andreoni, B. Erard, and J. Feinstein, "Tax Compliance," *Journal of Economic Literature* 36, no. 2 (June 1998): 818–60; Paul Weberly, ed., *Tax Evasion: An Experimental Approach* (Cambridge: Cambridge University Press, 1991).

127. Margaret Levi, *Of Rule and Revenue* (Berkeley: University of California Press, 1988), 52.

128. Eric Uslaner, *Corruption, Inequality and the Rule of Law* (Cambridge: Cambridge University Press, 2008); Lieberman, *Race and Regionalism in the Politics and Taxation of Brazil and South Africa.*

129. The concept of contingent consent is developed in the work of Margaret Levi, *Consent, Dissent and Patriotism* (New York: Cambridge University Press, 1997). Contingent consent in relation to taxation is a main theme in the essays found in Brautigam, Fjeldstad, and Moore, *Taxation and State-Building in Developing Countries.*

130. The findings are reported in the *Polish News Bulletin* (24 August 1993).

131. *Rzeczpospolita*, no. 201,31 August 1995, 7.

132. See remarks of Vice Minister of Interior Jan Widacki and Minister of Justice Wieslaw Czanowski to a special session on crime to the Sejm. *Polish News Bulletin* (23 April 1991). The Ministry of Interior reported that tax-related economic crimes in 1991 cost the Treasury over one hundred billion zloty, a more than 1,000% increase from the previous year.

133. Bielecki was the former prime minister and a minister without portfolio in Suchocka's government. His observations were drawn from a long personal report that he compiled for Waldemir Pawlak. Polish News Bulletin,6 August 1992.

134. Stanislaw Owsiak, "Taxes in Post-Communist Countries: Old and New Challenges," in *Tax Evasion, Trust and State Capacities*, ed. Nicolas Hayoz and Simon Hug (Bern: Peter Lang, 2007), 217. For a more extended discussion, see Stanislaw Owsiak, *Finanse publiczne: Teoria i praktyka*, 3rd ed. (Warsaw: WN PWN, 2005).

135. Poland's income threshold for small-business VAT exemption was high compared with most EU countries, such as Germany $16,000 and France $12,000, although the United Kingdom's $60,000 threshold was higher than Poland's. Grabowski and Smith, "The Taxation of Entrepreneurial Income in a Transition Economy," 108.

136. Owsiak, *Finanse Publiczyne*, 418, table 52.

137. The number of new pensioners averaged about one hundred thousand per year in the late 1980s, but shot up to five hundred thousand between 1990 and 1992, before settling back down to about 150,000 per year in the late 1990s. Robert Sierhej, "Pension Reforms in Central Eastern Europe: The Case of Poland," IMF Regional Office (Warsaw, 2008).

138. *Rocznik statystyczny, 1999* (Warsaw: GUS, 1999), 499, table 2:515.

139. Joanna Szczesna, "Tax Payers vs. Taxes," *East European Constitutional Review* 7, no. 1 (Winter 1998): 76. The poll was conducted by Poland's main public opinion survey agency, Centrum Badaniia Opinii Spolocznej (CBOS), located in Warsaw. CBOS conducted monthly survey findings of Polish public opinion on political and economic questions and current affairs.

140. Polish News Bulletin, 14 June 1997.

141. CBOS, *Polish Public Opinion*, June 1998, 3.

142. *OECD Economic Surveys: Poland, January 2000* (Paris, OECD: 2000), 123.

143. CBOS, *Polish Public Opinion* (June 1998), 3.

144. CBOS, "Reakcje na Zawetowanie Ustawy Podatkowej i Pozostanie Leszka Balcerowicza w Rzadzie," no. BS/93/99 (December 1999), 4, fig. 1.

145. *PAP News Agency* (Warsaw), 20 September 2002.

146 Constitutional Tribunal Ruling: K 41/02 (20 November 2002).

147. EBRD–World Bank, "Business Environment and Enterprise Performance Survey" (BEEPS), 2006, 2008.

148. Survey data, for example, found that the only social category in which support for a flat tax reached its highest level, 35%, was entrepreneurs/intelligentsia. CBOS, *Polish Public Opinion*, June 1998, 3.

149. Polish News Bulletin, 23 December 1993. Twenty-nine percent of respondents said that they had arrived at these opinions mainly from interactions with other businessmen.

150. *Prawo i gospodarka*, no. 7 (10–11 January 1998), 7.

151. Szczesna, "Tax Payers vs. Taxes," 79.

152. Uzar News Service, 13 March 2000 (http://newzar.wordpress.com/page/31/). Each donation was worth roughly a $50 deduction from one's personal income tax, up to 6% of total income.

153. The interest rate ordered by the courts reached as high as 43% annually. *Polish Business News* (13 July 2000).

154. *Rzeczpospolita*, no. 194, 21 August 1997, 7.

155. Owsiak, "Taxes in Post-Communist Countries," 218.

156. *Wprost*, no. 30, 26 July 1996, 34.

157. *Rzeczpospolita*, no. 253, 29 October 1996, 1.

158. *Gazeta Wyborcza*, no. 194, 21 August 1997, 1.

159. *Rzeczpospolita*, no. 253, 29 October 1996, 1; *Polish Business News*, 13 July 2000.

160. Polish News Bulletin, 28 August 1992.

161. Polish News Bulletin, 4 April 1996.

162. "Tax Administration and Tax System of Poland," 28.

163. M. Stankiewicz, "Niskie posatki wazniejsze od flagi narodowej," *Rzeczpospolita*, no. 266, 23 November 2005.

164. *Wprost*, 30 July 2006, 40–43.

165. *OECD Economic Surveys: Poland, 2000* (Paris, OECD: 2000), 120. One source estimated that the gray economy declined from 24% of the overall economy in 1990 to only 12% in 1995. Daniel Kaufman, "Corruption: The Facts," *Foreign Policy*, no. 107 (Summer 1997), 122. For the late 2000s, see *Warsaw Business Journal*, 5 May 2011. For European comparisons, see Friedrich Schneider, "Dimensions of the Shadow Economy," *Independent Review* 5, no. 1 (Summer 2000): 81–91; E. Tafenau, H. Herwatz, and F. Schneider, "Regional Estimates of the Shadow Economy in Europe," *International Economic Journal* 24, no. 4 (December 2010): 629–36.

166. In 1995, for example, the federal government tried to simplify tax compliance for small businesses by consolidating multiple taxes into a single, easy-to-calculate tax. But most regional governments obstructed or ignored the implementation of this reform. *OECD Economic Survey: Russian Federation, 1997* (Paris: OECD, 1997).

167. A. V. Perov, *Nalogi i mezhdurodnye soglasheniia Rossii* (Moscow: Iurist, 2000), 157.

168. Volkovskii, *Nalogoviie organy*, 104.

169. *Vedomosti*, 14 March 2002.

170. *OECD Economic Surveys: Russian Federation, 1997*, 226–28.

171. World Bank statistics reported in Luca Barbone and Rossana Polastri, "Hungary's Public Finances in an International Context," in *Public Finance Reform during the Transition: The Experience of Hungary*, ed. Laszlo Bokros and Jean-Jacques Dethier, 158 (Washington, D.C.: World Bank, 1998).

172. Volkovskii, *Nalogoviie organy*, 68–74.

173. *Rossiiskoe nalogovoe kurer*, no. 1 (2002). The poll was conducted in the first half of 2001 and included fifteen hundred respondents, two-thirds of whom had had no previous dealings with the tax agencies.

174. See, for example, the research findings of Mikhail Pryadilnikov, in conjunction with the World Bank, "Citizens (and Tax Inspectors) against the State: Tracking Changes in Attitudes towards Tax Compliance in Russia, 2001–2008," (unpublished paper, Harvard University, Davis Center, Postcommunist Workshop, September 2009), table 3.

175. *Uralskii rabochii*, 2 November 1993, 1.

176. See interview with former MVD chief Anatoly Kulikov. *Obshchaia gazeta* (30 July 1998).

177. *New York Times*, 8 August 1998.

178. Ivanova, Keen, and Klemm, "The Russian Flat Tax Reform,").

179. *Russian Economy: Trends and Outlooks*, 2002 (Moscow: Institute for the Economy in Transition, 2003), 60, table 7.

180. *Kommersant*, no. 31 (28 February 2007). The tax amnesty brought in more than $150 million in additional revenues to the treasury.

181. Military salaries were given an initial big boost of 150% in 2002 and 100% in 2003, before settling down to regular increases of roughly 25%. *Gazeta*, 18 March 2002.

182. *Kommersant*, 29 June 2008.

183. These performances were conducted with the likes of the governor of Arkhangelsk and business tycoon Oleg Deripaska of Russian Aluminum.

184. *Vedomosti*, 4 August 2009; *Nezavisimaia gazeta*, 4 August 2009.

185. Russian Public Opinion Foundation (October 2004), cited in Berenson, "Rationalizing or Empowering Bureaucrats?" 136–55.

186. IMF, "Russian Federation: Recent Economic Developments," 16, fig. 6.

187. *OECD Economic Surveys: Russian Federation, 1997* (Paris: OECD, 1997), 116, fig. 23.

188. David Woodruff, *Money Unmade: Barter and the Fate of Russian Capitalism* (Ithaca: Cornell University Press, 2000).

189. R. Ericson, "The Post-Soviet Russian Economic System: An Industrial Feudalism?" *BOFIT* (Helsinki), no. 8 (2000): 9.

190. Brian Aitken, "Falling Tax Compliance and the Rise of the Virtual Budget," *IMF Staff Papers*, no. 48 (2001), 186–87.

191. IMF, "Russian Federation: Recent Economic Developments," 60, fig. 13.

192. Tanzi, "Creating Tax Administration," 62–63.

193. *Kommersant*, 20–21 February 1997.

194. *Finansy v Rossii: Statisticheskii sbornik* (Moscow: Goskomstat, 2000), 24.

195. Aitken, "Falling Tax Compliance," 187.

196. V. N. Koshkin, "O dopolnitelnykh nalogakh i sborakh, vvodimykh organami vlasti sub'ektov RF," *Nalogovyi vestnik*, no. 28 (March 1997): 33–35. Vladimir Tikhomirov, *The Political Economy of Post-Soviet Russia* (London: Macmillan, 2000), 66.

197. Kokoshin, "O deponitelnykh nalogakh," 33–35.

198. In 1998, the top-ten tax delinquent regions were Tyumen, Moscow city, Moscow region, Bashkortostan, Samara, Sverdlovsk, Kemerov, Nizhegorod, Tatarstan, and Krasnoiarsk. *Finansy v Rossii, 2000*, 65–67, table 2:19.

199. *RFE/RF Business Watch*, 22 January 2002; Highfield and Baer, "Tax Administration for Russia," 1. The tax police believed that the shadow economy was sustained by as many as three thousand money-laundering operations.

200. Szczesna, "Tax Payers vs. Taxes," 76.

201. World Values Surveys: Poland (1989, 1999), http://www.worldvaluessurvey.org/index_html.

202. For survey results on tax levels, see CBOS, *Polish Public Opinion* (October 1999), 1. For an overview of public attitudes toward social assistance, see CBOS, *Polish Public Opinion* (August 2004), 3–4; CBOS, *Polish Public Opinion* (September 2008), 1.

203. CBOS, *Polish Public Opinion* (February 2003), 2.

204. More than two-thirds of respondents in a 2005 survey felt that it was "easy" to use money to influence an act of parliament. Osrodek Badania Opinii Publicznej (OBOP), "Corruption on the Eve of Political Change," no. 062/05 (Warsaw: September 2005), 3.

205. *Guardian*, 15 March 1994, 9.

206. CBOS, *Polish Public Opinion* (November 2004).

207. EBRD–World Bank, "Business Environment and Enterprise Performance Survey," (BEEPS), *Poland: Regulation and Tax* (2009): http://www.enterprisesurveys.org/ExploreEconomies/?economyid = 154&year = 2009.

208. EBRD–World Bank, BEEPS, "Poland-at-a-Glance" (Washington, D.C.: World Bank, 2006), 4.

209. Across all of postcommunist Eastern Europe and the former Soviet Union, the percentage of businessmen who said that "bribery is frequent" in dealings with tax administration was 16% in 2002 and 14% in 2005. EBRD–World Bank, BEEPS, "Poland-at-a-Glance," 8.

210. Polish News Bulletin, 12 August 1991.

211. Several studies confirm that the respectful behavior of tax officials in face-to-face meetings with taxpayers in several Swiss cantons has a positive effect on compliance. W. W. Pommerehne and H. Weck-Hannemann, "Tax Rates, Tax Administration and Income Tax Evasion in Switzerland," *Public Choice* 88 (1996): 161–70; and Lars Feld and Bruno Frey, "Trust Breeds Trust: How Taxpayers Are Treated," *Economics of Governance* 3, no. 2 (2002): 87–99.

212. World Values Survey: Russia (1990, 1995, 1999, 2006), http://www.worldvaluessurvey.org/index_html.

213. See, for example, Transparency International's Corruption Perception Index. Here is where Russia ranked throughout the 2000s, and where the lowest-scoring FSU state ranked as well: 2001—Russia (79 out of 91 countries); Azerbaijan (84/91); 2005—Russia (126/158); Turkmenistan (154/158); 2009—Russia (146/180); Uzbekistan (174/180).

214. EBRD–World Bank, BEEPS, "Russia at-a-Glance" (January 2010), 19–20.

215. *Rossiiskoe nalogovoe kurer*, no. 1 (2002).

216. A 1996 OECD survey of 887 SMEs found that 50% of managers said that "extortion by government officials" was a common occurrence. *Saint Petersburg Times*, no. 227, 6–12 January 1997. EBRD–World Bank, BEEPS, "Russia at-a-Glance" (Washington, D.C.: World Bank, 2006), 4; EBRD–World Bank, Business Environment and Enterprise Performance Survey (BEEPS), Russian Federation (2009).

217. E. L. Paneiakh, "Official against Entrepreneur: Manipulation of Law as the Basic Control Technique in Post-Soviet Russia," in *Russian Polity: The Russian Political Science Yearbook*, 118–37 (Moscow: Politeia, 2009).

218. *OECD Economic Surveys: Russian Federation, 2001–2002* (Paris: OECD, 2002), 90 (table 20). The survey was conducted in Irkutsk, Tula, and Udmurtia.

219. *Nalogovaia politsiia*, no. 7 (April 2001).

220. Interviews conducted by author with six tax police officers in Ekaterinburg, September–October 1998.

221. Ibid.

222. *New York Times*, 8 August 1998.

5. BUILDING FISCAL CAPACITY IN POSTCOMMUNIST STATES

1. Hendrick Spruyt, *The Sovereign State and Its Competitors* (Princeton: Princeton University Press, 1994).

2. John Norwich, *A History of Venice* (New York: Vintage Books, 1989), pt. 2.

3. Brewer, *The Sinews of Power: War, Money and the English State, 1688–1783*; Jan Glete, *War and the State in Early Modern Europe: Spain, the Dutch Republic and Sweden as Fiscal-Military States* (London: Routledge, 2002). Downing's fiscal reforms, particularly the use of short-term public debt offerings, had already been developed by the Dutch Republic, whose merchant elite was very good at raising capital but less committed than England to expensive long-term investment in coercion.

4. Belka, Krajewska, Krajewski, and Santos, "Poland: Country Overview Study," 24.

5. Ibid., 26.

6. Andrej Bratkowski, "Macroeconomic Performance," *Russian and East European Finance and Trade* 33, no. 6 (November–December 1997): 18–30.

7. Alain de Crombrugghe and David Lipton, "The Government Budget and Economic Performance in Poland," in *The Transition in Eastern Europe*, ed. Oliver Jean Blanchard, Kenneth A. Froot, and Jeffrey D. Sachs, 117 (Chicago: University of Chicago Press, 1994).

8. *Poland: International Economic Report, 1991/92* (Warsaw: World Economy Research Institute, 1992), 51, table 8. The dividend tax was another of Balcerowicz's punitive taxes on the state sector.

9. Ibid., table 7.

10. Belka et al., "Poland," 38.

11. *Zycie Gospodarcze*, no. 26 (30 July 1991).

12. *OECD Economic Surveys: Poland, 1998*, 13.

13. *OECD Economic Surveys: Poland, 2000*, 25.

14. *OECD Economic Surveys: Poland, 1994*, 37.

15. Ibid. These figures are for total tax take, and do not include social security contributions.

16. *OECD Economic Surveys: Poland, 2001*, 75.

17. *OECD Economic Surveys: Poland, 1994*, 37.

18. Aslund, *Building Capitalism*, 286, table 7.3.

19. Grabowski and Smith, "The Taxation of Entrepreneurial Income in a Transition Economy: Issues Raised by the Experience of Poland," 111.

20. Total tax revenues include direct and indirect taxes on the corporate sector as well as social insurance taxes for 1988. Peter Mieszkowski, Izabela Bolkowiak, Donald Lubick, and Hanna Sochacka-Krysiak, "Tax Reform," in *Stabilization and Structural Adjustment in Poland*, ed. Henryk Kierzkowzski, Marek Okolski, and Stanislaw Wellisz, 93–95 (London: Routledge, 1993).

21. *OECD Economic Surveys: Poland* (Paris: OECD, 2000), 125.

22. Polish News Bulletin, 20 May 1994.

23. Lenain and Bartoszuk, "The Polish Tax Reform," 5.

24. Lenain and Bartoszuk, "The Polish Tax Reform," 28, 30 (figures 2, 4).

25. *OECD Economic Surveys: Poland, 2000*, 127.

26. *OECD Economic Surveys: Poland, 2000*, 30, 31; Henryk Kierzkowski, Marek Okolski, and Stanislaw Wellisz, "The Polish Economy 1989–1991," in *Stabilization and Structural Adjustment*, ed. Kierzkowski, Okolski, and Wellisz, 29–33.

27. *Poland: International Economic Report, 1997/98*, 170.

28. *Poland: International Economic Report, 1997/98*, 139, table 30). The figures include both principal and interest.

29. *Poland: International Economic Report, 1997/98*, 100, table 15.

30. Gaidar, *Dni porazhenii pobed*, 100.

31. Nagy, "The Fiscal Component of the First Russian Stabilization Effort, 1992–93," 235.

32. Interview with Aleksandr Pochinok, head of the State Tax Service in *Ekspert*, 1 December 1997.

33. *Russian Economic Trends* (December 1997), figure 5.

34. *OECD Economic Surveys: Russian Federation, 1997/98* (Paris: OECD, 1997), 29, figure 1.

35. *Rossiia v tsifrakh: Ofitsial'noe izdanie* (Moscow: Goskomstat, 1999), 315, table 22.12.

36. *Nalogovyi vestnik*, no. 1 (1997).

37. Ibid.

38. *OECD Economic Surveys: Russian Federation, 1997/98*, 66, figure 17.

39. *Russian Economy in 2000: Trends and Outlook* (Moscow: Institute for the Economy in Transition, 2001), 196, table 2.4.

40. *OECD Economic Surveys: Russian Federation, 1997/98*, 136, table 20.

41. *OECD Economic Surveys: Russian Federation, 2001–02*, 77, table 15.

42. *OECD Economic Surveys: Russian Federation, 1997/98*, 135.

43. *Segodnia*, 5 February 1997; *Finansovaia izvestiia*, 6 February 1997.

44. *Russian Economy in 2000: Trends and Outlook*, 227, table 2.12.

45. *OECD Economic Surveys: Russian Federation, 1997*, 137.

46. *OECD Economic Surveys: Russian Federation, 2001–02*, 167, figure 31.

47. Gilman, *No Precedent, No Plan*, 11, 54.

48. *OECD Economic Surveys: Russian Federation, 1997*, 230.

49. Ibid., 71.

50. Ibid., 72, table 5. Debt figures include official creditors, commercial lenders, and bonds sales.

51. The state savings bank, Sberbank, held the largest amount of government-issued short-term debt, accounting for over one-third of the total debt in circulation in the spring of 1996. Schleifer and Treisman, *Without a Map*, 63.

52. Ibid., 64.

53. Miles Kahler, ed., *Capital Flows and Financial Crises* (Ithaca: Cornell University Press, 1998).

54. *Rzeczpospolita*, no. 25, 30 January 1997, 2.

55. *Nowa Europa*, no. 36, 12 February 1997, 8.

56. *Gazeta wyborcza*, no. 52, 3 March 1997, 3.

57. Interview with Stanislaw Owsiak, member of the Monetary Policy Council, Krakow, 6 July 2005.

58. *OECD Economic Surveys: Poland, 2001*, 52, 53.

59. *Gazeta wyborcza*, no. 20, 29 January 1998, 21.

60. *Rzeczpospolita*, no. 10, 12 May 1998, 7; *Prawo i gospodarka*, no. 114, 3 June 1998.

61. *Rzeczpospolita*, no. 198, 22–23 August 1998, 7.

62. Polish News Bulletin, 18 August 1998.

63. *Rzeczpospolita*, no. 192, 18 August 1998, 1; no. 200, 27 August 1998, 16.

64. *OECD Economic Surveys: Poland, 2000*, 53, table 6.

65. *Prawo i gospodarka*, no. 167, 18 August 1998, 1.

66. See table 5.3.

67. *OECD Economic Surveys: Poland, 2004* (Paris: OECD, 2004), 84.

68. *Rzeczpospolita*, no. 198, 22–23 August 1998, 7.

69. *Rzeczpospolita*, no. 161, 17 July 1998, 1.

70. *Rzeczpospolita*, no. 214, 12–13 September 1998, 8.

71. *The Warsaw Voice: Business and Economy Yearbook, 1998* (Warsaw: Warsaw Voice, 1998), 22–23.

72. Yeltsin, *Midnight Diaries*, 90.

73. Pavel Kuznetsov and Alesandr Fomin, "Osushchestvlenie vlastnykh polnomochii koordinatsionnymi organami: Na primere operativnoi kommissii," in *Effektivnost' osushchestvleniia gosudarstvennogo upravlennia v Rossii: Period prezidentsva el'tsina* (Moscow: Institut prava i publichnoi politiki, 2002), 220–37. The Tax Cheka was formally chaired by Chernomyrdin, but it was actually run by Chubais, who headed the commission's Operational Committee. In March 1998, Chubais was forced out of the government, tainted by a corruption scandal. His portfolio, including the Tax Cheka, was assumed by Viktor Khristenko.

74. Tanzi, "Creating Tax Administration," 62–63.

75. The four firms were Severonikel (subsidiary of Noril'sk Nikel), R250 million; Vostsibugol (coal), R400 million; Chepetsk Mechanical Plant, R175 million; Rosenergoatom (nuclear energy), R329 million. *RFE/RL: Newsline* 2, no. 102, pt. 1 (2 June 1998).

76. These were the findings of the Interdepartmental Balances Commission, formed in 1997 to get to the bottom of corporate tax arrears problem. Aitken, "Falling Tax Compliance," 191.

77. *Obshchaia gazeta*, no. 23, June 1998; Fedorov, *10 bezumnykh let*, 196.

78. *Kommersant*, 5 June 1998.

79. *RFE/RL: Newsline* 2, no. 116 (18 June 1998).

80. *Kommersant*, 18 June 1998.

81. *RFE/RL: Newsline* 2, no. 129, pt. 1 (8 July 1998).

82. *RFE/RL: Newsline* 2, no. 123, pt. 1 (3 July 1998).

83. *RFE/RL: Newsline* 2, no. 127, pt. 1 (3 July 1998).

84. *Komsomolskaia Pravda*, 5 August 1998.

85. Gilman, *No Precedent, No Plan*, chaps. 5, 6.

86. Interview with Sergei Kiriyenko, *Itogi*, 24 August 1998.

87. *Komsomolskaia pravda*, 29 August 1998; *Nezavisimaia gazeta*, 29 August 1998.

88. Yegor Gaidar, "Lessons of the Russian Crisis for Transition Economies," *Finance and Development* (June 1999): 8.

89. *Komsomolskaia pravda,* 25 August 1998.

90. *OECD Observer,* no. 273 (June 2009), 8.

91. *Dziennik,* 10–11 May 2008, 20–21.

92. Rostowski's main nemeses were Aleksandra Natalii-Swiat of the conservative-populist Law and Justice Party, the deputy head of the Sejm's finance committee; and Zbigniew Clebowski of the market-liberal Civic Platform party, who fancied himself as finance minister and made the elimination of the capital gains tax his personal mission.

93. *Polityka,* 23 May 2008, 16, 18.

94. Rostowski's policy agenda is summarized in an interview in *Polityka,* 23 May 2008, 16, 18.

95. The Law and Justice Party was led by former child actors and later Solidarity activists, the Kaczynski twins, Lech and Jaroslaw, who held the offices of president and prime minister respectively in the second half of the 2000s.

96. Ibid.

97. *Rzeczpospolita,* 13 June 2008, 4.

98. *Wall Street Journal Polska,* 31 May–1 June 2008, 3.

99. *Gazeta wyborcza,* 14–15 June 2008.

100. *Gazeta wyborcza,* 23 May 2009.

101. Polish News Bulletin, 26 June 2009.

102. The honor was bestowed by the *Banker,* a subsidiary publication of the *Financial Times.*

103. See interview with Rostowski in the *Financial Times,* 23 October 2009.

104. *Warsaw Voice,* 5 August 2010.

105. The interest rates on long-term government issues actually dropped in 2009. *OECD: Policy Briefs, Poland 2010* (April 2010), 4–7.

106. See World Economic Forum website: http://www.gowarsaw.eu/en/news/poland-advances-to-39th-in-world-economic-forums-competitiveness.

107. *Finansy v Rossii: Statisticheskii sbornik* (Moscow: Goskomstat, 2002), table 1.1.

108. Ibid.

109. See World Bank website: http://www.worldbank.org/html/prddr/trans/december_2004/pgs4–5.htm.

110. *St. Petersburg Times,* 18 February 2003, 8.

111. *Kommersant,* 2 April 2003, 1, 11.

112. *Finansy v Rossii: Statisticheskii sbornik, 2006* (Moscow: Goskomstat, 2006), table 2.3, 2.4.

113. *Kommersant,* 18 October 2006.

114. *Kommersant,* 29 August 2005.

115. *Kommersant,* 9 February 2006.

116. *Telegraph,* 22 August 2006.

117. *OECD Economic Surveys: Russian Federation, 2009* (Paris: OECD, 2009), chap. 2.

118. *Finansy v Rossii: Statisticheskii sbornik, 2006* (Moscow: Goskomstat, 2006), table 2.9; (2008), table 1.2. On the eve of the 2008 international financial crisis, the foreign reserve held more than $386 billion.

119. *Finansy v Rossii,2006,* table 2.9.

120. *RFE/RL—Newsline* (1 February 2008).

121. Ibid.

122. *Sunday Times (London),* 17 September 2008.

123. The World Bank: Economic Management and Policy Unit, "Russian Economic Report," no. 18 (March 2009), 5.

124. Ibid.

125. Ibid.

126. *Moscow Times*, no. 4378, 23 April 2010. Oil-rich Qatar held the record for the largest debt offering, $7 billion, in November 2009.

6. TAXATION AND THE RECONFIGURATION OF STATE AND SOCIETY

1. See, for example, Marc Howard, *The Weakness of Civil Society in Post-Communist Europe* (New York: Cambridge University Press, 2003); Peter Kopecky and Cas Mudde, eds., *Uncivil Society? Contentious Politics in Post-Communist Europe* (London: Routledge, 2003).

2. Adam Smith, *Lectures on Justice, Police, Revenue and Arms* (New York: Augustus M. Kekkey, 1964), 154.

3. Renate Weber, "Police Organization and Accountability: A Comparative Study," in *Police in Transition*, ed. Andras Kadar (Budapest: Central European University Press, 2001).

4. Andrzeij Rzeplinski, "The Police in the Constitutional Framework: The Limits of Policing," in Kadar, *Police in Transition*, 339–88.

5. Tomasz Inglot, *Welfare States in East Central Europe, 1919–2004* (New York: Cambridge University Press, 2008), 270, 271, table 4.9. The annual percentage increases of the special social insurance fund for "uniformed" retirees were consistently high—1991: 118%; 1992: 56%; 1993: 48%;1994: 82%; 1995: 50%. By contrast, over the same years the general social insurance fund increased more modestly—1991: 60%; 1992: 42%; 1991: 31%; 1994: 32%; 1995: 8%.

6. Kurowski, Ruskowski, and Sochacka-Krysiak, *Kontrola finansowa w sektorze publyczym*, 239–50.

7. *Rzeczpospolita*, 2 May 2001, B1.

8. In the 1997 Constitution the organization of the office of Ombudsman is covered in Article 80; the rights of citizens to contest unlawful state power by petitioning the Ombudsman is covered in Article 208. In 1996, tax disputes occupied 12.5% of the Ombudsman office's total caseload; see Piotr Przybysz, "Polish Ombudsman Works for a Democratic Society," *OECD: Public Management Forum* 2, no. 3 (1996): 6.

9. For an extensive discussion of the role of the Ombudsman and the Constitutional Tribunal in postcommunist Poland, see Mark Brzezinski, *The Struggle for Constitutionalism in Poland* (London: Macmillan, 2000).

10. In the 1997 Constitution, the organization and powers of the Constitutional Tribunal are covered in Article 79 and Article 188, and the Constitutional Tribunal Act (7 August 1997).

11. In the first five years of the transition, the Sejm was able to muster the necessary three-fifths majority to overrule the Tribunal only six times. *Polish News Bulletin* (26 July 1996).

12. Polish News Bulletin, 8 December 1993.

13. Polish News Bulletin, 25 August 1993.

14. Polish News Bulletin, 30 March 1994.

15. *Orzecznistwo Tribunalu Konstytucyjnego Zbior Urzedowy* (K 4/03), 11 May 2004.

16. A poll conducted by Centrum Badaniia Opinii Spolocznej (CBOS) in February 2006 found that 69% of respondents "trusted" the Ombudsman, which was higher than NATO, 65%, and lower than the Boy Scouts, 75%. CBOS, Public Opinion Survey, no. 2 (February 2006), 3. Whereas the Ombudsman rated highly, the Polish court system was not trusted by society in general or by the business community in particular. For example, in November 2000, respondents to the question "whom do you trust?" answered: president, 56% trust/16% distrust; Church, 47% trust/24% distrust; the courts, 22% trust/35% distrust. CBOS, Public Opinion Survey (November 2000), 1–2.

17. Polish News Bulletin, 9 January 1995.

18. Polish News Bulletin, 5 March 1996.

19. Polish News Bulletin, 21 December 2005.

20. The film was supposed to be produced by Stanley Kramer, famous for the films *The Caine Mutiny* and *The Wild Ones*.

21. *Gazeta wyborcza*, 12 June 1997 (no. 135), 3.

22. Onet.pl was Poland's largest domestic Internet service provider and information-based website; its operation later extended to include the ownership of half a dozen television stations and a movie theater chain; exclusive distribution deals with Microsoft and Lockheed Martin; exclusive distribution deals with Disney, Miramax, and Touchstone studios. It later bought up CD Projekt, East Central Europe's largest computer game company and maker of *The Witcher*, Poland's most popular computer game.

23. *Wprost 24*, no. 46 (2007), http://www.wprost.pl/ar/117482/Boscy-sponsorzy/?I = 1299.

24. *Rzeczpospolita*, 3 July 2002, A1

25. *Puls biznesu*, 28 April 2004, 5.

26. *Rzeczpospolita*, 7 February 2003, A3.

27. *Gazeta wyborcza*, 25 February 2003, 3; *Rzeczpospolita*, 25 February 2003, A1; *Rzeczpospolita*, 24 January 2003, A1.

28. *Puls biznesu*, 26 September 2003, 9.

29. *Gazeta wyborcza*, 3 December 2003, 1.

30. *Gazeta wyborcza*, 18 October 2005; *Puls biznesu*, 20 September 2005, 5.

31. *Rzeczpospolita*, 24 June 2003, A4.

32. *Puls biznesu*, 20 September 2005, 5.

33. *Rzeczpospolita*, 17 October 2003, B1.

34. *Puls biznesu*, 30 May 2007, 4–5.

35. Vadim Volkov, *Violent Entrepreneurs*, 138. Volkov counted 11,652 newly registered private security firms by 1999.

36. Amy Knight, *Spies without Cloaks: The KGB's Successors* (Princeton: Princeton University Press, 1996), 40.

37. *Rossiiskaia gazeta*, 14 April 1999; *Rossiiskaia gazeta*, 14 March 2002. The two main articles of the criminal code dealing with tax evasion were nos. 198 and 199.

38. *Kommersant*, 12 November 2004. The comments were made respectively by Economic Development Minister German Gref, Finance Minister Aleksei Kudrin, and Deputy Head Igor Shugalov.

39. Ibid. Tax exemption for cities in Russia and the CIS ended in 2001. The national autonomous republic tax havens (Mordovia, utilized by Yukos; Chukotka, utilized by Sibneft; and Kalmykia, utilized by everybody) were finally shut down in 2004.

40. Ibid.

41. *St Petersburg Times*, no. 983, 6 July 2004.

42. Kathryn Hendley, Peter Murrell, and Randi Ryterman, "Law, Relationships and Private Enforcement: Transactional Strategies of Russian Enterprises," *Europe-Asia Studies* 52, no. 4 (2000): 627–56; Timothy Frye, "The Two Faces of Russian Courts: Evidence from a Survey of Company Managers," *East European Constitutional Review* 11 (2002): 125–35.

43. Courts of arbitration existed in the Soviet period as far back as the 1920s. They acted in two ways: to resolve disputes between enterprises and to enforce central state authority over economic enterprises. The existing network of arbitration courts was reorganized in December 1992 in order to provide a legal forum for conflict resolution in the transition economy.

44. *Kommersant*, no. 25, 16 February 2007.

45. Volkovskii, *Nalogovyie organy*, 104.

46. *Moscow Times*, 8 August 2000. In the Avtovaz case, the giant carmaker was accused of manufacturing 280,000 cars with the same identification number so to not have to account for the vehicles to the tax administration.

47. *Vedomosti*, 14 March 2002. The Russian chapter of an international NGO, Society of Taxpayers, maintains that the tax police have won fewer than 5% of the criminal cases that have actually gone to trial.

48. Ibid.

49. Kozyrin, A. N., ed., *O federal'nykh organakh nalogovoi politsii: S postateinimi materialami* (Moscow: Statut, 2000), 21, 30, 68–70.

50. Article 169 was successfully used in cases against large oil companies Yukos and Russneft and a collection of Bashkortastan-based financial and energy firms. The arbitrage courts did not always accept the tax authorities' attempts to apply this controversial article, although it was used in tax evasion cases prosecuted against targeted corporate and regional elites. In April 2008, the Higher Arbitrage Court, in Resolution 22, finally defined a limited range of tax-related behavior to which this article could be applied, and urged tax authorities to use the tax code, not the civil code, in tax evasion cases.

51. *Moscow Times*, no. 2161, 15 March 2001.

52. *Kommersant*, no. 25, 16 February 2007.

53. *Moscow Times*, 1 November 2001, 6 November 2001, 16 April 2002.

54. *Nevskoe Vremia*, 11 February 2003, 1; *St Petersburg Times*, 14 February 2003, 6. In 2003, for example, Stepashin exposed the fiscal shenanigans of the St. Petersburg city administration, including an unaccounted half billion rubles that was supposed to be spent on the city's glitzy three hundredth anniversary festival and the fishy privatization sale of the state's shares in the Grand Hotel.

55. Vadim Volkov, "The Yukos Affair: Terminating the Implicit Contract," *PONARS Policy Memo*, no. 137 (November 2003); Marshall Goldman, "Putin and the Oligarchs," *Foreign Affairs* 83, no. 6 (2004): 33–44.

56. *Kommersant*, 28 March 2003, 3.

57. *Kommersant*, 20 February 2003.

58. *New York Times*, 2 January 2004.

59. The judge was Olga Kudeshkina, who in a later interview said that she had been given orders from a superior to manipulate the proceedings to the advantage of the prosecution. *Wall Street Journal*, 5 August 2004.

60. *Kommersant*, 9 August 2007.

61. Joseph Schumpeter, "The Crisis of the Tax State," quoted in W. Elliot Brownlee, *Federal Taxation in America: A Short History* (New York: Cambridge University Press: 1996), 169.

62. "The Constitution of the Republic of Poland," published in *Dziennik ustaw*, no. 78 (483), chap. 1, art. 20.

63. On the varieties of European welfare capitalism, see Gosta Esping-Andersen, *The Three Worlds of Welfare Capitalism* (Cambridge: Polity Press, 1990). Of the three types of welfare capitalism identified by Esping-Andersen (Anglo-minimalist, Scando-social democrat, Germano-Franco-conservative corporatist), Polish welfare capitalism more closely resembled the conservative corporatist type, but without the wealth.

64. See, for example, Grzegorz Kolodko, "Institutions, Policies, Growth," in *The Polish Miracle: Lessons for the Emerging Markets*, ed. Kolodko (Aldershot, U.K.: Ashgate, 2005), 3–26.

65. The manifesto, "In Search of the Polish Model of Social Economy" (article 3), is posted on the website for Social Economy in Poland: http://www.ekonomiaspoleczna.pl/ files/ekonomiaspoleczna.pl/public/gk/panele/Polish_social_economy_manifesto.pdf.

66. Kolodko, "Institutions, Policies, Growth," 3–26.

67. "In Search of the Polish Model of Social Economy," (article. 2).

68. Wladyslaw Baka, "The Economic Agenda of the Polish Round Table 15 Years Later: Implications for the Future," in Kolodko, *Polish Miracle*, 51–60.

69. Inglot, *Welfare States in East Central Europe*, 78–96.

70. CBOS, *Polish Public Opinion* (June 1997), 4. The survey showed 32% support for "economic efficiency," 60% for "no one should get hurt," and 8% for "don't know."

71. CBOS, *Polish Public Opinion* (February 1998), 3; (August 2004), 3–4; and (September 2008), 1.

72. CBOS, *Polish Public Opinion* (June 2003), 1.

73. CBOS, *Polish Public Opinion* (July–August 2002), nos. 7–8, 2.

74. Concessions are not unfamiliar to capitalist economies. The owner of a sports stadium concedes a space or privilege to a private firm to sell popcorn and soda. The concessionaire profits from the noncompetitive market and in exchange pays the stadium owner a fee and share of the profits. The concessionaire does not own the space; it is a paid-for privilege subject to a contractual agreement. Of course, Russian state concessions are not regulated by the terms of legally enforceable contracts, so the popcorn vendor has more rights than the oil baron.

75. The concessions economy is one of the major recurring structural patterns in Russia: Stefan Hedlund, *Russian Path Dependence: A People with a Troubled History* (New York: Routledge, 2005).

76. Martin, *Medieval Russia* ; Marc Raeff, *Understanding Imperial Russia* (New York: Columbia University Press, 1984); John LeDonne, *Absolutism and Ruling Class: The Formation of the Russian Political Order, 1700–1825* (New York: Oxford University Press, 1991).

77. David McDonald, *United Government and Foreign Policy in Russia, 1900–1914* (Cambridge: Harvard University Press, 1992).

78. *Moscow Times*, 30 October 2003, 1.

79. *Kommersant*, 17 November 2003.

80. Vserossiikii tsentr izucheniia obshchestvennogo mneniia (VTsIOM) (August 2001), nationwide survey, 1,600 respondents; VTsIOM (July 2003), nationwide survey, 1,585 respondents. See website Russia Votes: http://www.russiavotes.org/national_issues/privatisation.php?S776173303132 = 526aef939a2e832997dc200e09c691f3#284.

81. David Woodruff, "The Expansion of State Ownership in Russia: Cause for Concern?" *Development and Transition* 7, nos. 11–13 (July 2007): 11–13.

82. *Kommersant*, 13 January 2006.

83. *Kommersant*, 17 March 2003, 2; 20 March 2003, 10.

84. *Kommersant*, 23 April 2003, 9–10.

85. *Moscow Times*, 5 May 2003, 7.

86. *Kommersant*, 30 November 2007, 1

87. *Wprost*, 27 June 2003. Russia's richest individual at this time was Mikhail Khodorkovsky.

88. *Wprost*, no. 619, 25 September 2007. The highest spot went to Ryszard Krauze, with an estimated wealth of $600 million.

89. "Najbogatszy Polak 2009," *Forbes Polska* (March 2009): 62–74.

90. *Krakow Post*, 26 July 2007.

91. Interview with A. Andarski in *Prawo i gospodarki—magazyn finansowy*, 6 August 2001, 10; Polish News Bulletin, 10 June 1995.

92. Interview with A. Sadowski in *Puls biznesu*, 25 September 2004, 20–23; Polish News Bulletin, 10 June 1995.

93. Iain McMenamin, "Polish Business Associations: Flattened Society or Super Lobbies," *Business and Politics* 4, no. 3 (2002): 301–17. The five largest business associations

were the Confederation of Polish Employers, Business Centre Club, the Polish Chamber of Commerce, the Polish Business Roundtable, and the Polish Confederation of Private Employers.

94. The dinners were held in January and June 2008; see the archive of events at the Polish Business Roundtable website: http://www.prb.pl/index.php?topic = archiwum&lang = en.

95. *Rzeczpospolita*, 2 May 2001, A1.

96. The Taxpayers Association of Poland is a national branch office of the Taxpayers Association of Europe. For an overview of its activities, see the PAT program at their website: http://www.podatnicy.org/index.php?strona = 3.

97. *Puls biznesu*, 11 September 2003, 5.

98. Polish News Bulletin, 21 May 2008.

99. One notable exception to this trend was the attempt by the tax administration to tax the invested funds of the nonprofit foundation Society for Polish Science for an amount in excess of $20 million. On appeal, the Supreme Administrative Court sided with the tax administration, but in the ultimate appeal the Polish Supreme Court overturned the tax administration's claim. *Gazeta Wyborcza*, 14 March 2002.

100. "Survey of Tax Laws Affecting Non-Governmental Organizations in Central and Eastern Europe" (Washington, D.C.: International Center for Not-for-Profit Law, 2002). Among postcommunist states, Hungary took the lead in 1996, followed by Lithuania and Slovakia. The Hungarian "1 percent" reform raised more than $9 million in revenue for the NGO sector.

101. One of the main contributors to this effort was Igor Golinski, a young tax lawyer who had previously served as an intern in the Department of Taxes in MinFin. Igor Golinski, "Polish Parliament Adopts New Law on Public Benefit Activities and Volunteerism," *Social Economy and Law Journal* 6, no. 1 (Summer 2003).

102. "Survey of Tax Laws," 14.

103. Golinski, "Polish Parliament Adopts New Law."

104. Marta Gumkowska and Jan Herbst, "Basic Facts about NGOs: Report on 2006 Survey," *Klon/Jowar Association* (2006): 4.

105. Ibid.

106. Ibid. The number of foundations increased as well, from five thousand in 2002 to eight thousand in 2006; 29, table 10.

107. Hanna Diskin, *The Seeds of Triumph: Church and State in Gomulka's Poland* (Budapest: Central European University Press, 2001).

108. *Gazeta Wyborcza*, 9 December 1993.

109. Polish News Bulletin, 21 December 1993.

110. Polish News Bulletin, 14 June 1997. A survey taken at the time showed 70% of Poles against the tax boycott.

111. *Trybuna*, no. 190, 14–15 August 1996, 1.

112. *Rzeczpospolita*, no. 82, 7 April 1998, 1; *Gazeta Wyborcza*, no. 52, 3 March 1998, 5.

113. *Gazeta Wyborcza*, 13 March 2001, 4.

114. Based on the annual *Forbes* list, the ten were Vladimir Lisin (steel), Mikhail Prokhorov (metallurgy), Mikhail Fridman (energy, metallurgy), Roman Abramovich (energy), Oleg Derispaka (metallurgy), Vagit Alekperov (energy), Vladimir Potanin (energy, metallurgy), Alexei Mordashev (steel), Viktor Rashnikov (metallurgy), and Dmitry Rybolovlev (petrochemical). *Daily Mail*, 16 April 2010.

115. The main professional association for small businesses was the All-Russian Nongovernmental Organization of Small and Medium Businesses (OPORA). *St. Petersburg Times*, 18 February 2003, p. 8.

116. Most of the big business tycoons joined RUIE at its 11th Congress, when they displaced the union's existing "red director" board members. *Vedomosti*, 28 February 2001.

117. *Ogonek*, no. 21 (May 2002), 17–21.

118. *St. Petersburg Times*, 28 January 2003, 4.

119. Ibid.

120. *Moscow Times*, 25 February 2005, 3.

121. "2009 NGO Sustainability Index in Central and Eastern Europe," (Washington, DC: USAID, 2010), p. 182.

122. Lyubov Alenicheva, "Donor and Non-Profit Organizations: What Do We Know about Them" (Moscow, Donors Forum, 2005). The statistics are drawn from tables 2, 3 and diagrams 3, 4. The Donors Forum, founded in 1996, is an umbrella group that includes both Russian and foreign grant-making organizations, dedicated to the development of democratic civil society in Russia.

123. Alfred Evans Jr., "The First Steps of Russia's Public Chamber: Representation or Coordination?" *Demokratizatsiya* (Fall 2008).

124. Ibid.

125. James Richter, "Putin and Public Chamber," *Post-Soviet Affairs* 25, no. 1 (January–March 2009): 39–65; *Johnson's Russia List* (#17-JRL-2007-171).

126. *Kommersant*, no. 48/3379 (21 March 2006).

127. Interfax: News Headlines (29 December 2009). See the Interfax website, http://www.interfax.com/newsinf.asp?id = 138881.

128. *Nezavismaia gazeta*, 17 May 2000.

129. *Segodnia*, 30 November 2000; *Nalogovaia politsiia*, no. 19 (October 2001).

130. *Moskovskie novosti*, 22 January 2002.

Selected Bibliography

FINANCIAL AND STATISTICAL COMPILATIONS, PUBLIC OPINION SOURCES

Business and Economic Outlook: 1998. Warsaw: Warsaw Voice, 1998.

CIA: "USSR: Sharply Higher Deficits Threaten Perestroika: A Research Paper." CIA: Sov-88-10043U (September 1988).

Centrum Badaniia Opinii Spolocznej (CBOS), *Polish Public Opinion.*

EBRD–World Bank. "Business Environment and Enterprise Performance Survey" (BEEPS), 2006, 2008.

EBRD–World Bank. "Business Environment and Enterprise Performance Survey" BEEPS, "Poland-at-a-Glance" (Washington, D.C.: World Bank, 2006).

Finansy v Rossii: Statisticheskii sbornik. Moscow: Goskomstat Rossii, 1996.

Finansy v Rossii: Statisticheskii sbornik. Moscow: Goskomstat Rossii, 2000.

Finansy v Rossii: Statisticheskii sbornik. Moscow: Goskomstat Rossii, 2002.

Finansy v Rossii: Statisticheskii sbornik. Moscow: Goskomstat Rossii, 2006.

OECD Economic Surveys of the Czech Republic, 2008. Paris: OECD, 2008.

OECD Economic Surveys: Poland. Paris: OECD, 1992.

OECD Economic Surveys: Poland. Paris: OECD, 1994.

OECD Economic Surveys: Poland. Paris: OECD, 1997.

OECD Economic Surveys: Poland, 1998. Paris: OECD, 1998.

OECD Economic Surveys: Poland, 2000. Paris: OECD, 2000.

OECD Economic Surveys: Poland: 2000–2001. Paris: OECD, 2001.

OECD Economic Surveys: Poland, 2004. Paris: OECD, 2004.

OECD Economic Surveys: Russian Federation, 1995. Paris: OECD, 1995.

OECD Economic Surveys: Russian Federation, 1997/98. Paris: OECD, 1997.

OECD: Economic Surveys: Russian Federation, 2001/2002. Paris: OECD, 2002.

Osrodek Badania Opinii Publicznej (OBOP). "Corruption on the Eve of Political Change," no. 062/05. Warsaw: September 2005.

Poland: International Economic Report, 1991/1992. Warsaw: World Economy Research Institute, 1992.

Poland: International Economic Report, 1997/1998. Warsaw: World Economy Research Institute, 1998.

Rocznyk Statystyczny, 1992. Warsaw: GUS, 1992.

Rocznyk Statystyczny, 1993. Warsaw: GUS, 1993.

Rocznyk Statystyczny, 1995. Warsaw: GUS, 1995.

Rocznik statystyczny, 1999. Warsaw: GUS, 1999.

Rocznik statystychny, 2000. Warsaw: GUS, 2000.

Rocznik statystyczny handlu zagranicznego 1983. Warsaw: GUS, 1983.

Rossiia v tsifrakh: Ofitsial'noe izdanie. Moscow: Goskomstat, 1999.

Russian Economy: Trends and Outlook, 2000. Moscow: Institute for the Economy in Transition, 2001.

Russian Economy: Trends and Outlooks, 2002. Moscow: Institute for the Economy in Transition, 2003.

World Values Surveys: Poland (1989, 1999), http://www.worldvaluessurvey.org/index_html.

World Values Surveys: Russia (1990, 1995, 1999, 2006), http://www.worldvaluessurvey.org/index_html.

Wybory 1993: Partie i ich programy. Warsaw: Institute of Political Studies, Polish Academy of Science, 2003.

Wybory 1997: Partie i ich programy: Warsaw: Institute of Political Studies, Polish Academy of Science, 2004.

Wybory 2001: Partie i ich programy. Warsaw: Institute of Polish Studies, Polish Academy of Sciences, 2002.

Wybory 1991: Programy Partii i Ugrupowan Politychnych. Warsaw: Institute of Political Studies, Polish Academy of Science, 2001.

Index